Antique Toys and their Background

Written and illustrated by the same author:

Ancient and Modern Dolls
Toys' Adventures at the Zoo
Ladybird, Ladybird
A Book of Toys
Eight Little Frogs
A Book of Dolls
A Book of Pictorial Perspective
A World of Pattern
Dolls of the World
European and American Dolls
Perspective: A Guide for Artists,
    Architects and Designers

1 Poupard, wood and cloth. 2 Doll's house, wood and printed paper. 3 Snow-storm novelty, glass and shells.
4 Spinning-top, metal and thread. 5 Laying goose, plastic and elastic

Antique Toys
and their background

Gwen White

arco
New York

Published by ARCO PUBLISHING COMPANY, INC.
219 Park Avenue South, New York, N.Y. 10003

Library of Congress Number 74-153651
ISBN 0-668-02484-4

Printed in Great Britain

Contents

Acknowledgments

The author thanks the curators for making toys available in the various museums in which she has made drawings, and the collectors and others who have let her sketch their toys. In particular Mr J. D. Fordham of the Bethnal Green Museum, Miss Ilid Anthony of the City Museum, St Albans, Mrs J. C. Bishop, Miss Janet Dunbar, Mrs Fawdry of Pollock's Toy Museum, Mrs Estrid Faurholt, Mrs Heather Fox, the Lord Grantley, Mr A. E. D. Lott, Mr Edward Pinto, the Marquess of Salisbury, and Miss Ruth Wainwright.

She also thanks Mr Nicolas Bentley, Mr W. A. Butcher, Mr H. E. Cox of the *Daily Mirror*, Miss Joy Gawne of the Budleigh Salterton Museum, Mr C. Rupert Moore for information on model aeroplanes, the Comptroller of the Patent Office Library, Messrs Warnes for permission to use the Kate Greenaway initial, the Imperial War Museum, and Miss Jennie Polley of the Youngstown Doll Club, U.S.A.

She would like to thank all the small children who have kept their eye on her while sketching their valuable belongings, and last but not least she thanks her three sons, Richard, Moreton and Guy for treasuring some of their toys.

Preface

Many of the pristine toys which belong to past ages have never been played with by children, but have spent their time in cabinets in the drawing-room or farther back still, in the graves of their owners. Dolls may only have been touched now and again and then returned to a box lined with tissue paper for fear they should be spoilt.

Some toys survive whose origins are difficult to trace. On the other hand, stuffed pandas are still seen riding in prams whereas the original panda at the Zoo is hardly noticed. The white bear Brumas has grown up, from 1968 the white bear tucked up at night is known as Pipaluk. Today we have the Aldermaston doll and the Beatle doll and these too will probably outlive their prototypes. In this manner toys help history and give examples to future generations of the playthings of the present.

There are toys with which the child can play and there are those with which a doll can play and between these two extremes of scale come other sizes. The large horse or engine on which a child might ride, the tea cups from which a child may drink, and the tiny horse or tea-set to go in a doll's house, or a miniature train to run on lines.

How interesting history would be if one realized that the world has grown up everywhere every day. In some parts more has happened than in others but it has all been on the same day of the week, month, year or century. Even Biblical days seem a thing apart and yet at the time of Christ, tin was being used in Britain and boys were playing with marbles.

Little toy animals of ancient times show where that kind of animal might have been found, and miniature carts show the evolution of the wheel. Balls and rattles come from the Stone Age, bronze toys denote methods of casting, and even the coming of the potter's wheel can be discovered by studying playthings.

Miniature soldiers show how armies were dressed and many historical events have been commemorated by games. The disappearance of rag-books in wartime indicates the rationing of cloth and when peace came, the Plastic Age began with free gifts and space toys.

Today's giants of the Toy World are the big firms like Lines Bros., Lesney, Mattel and Fisher Price, firms making all kinds of things, some beautiful, some funny, and some almost as frightening as the Salisbury giant of A.D. 1496.

1   Italian Sweetnik

2   The Salisbury Giant. England

7

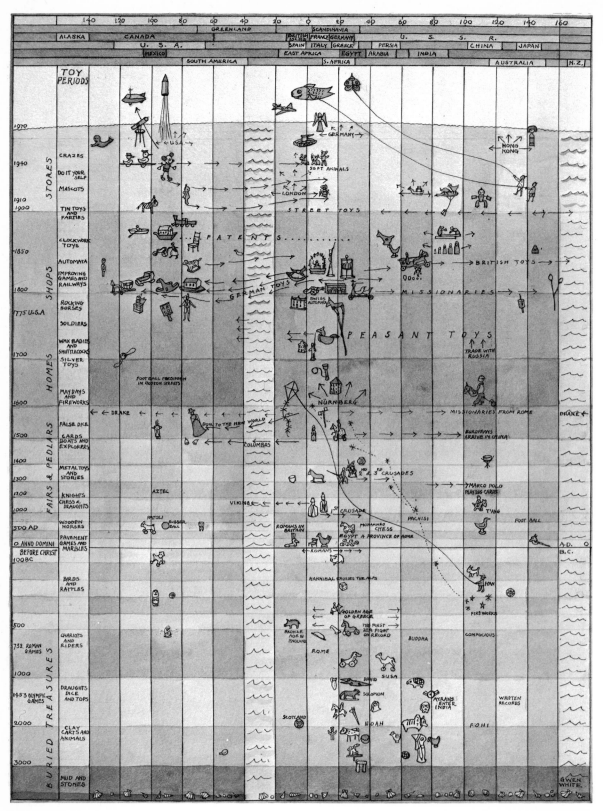

Chart showing place and time

1 Historical outline

A long time ago, 4,000 years and more, children played with much the same kind of things as they do today. There were plenty of pebbles to throw into water, plenty of sticks to float and mud to scoop.

Their parents looked for caves in which to dwell, and hunted for food. They lived on berries, fruits and nuts, so almost the first thing they needed was a basket in which to stow what they had picked.

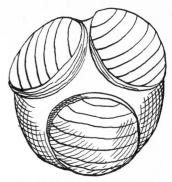

3 Ball of stone. Scotland

They needed stones to throw at the wild animals and flints for shaping other flints, bones, horns and tusks, and they made sharp tools with which to carve and chip the things they wanted. Because of using all these stones, these early people were known as the 'Stone Age' men, and one of the earliest toys known is a stone ball. Perhaps it is not a plaything, no one knows why it was made, but it is a convenient size to hold in the hand.

The Stone Age men buried their dead together with their belongings, things they had loved when they were alive, or things they might need when they went to another world. Sometimes a person would have a round mound all to himself for a grave, or sometimes a family would share a long-shaped mound or a tomb. Years and years later, when some of these mounds were dug up, toys and dolls and games were discovered in the graves of the children, and in parts of Europe and America small stone figures made by early man have been found.

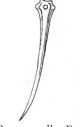

4 Bone needle. Egypt

Later on, tribes and settled communities began to develop, particularly in self-sufficient areas where there was no need to travel, such as Egypt with its river and its warm climate. The longer one stays in one place the more possessions are accumulated, so it was natural that the people of Egypt occupied themselves by making things with their hands and that they made many toys for their children.

Apart from the Nile, people lived on other river-banks such as the Jordan, the Tigris and the Euphrates. There was clay for making pots, figurines and little animals and plenty of sand for the children to play with. Carts were made in Egypt and Mesopotamia and asses and oxen trained to pull them along, and there were toy carts and pull-along toys in the Early Dynastic period of 3100–2686 B.C.

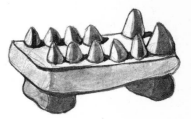

5 Mud gaming board with pieces. Egypt

In India, a city called Chanhudaro, near the River Indus, seems to have specialised in toy-making. Here bird whistles were made and bulls with nodding heads and little earthenware scale-pans. Two infants were found in a grave wearing bead necklaces. Often a child would wear a blue bead, for the colour was considered to be lucky.

When pavements were marked out, they were soon used for games, in Egypt and in India, and there were also bricks incised with lines and boards on which to play.

Bronze was used for figurines and little animals, and articles were sold in various bazaars or exchanged by barter. In China people played with shadow figures made from wax.

Men played games of chance with nuts, bets were laid and later on they had dice.

6 Clay bull. Kulli, Western India

At a time when Joseph was arrayed in fine linen, it was the Early Bronze Age in England, and men and boys threw knives at blocks of wood like the more modern game of darts.

By 1453 B.C. the Phoenicians were bartering their toys and trifles on the River Nile, a toy being perhaps a glass trinket or some little ornament, and by 1100 B.C. they traded with England for tin. Potters from Asia used the potter's wheel in Crete, and there were organised games in Greece.

During excavations in ancient Jerusalem, rattles and whistles were found of a period about 1050 B.C. when David might have been there. Pottery models of furniture, animals and cooking utensils were also unearthed.

Although copper had been found in the Americas, stone axes were still in general use, for iron had not been discovered. By 1000 B.C. there were civilised people living in Mexico, Yucatan and Peru.

From Greece organised games spread to other parts and travellers to and fro would tell one another the latest news. In 664 B.C. the first recorded sea fight took place, and on the land there were various kinds of chariots for racing and for warfare.

7 Boy with toy cart. Greece

Most trade was done in kind and where the articles had to be weighed, the traders carried their scales and their weights with them. (In 1970 even in London there are still vegetable carts with their scales and weights and periodically these carts are stopped by the Weights and Measures men in order to have their scales checked.)

Balls were mentioned in the Bible, goods were purchased by coins and Africa exported bows and arrows.

By 120 B.C. the Tartar used the horse for hunting, the Arab rode on the camel, the people of Lapland subdued the reindeer, and those of Kamchatka trained their dogs for labour. Travellers along the incense route could purchase small figures and gifties for their friends at home, and by 27 B.C. all travellers to and from the Olympic Games were protected by a truce, so important had the Games become.

Bronze was used for making many of the little toy animals, and in Rome rich men amused their guests with automata, and children played with clay birds.

★

The early Christians were persecuted because they refused to worship the images of the Roman Emperor, and while in hiding they would make toys to amuse the children and keep them quiet. Later when the Roman Empire became too large to be protected by Roman soldiers only, they had to recruit 'barbarians' to help them, but eventually the Romans had to withdraw in order to keep an eye on their own country.

The majority of English towns were in ruins by this time. However, the Romans left behind many bone dice, counters, roundels, alabaster balls and glass marbles which have since been unearthed. The Dark Ages loomed over Europe and the long straight roads were over-

8 Bone doll. Roman

grown with grass just at the period when the Mayan culture was flourishing.

Gradually things improved. The people in Britain built and lived in wooden huts, the lords in wooden halls. Some played at archery and a few added newfangled stirrups to their horses.

The Anglo-Saxons became Christians and scholars wrote on parchment with quill pens, little decorations showed a Punch and Judy show and a horse with a saddle. Draughtsmen were made from horses' teeth and in Germany from stags' horns. Chess was played by the Persians and other learned men in the East where by A.D. 618 China had become the most civilised State.

Few western European toys have survived the first 100 years of the Christian era. There were many fires and plagues in these Dark Ages, and in A.D. 430 in Britain alone there was such a dreadful plague in which so many people died that there were hardly enough left to bury them.

When Canute sailed up the Thames from Denmark in the eleventh century, he played dice and chess with his courtiers and forbade the English from selling their children to the Irish as slaves. Toys were on sale at the many fairs, and pedlars travelled from place to place. There were dancing bears and jugglers and in gaming the loser was often made a slave to the winner.

By 1150 in England there were merry-go-rounds and beargardens on the south bank of the Thames. Young men played upon the ice and Fitz-Stephen said 'they do slide as swiftly as a bird flieth in the air, or an arrow out of a crossbow'.

In China where it was the Sung dynasty, people played with kites which hummed with vibrating cords, and they dressed their dolls in paper. Playing-cards mentioned for the first time were exported to the West.

Toys could be purchased in shops with halfpennies and farthings, for round pennies were quartered with a cross and could be broken by an order of Henry I. Goods were transported by pack-horses, and a stationer's was simply a stall which stayed in one place.

In the twelfth century toy knights appeared in England and there were also board games. A favourite place in which to play on summer evenings was the Priory churchyard at Smithfield, and here between 1133 and 1300 would be seen people sitting on seats under the trees

9   Chess piece of carved bone. Probably Roman

10   Draughtsman made from a horse's tooth

11   Chinese child at play

13   Figure with animal. German

12   Juggler

playing dice or board games, while on the grass around would be boys tossing a ball or playing at kayles, i.e. throwing a stick at ninepins.

Life in the medieval castles was boring, and whenever the weather was suitable the lords gave up their chess and their dice and went off fighting, for this was their chief amusement in the Middle Ages, apart from tournaments.

Boys played the game of quintain, riding on a stick or a hobby-horse and tilting at some kind of target, usually with a lance or a cane, in which case it was called the 'cane game'. In the fourteenth century it could be played on water. Quintain was played on horseback by men, often tilting at a ring attached to a post, or in later times to a sandbag suspended from a pole. There is an old quintain at the village of Offham, in Kent.

14　Water Quintain. England

On Easter Monday, 14 April 1360, 'it was so full dark of mist and hail and so bitter cold, that many men died on their horsebacks with the cold'.

Bowls were played outdoors and there were metal toys both here and in Holland and Germany. The majority of toys were home-made, miniature crossbows and little wooden models such as windmills and kites which were glued together and painted. The children of Edward I had a small cart and a model of a plough.

15　Toy bean-shooter. Choroti, South American

There were shops in the towns and houses where cards were played, while in the country there were 'neterludes, maye games, wakes and revells'. In the winter people used skates made from sheep's bones and boys played handball, football and a kind of hockey.

About 1490 there were toy windmills with sails, tigers with wagging heads, falcons beating their wings, and miniature churches with ringing bells. Leonardo da Vinci made models of flying birds.

The seas were gradually explored and in 1498 Columbus, on his third voyage, reached Trinidad, and on the mainland of America the natives exchanged solid gold ornaments and pearls for European 'toys' such as trinkets, knives and little bells.

Many playthings in the Grand Chaco were similar to those in North America such as their bean-shooters and bows, the ones from the Rio Parapiti being much like those of the Zuni Indians. In Europe and Asia, children had walking aids and small chairs, bigger children played on hobby-horses. Bows and arrows were used for amusement apart from fighting, and in England a plain field was kept at Finsbury for archers. There were bowling-alleys and dicing-houses which according to Stow were 'too much frequented'. Quoits and football were played and there was 'Tenysplaye with a ball full of wynde'. There was also a complaint, 'he hit me in the yie with a tenys-ball'.

16　Figure of carved boxwood. Bavarian

It was the fashion in sixteenth-century Europe to have cabinets in which 'toy collections' were housed and carved cabinets, many from Augsburg in 1519, opened to reveal drawers and cupboards, some showing buildings in perspective, ruins with people and animals and insects. When a cabinet was damaged these little carvings in the round could be mistaken for toys, and the little knights in armour when fixed to stands could become playthings.

When Nuremberg was an Imperial city, the making and selling of toys was an established craft. By 1532 the so-called 'Nuremberger Tand' (*tand* meaning 'toy', 'trifle', 'bauble') made Nuremberg one of the greatest trading centres in medieval Europe. Local toys and foreign toys brought in by merchants were traded, such as watches, carvings in wood, metal and bone.

> *Toys from Nürnberg hand*
> *Go to every land.*

In the U.S.A., an old engraving by van der Venne shows children playing with hoops, kites, windmills, whip-tops and what looks like a live bird on a string. Some girls are shown skipping, boys have bladders and stilts and one child has one of those toys which open like a continuous pair of scissors with something on the end, such as could be purchased at fairs.

17   Detail from a Rubens painting. Flemish

18   Rider of pipe-clay. Made near tobacco factories on River Sieg. Germany

In 1568 toys such as moving jacks and puppets were on sale in the numerous English markets. Cambridge was famous for its fair, and the nobility travelled in crude carriages which were known as 'whirlicotes' and were made without 'straps or strings'.

Shakespeare, aged 11, was taken to see pageants and firework displays, children learnt their ABC from hornbooks and at Harrow the boys had to talk Latin even when tossing the handball, whipping their tops or practising archery.

In Italy, apart from fairs, children might be taken to see elaborate grottoes crowded with automata made by Thomas de Francici, and wooden toys which were marketed from Venice.

In 1577 toys and trifles were bestowed upon the natives by the expedition of Captain Yorke when he explored the 'Icie Seas'. In George Beste's account of the Third Voyage he mentions that 'to allure the brutish and uncivil people we left therein divers of our country's toys as bells and knives (wherein they specially delight), also pictures of men and women in lead, men on horseback, looking glasses, whistles and pipes. Also in the house was made an oven, and bread left baked therein for them to see and taste.'

Shakespeare, when in London, wrote about pastimes in England and the naughty boy who instead of going to school 'did scourge his top, play for pennies, cherie stones, counters, dice and cards'.

Fynes Moryson remarked that 'the English are so naturally inclined to pleasure as there is no country wherein the gentlemen and lords have so many and large parks only reserved for the pleasure of hunting, or where all sorts of men allot so much ground about their homes for pleasure of gardens and orchards'.

In 1610 during Henry Hudson's fateful voyage it was found that the savages had bows and arrows, and the 'toys' which were given to the natives consisted of looking-glasses, whistles and pipes.

John Earle noted in 1625 that children had whipping-tops and kites: 'we laugh at his foolish sports, but his game is our earnest, and his drums, rattles and hobby-horses but the emblems and mockings of men's business'.

Here are a few rareties from the Tradescant Collection of around 1620 which give an idea of the toys at this time:

A Hand of Jet usually given to Children, in Turky, to preserve them from Witchcraft.

A nest of 52 wooden-cups turned within each other as thin as paper.

Divers sorts of ivory balls turned one within another, some 6, some 12 folds, very excellent work.

Indian Conjurors rattle, wherewith he calls up Spirits.

Pictures to be seene by a Celinder which otherwise appeare like confused blotts.

Beads strung upon stiffe wyers, and set in four-square frames wherewith the Indians cast account.

A Set of Chesse-men in a peppercorn turned in ivory.

Bowls were played at the Court of Charles 1 and children played with toys made from pipeclay.

Noah's arks came early in the seventeenth century, and rocking-horses and toys which could be made by carpenters living on the large estates, often for the children of the nobility. Dolls' houses and miniature furniture were made by craftsmen and wonderful silver toys made by silversmiths in England and Holland. The word 'toy' being used by the craft guilds to describe any tiny copy of the real thing in seventeenth- and eighteenth-century Europe.

Races were run in England by country girls as well as boys during the seventeenth century – according to Ashton in his *Ballads of the 17th Century.*

14

1 Baby's coral rattle. Italian. 2 Tarocco counters with box. 3 Lead soldier. German. 4 Animated bone figures. French. 5 Paper soldiers on wood. English. 6 Lottery board. Danish. 7 Peacock boat. Indian. 8 Terracotta soldiers. English.

In half-shirts and drawers these Maids did run
But bonny Nan the race hath won.

One of the first books to show children at play was that of Jacques Stella, *Les Jeux et Plaisirs de l'Enfance*, published in Paris in 1657 with engraved plates, but there were many fires at this time, including the Great Fire of London, when numerous books, wooden toys and dolls must have been turned to ashes.

19 'Boyes-sports', from Comenius's *Visible World*. Czechoslovakia

Tops, ninepins, stilts, swings and toy guns were playthings coming from the districts round Berchtesgaden, Oberammergau, Grödner Valley and Sonneberg. The material known as 'baize', used for card- and billiard-tables, came from the Flemish and Dutch emigrants who settled in Colchester.

Bone skates were still used by boys skating on the ponds, though both Evelyn and Pepys noticed that some had blade skates.

Away in the north, the Eskimo people traded their clothes to the French for knives, scissors, needles, bells, farthings, playing-cards and old sheet music, these goods still being commonly referred to as toys.

In the New World the beautiful home-made playthings gradually found their way into the shops and English toys were sold in America in 1695. In New England and in Pennsylvania where there were German settlers, the toys of the Old World and the New were similar and many of these toys have been handed down from generation to generation.

Matthias Schultz made and repaired playthings for the princes of the Court at Munich, and Perrault in France wrote stories about Cinderella, Bluebeard, Little Red Riding Hood and the Sleeping Beauty in his *Contes*.

'A humming-top and a box of Antick Pictures in a roll under a Glass', were purchased in 1701 by Dr Claver Morris of Wells when he visited London, according to the *Somerset and Dorset Notes and Queries* of June 1938. Children found time to play darts, battledore and shuttlecock, and a game called 'hot cockles', when not embroidering samplers or doing paper-cutting or rolled paperwork.

In the 1700s cheapmen or chapmen travelled the countryside far into the places remote from shops. The little chap-books for children were included in their wares, also broadsides and lottery pictures apart from all kinds of household remedies. Women and children spun at home in their cottages while in the towns children were employed in the factories.

Valuable toys were derived from Meissen novelties, the Chelsea toys being of porcelain and consisting of 'snuff boxes, smelling bottles, etwees and trinkets for watches'. Model tea-sets and beautiful miniature dinner-services were often made specially as gifts for royalty by other potteries because the royal families of Europe were particularly interested in toys, and on their various visits presents would be exchanged between their large families of children.

Henry Crouch, in 1724, published the *Complete View of British Customs*, and in 1732 his *Complete Guide to Officers*. In England since 1660, and all through the eighteenth century, a tax upon toys was 16 pence in every 20 shillings of their value upon oath. In 1747 painted toys were prohibited from being imported. (See page 135.)

20   Toy booth at Bartholomew Fair. London

Tin soldiers and rag dolls were sold in a small toyshop called the Noah's Ark, in High Holborn, London, which had been opened by a Cornishman in 1760. The Cornishman was William Hamley.

Educational pastimes became popular and lettered bricks helped children to spell both in America and in England. By 1767 most nurseries had a horse on wheels and a game of cup and ball.

Maria Edgeworth suggested that children should be taught to use their hands and that toyshops should be stocked with miniature carpenter's tools, with nails and screws, and pieces of wood prepared ready for use.

Southern German toy-makers showed their wares at Leipzig in 1775, a town now more important than Nuremberg, where the annual trade fairs were held.

In 1771 and 1775 advertisements for tin drums, rattles, 'drest and naked' dolls and other toys appeared in the American newspapers. In 1785 was Long's advertisement for rocking-horses. Coach-builders, sign-writers and furniture-makers were there in the mid eighteenth century and they would have known how to carve horses, make wagon wheels and miniature furniture, many of them having arrived from England and the continent of Europe.

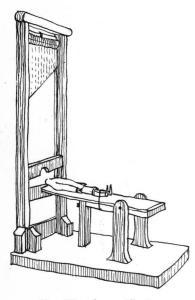

21   Wooden guillotine

During the French Revolution, women wore tiny guillotines as ornaments, and children were given toy guillotines with which they could decapitate the toy figures of aristocrats, according to J. H. Robinson in *Medieval and Modern Times*.

Small models of furniture decorated with straw were made by French prisoners-of-war at Porchester Castle, Hampshire, in 1794. The straw was taken from their beds when the castle was used as a prison.

Coleridge, the English poet, when travelling in Germany in 1798 noted the custom of erecting great boughs of yew at Christmas-time, laden with little tapers so that the twigs and needles snapped as the flames reached them.

On Christmas Day 1800, Queen Charlotte, wife of George III, was staying at Queen's Lodge, Windsor. In the evenings children from the principal families in the neighbourhood were invited for entertainment at the Lodge. This year there was an immense tub in the centre of the room containing a yew tree, and from the branches hung bunches of sweetmeats, almonds, raisins in paper, and fruits and toys 'most tastefully arranged, and the whole illuminated by small wax candles'. Each child was given some sweets and a toy after the whole company had walked round and admired the tree.

At the beginning of the nineteenth century, wooden toys predominated but metal toys could be more realistic. Gradually brass and tin playthings increased in number, mechanical toys became popular and later when the technique of stamping from sheet-metal was discovered, toys were turned out in their thousands by this method.

The little King of Rome, son of Napoleon I, born in March 1811, and later to become Napoleon II, had many toys made especially for him by Cacheleux in 1812. In August there was a list containing tops, drums, a nest of 15 boxes, a velvet football, a wheelbarrow of cherry-tree wood, a spade and shovel also of this wood, a Noah's ark with 52 carved pieces, wooden guns, a cannon and a game of ninepins. This was a vast amount of toys for a baby of 17 months.

In October 1812, Cacheleux entered the following: 'two wooden guns adorned with velvet and embroidered with spangles, and an item for repairing the clasps of two mechanical toys'. In November, again for the royal child, Cacheleux made two guns, two clasp-knives, a cradle of pink satin containing a doll with enamel eyes and a cage containing four mechanical birds.

Victoria of England, born 1819, was another royal child who must have been inundated with toys. Many of hers came from her numerous relations in Germany, but Victoria had a strict upbringing and like so many children of her class there was not much time for play. They would work samplers at an early age with such rhymes as

> *Let not the Morrow*
> *Your vain thoughts employ*
> *But think this Day*
> *The last you shall enjoy.*
> (From a child's sampler, Cirencester Museum)

It was left to other children to play tops, hoops and marbles in the streets of the towns or in the country.

22   Child with a butterfly-net. English

In 1830 the old Argyll Rooms, in which stalls had displayed dolls and toys, were burnt down while M. Chabert, known as the 'Fire King', was holding a show. The new building in its place was eventually converted into shops.

On Christmas Eve 1832, at Kensington Palace, the future Queen Victoria, then aged 13, wrote in her *Journal*, 'we then went into the drawing room near the dining room. After Mama had rung a bell three times we went in. There were two large round tables on which were placed two trees hung with lights and sugar ornaments. All the presents being placed round the tree. I had one table for myself.'

A picture of the 1830s shows an American family group with a doll, a miniature tallboy, a skipping-rope, a battledore and a shuttlecock. Dissected maps, china toy tea-sets, battledores and jumping-ropes were advertised in 1833, and the metal toys of 1840 were made at the Philadelphia Tin Toy Manufactory.

23 German bandsman. Biberach, Germany

At this time much of the juvenile reading was what we now call the 'Penny Dreadfuls'. These were read by others than children, especially little servants in their garrets, and nannies who would tell the children in their charge hair-raising stories. It is no wonder that so many of the children were afraid of the dark, what with stories of foul deeds on dark nights, murders and ghosts, and large rooms with recesses and many-curtained doorways to keep out the draughts. The huge chimneys in which a man might hide were plenty big enough for Father Christmas to come down at Christmas-time.

Exhibitions always produce something new and the one held in Paris in 1844 was no exception. Novelty dolls, toys, model carriages and furniture appeared. By 1851, the Crystal Palace Exhibition year, there were many Punch and Judy shows, dancing dolls, the Fantoccini and mechanical figures.

Queen Victoria and other members of the Royal Family would order toys from Whiteley's for their numerous children and the Duke of Edinburgh used to visit the Christmas Bazaar and buy toys and other gifts, thus adding a fillip to trade.

In 1852 there were toys made of copper, and in the same year rubber dolls and toys came from the U.S.A.

'Baby has got an India rubber rattle and a small fat tumbler. I have found a large beautiful toyshop at Newcastle and if you like I will send you a doll from it', so wrote 'Cecilia' on 5 December 1858, but so far the author has not been able to ascertain who Cecilia was.

In 1851 Livingstone discovered the Zambezi River in Africa and at this time many travellers, missionaries and even soldiers returned from distant lands with primitive toys, many of which, fortunately, may be seen in museums.

In the *Illustrated London News* for January 1855, there is an interesting item regarding New Year gifts in France:

'. . . except in the lowest booths, and scarcely even there, you seek in vain the modest dolls, the small puppets, the minutest horses of wood, the lines of fierce soldiers in lead of other days. Objects of

18

far greater value, playthings unknown to the past generation, articles of complicated mechanism and of fabulous prices have replaced them. . . . Toys of 1,200f or 2,000f, or even more, must sooner or later, disappear from the places where they are now exhibited so temptingly, for no means will suffice to purchase them.'

When in Paris, in 1855, Queen Victoria mentioned that the 'Emperor and Empress of France had a table covered with toys they had brought for the children; a doll and trousseau, beautiful soldiers for Arthur, a panarama [sic], games, a beautiful little picture of a dog en gobelin, for Vicky and, finally two beautiful models of the nine-pounders the Emperor has himself invented, and which he showed off with great pleasure.'

In 1863 it was noted that Princess Beatrice was brought up in an atmosphere of simplicity, and when at Balmoral she slept in a little iron bedstead and in one corner of her room was a china doll with sawdust-filled legs.

In 1860 there were aluminium toys, and in 1869 came the invention of celluloid, and some time after this toys of this highly inflammable material were manufactured.

The roller-skating craze came in 1870 and for a few years the Patent Office was flooded with applications for patents for skates. The toys in the U.S.A. were similar to those of Europe, many of the makers being youths from Germany who had crossed the water in order to avoid conscription in 1872.

24   Child with skipping-rope. English

Small toys and watches were made of an alloy consisting of 25 per cent zinc and 75 per cent copper, known as 'pinchbeck'. It was named after Christopher Pinchbeck, a toy-seller in Cockburn Street who died in 1873. McKensie and McBurney had their 'one shilling store' at Dundee, in Scotland in 1876.

Renoir, a painter of the Second Empire, 1878, painted many pictures of French children at play. Not only do they show the costume they also show dolls and hoops and little dinner-services.

At the beginning of the twentieth century Queen Victoria died and everyone wore black including the children. From 1900 to 1910, it was the Edwardian era, a time of peace in England.

In 1910 the chief warehouses for toys were in Houndsditch. In stocking a toyshop '£100 worth of stock goes a long way towards making a brave show. Toys to retail at one penny to sixpence cost 7/6 to 8/6 per gross, toy picture books 2/- to 8/- per dozen, Snap and Happy Families sell from 6d to 3/- per pack, and mechanical toys are splendid sellers, including trams, rolling stock operated by clockwork, steam, and even the electric current on the three-rail plan of the District Railway.'

Proprietors were advised to have something working in their window 'for this was sure *to attract the attention of the fathers*'.

Wooden toys were universal for many parents considered tin toys to be dangerous and beautifully carved painted toys from India found a ready market.

In the early twentieth century, the most popular toys were the rocking-horse, the doll's house, nested blocks, soldiers, ninepins, perhaps a musical-box and a humming-top, and a boat for the summer holidays, when both boys and girls wore 'sailor suits'.

All manner of toys could be bought in shops known as the D.B.C., that was the Domestic Bazaar Company, where prices ranged from one penny to sixpence and not so very much more. Ninepins, hoops, drums, tambourines, dolls, dolls' straw hats and little kitchen stoves lined the shelves or hung from the ceilings of these packed shops.

With two pennies a week pocket-money, there seemed to be no end to the delights and time well spent in gazing around. If parents visited London they returned with toys from Gamages, Hamley's or Selfridge's, and from Paris from Le Nain Bleu.

When war came in 1914 celluloid dolls marked 'Made in Germany' were squashed underfoot by French children and the cryptic letters D.R.G.M. were said by patriotic schoolboys to stand for 'Dirty Rotten German Muck', instead of *Deutsches-Reichs Gebrauchs Muster*. Celluloid and rubber toys arrived from the U.S.A., wooden toys were made by disabled soldiers and sandbags were included in boxes of toy soldiers for playing at trench warfare. Board games were brought up to date including Snakes and Ladders, where hazards such as submarines and mines were added.

The material Bakelite had been invented in 1909, but toys of this man-made substance did not come for a long while and it was not until 1925 that people became plastic-conscious.

It was some time before the German toys returned, but during the 1920s and 1930s toys were cheap and plentiful.

The pogo-stick craze was in 1924, a kind of stick with a wheel and a spring, on which people could leap about like kangaroos. There was a dance tune and a song, 'Oh, the Ogo, Ogo Pogo Man'. The only German toys to bear arms in the 1930s were Crusaders, medieval archers and later on, cowboys. There were diesel locomotives, Siebengebirge dwarfs, cuddly animals and of course, dolls. The first Rustler and Lone Star pistols sold in Germany were made in Britain and small boys sniped at passers-by with British-made colts.

Blue pillar-boxes in which to post airmail letters were made by Dinky Toys, and in 1935 there was a model van, also blue, which was used to collect the mail from the special boxes.

When war came again in 1939, the toyshops gradually emptied, and people took to making toys at home. Paper patterns were sold for making stuffed animals and masks were sold to make faces for rag dolls. These thin linen masks were not pretty but if one hunted around, glass eyes could still be purchased for the stuffed animals. Owing to coupons being necessary for new material, old stuff was used. Stripy cows were assembled, spotted dogs covered with flowers, patchwork Humpty Dumptys and curious cows, animals which had never been seen on earth. Rag books disappeared, the first Puffins arrived and most books were printed on poor-quality paper with restricted margins.

25   Tin lid toy. English

Children were warned not to pick anything up when outdoors because bombs made like butterflies were dropped by the Germans, which would explode in the hands if touched, but strips and strips of silver shavings lying about on the ground (to confuse Radar and called 'window') were saved to decorate Christmas-trees. In 1943, in November, the ban on metal toys was lifted for Christmas but no toy was to cost more than 34s. 6d.

In 1944, Anne Frank wrote in her diary that 'Miep sent us a currant cake made up in the shape of a doll, with the words Happy Whitsun on the note attached to it.' A small collection of stuffed toys has been preserved which were made by Polish women in Belsen for the first children's party held after the liberation.

In 1829 Commander Ross had written, 'Let no man imagine that he knows what a present is worth till he has found what happiness can be produced by a blue bead, a needle, or a piece of an old iron hoop', and the same was true 110 years later.

During the war the wood and metal toys which had gradually disappeared, along with many garden railings, did not appear again in the same form. The Plastic Age had begun. It was no longer possible to buy a metal man, a ladder and a lamp-post all in a box for sixpence. Not only had the toys changed, but also the manner in which they were wrapped.

Transparent plastic bags or pretty coloured nets took the place of the cardboard boxes which in their turn had replaced those of chip and bast, just as matches are now in cardboard boxes and strawberries in synthetic punnets instead of baskets. (Reels of cotton purchased in 1968 were plastic instead of the wooden ones which had been in use since the beginning of the twentieth century when spools were discarded.)

Japanese toys returned to the shops, shuttlecocks, flying birds and kites which still play an important part in festivals both in India and Africa, where intricate paper houses were made by Muslim children for their New Year festivals.

However, the toy-makers seemed to think that the children themselves had changed during the war years. Nursery cocktail sets appeared with non-alcoholic drinks and miniature electric shavers, but tiny children could be comforted by dolls which glowed faintly in the dark. In 1958, on the top of a Christmas-tree made of goose feathers was a plastic spaceman in Martian-style helmet instead of the traditional fairy.

In a road safety campaign in the U.S.A., toy British policemen were awarded as prizes to the American children. Toys were also given away as free gifts, especially in packets containing cereals – plastic aeroplanes, missiles, boomerangs, spacemen with transparent hoods, plastic horses with weights, and puzzle motor cars, the majority of these coming from Hong Kong.

Another change was the disappointing fact that toys were no longer so well made. Some on Christmas morning being already

26 Horse and man, weighted. Probably Hong Kong

21

broken by lunchtime, a far cry from those which had been passed down from generation to generation.

When the World's Fair was held in Brussels in 1958, models of the Sputnik, launched the year before, were given away in the Russian Pavilion. Early one morning, while staying in Paris, Mr Khrushchev rose and went out in the parks where he distributed model Sputniks to the playing children. These were the very latest thing in the toy world and could 'bleep, bleep' almost continuously. Needless to say there was great consternation in the hotel when Mr Khrushchev was discovered to be missing.

Miniature guitars, tape recorders, headphones, walkie-talkie sets, moonscopes with which to follow the latest Lunik, all show how grown-up the toys were becoming, not to mention that by 1960 little nurses and boys playing doctors had hypodermic needles included in their outfits. By 1967, these children had become what were known as 'teenagers'.

After November 1967, the making of celluloid toys was banned.

Just to show how important toys have become in the present age, exports to Germany from Britain were worth over £1,630,000 during 1966 and 1967, but a toy has to be about 30 years old before a collector begins to take notice.

Anything before 1890 is now considered antique, so when a person of today reaches the age of 70, the toys of their childhood have reached this category and their price has risen accordingly.

Sometimes a toy will have been handed down from generation to generation, others may have changed owners many times. Some are as old as Methuselah, even older, for he was only 969 when he died. Others will be as short-lived as a toy balloon which gives so much pleasure and looks so pretty until it bursts.

This makes me think of all the toys I have omitted, such as the white clay pipes, with ends of sealing-wax, for blowing soap bubbles in the early twentieth century, and the present-day wire rings through which one blows effortlessly a multitude of bubbles, which even the most ardent toy-collector could never hope to keep.

Punch, 1891. 'O, Mammy darling, why can't the Toyshop man call for orders every morning, like the Baker?'

27 Stone ball. North-east Scotland

28 Ball of twisted rushes. Egypt

29 Leather ball. Egypt

2 Balls, marbles, rattles, poupards, ninepins, tops

BALLS

A lump of clay thrown from hand to hand soon assumes a more perfect shape, a tuft of grass when thrown to and fro becomes round by merely pressing it in the hand, and thus we have a ball, the earliest known toy.

Why stone balls were made and carved it is difficult to imagine, but they have been found and a date given somewhere about 3000 to 2000 B.C. Those found in Scotland were almost black with age, decorated with raised marks and stripes, a few with traces of red paint and a circular design carved in relief, and all very heavy to handle.

Two and a half inches in diameter is a convenient size for a ball when held in the hand, and most tossing balls, whether of plaited rushes, leather or wood, are about this size.

Among playthings, balls have a long history; stuffed leather and plaited rush balls were found at Chanhudaro dating from about 2500 B.C., and balls of these materials seem to have been used all over the world, each different country using local materials, and down through the centuries various games with balls have been played, from the baby crawling along the ground to the old-age pensioner stooping on the bowling-green.

Plaited rush balls are seen on wall-paintings in Egypt belonging to the Twelfth dynasty, that is about 1786 B.C. They were sometimes of papyrus fibre or of flax, and being light were probably for girls who played catch. In one game, should a girl miss a catch she had to take another girl on her back until she also missed.

30 Putting the stone

31 Girls playing catch. Egypt

23

Heavier balls were used to bowl along the ground, simple ones of grey pottery or porcelain balls beautifully striped in blue and white and glazed.

Most ancient ball games seemed to be either tossing or bowling without the aid of a stick or bat, but about 1100 B.C. the Persians played ball on horseback using a mallet or malet, and in Tibet this game was called *pulu*, meaning ball. Homer mentions balls in the *Odyssey*, 860 B.C., and, in the Bible, Isaiah, about 550 B.C., says 'he will surely toss thee like a ball'.

In 400 B.C. balls were made from 12 pieces of skin, each piece being in the shape of a regular pentagon. These, when sewn together, would form a regular dodecahedron which became reasonably spherical when made from fairly pliable leather and stuffed with papyrus grass, chopped straw, hair or thread.

According to Phaedo, Socrates talking to Simmias said, 'Well, my dear boy, the real earth when viewed from above is supposed to look like one of these balls made from 12 pieces of skin, variegated and marked out in different colours, of which the colours we know are only limited samples like the paints which artists use.'

The baby Zeus had a multi-coloured ball with which to play, and light balls were made of wool, but were not so strong as those of leather. In one game the Greeks rolled a ball down a sloping board into a hole in the ground a few feet away.

Balls were dedicated to the infant Dionysus in Greece, where they were made of various materials including wool and clay, those of pottery being usually used for bowling along the ground. Bouncing balls were made of split cane and were similar to those made in the Malay Peninsula today. Those in Rome, 27 B.C., were made of cloth or hide and could be stuffed with feathers, hair or even fig seeds. A statue was erected to Aristonicus for his skill in playing ball, for it was a pastime for people of all ages, not just for the young.

In England during the years of the Roman occupation, balls of alabaster were used in play. These may have been bowled along the ground by children or tossed by sporting youths.

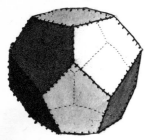

32　Ball with 12 sides

33　Ball game. Greece

34　Porcelain ball. Egypt

35　Ball of split cane. Malay Peninsula

36　Stone ball. Romano-British

In France, in the fourth century A.D., a bishop named Sidonius Apollinaris described how after a religious ceremony, the clerics and the laymen lay stretched out on the grass in the shade and talked animatedly about literature, and after this they played long games of handball.

Bigger balls were made for kicking with the foot, and in the seventh century football was played in Japan at Tai-ho.

Much has been written about the ball game known as 'tlachtli' played by the Aztecs, partly because it was the first time that a hard ball of rubber was used. About A.D. 700 the game was played in a court shaped rather like the capital letter 'I' and with walls extended all round. In the middle of each 'stem' a stone or wooden ring was set vertically and through this the players tried to pass the ball. They were allowed to hit it only with their elbows, hips or legs. The game was played far and wide, and courts have been found from the republic of Honduras to south-eastern Arizona.

This use of a rubber ball is especially interesting, for not until the sixteenth century was it mentioned when Oviedo described the game and its players. Montezuma II played a game of basketball with the Chief of Texcoco for a wager, but he lost and all kinds of woes followed which upset the inhabitants of the Mexican valley, making them superstitious.

The Anglo-Saxons played ball, and throughout the Middle Ages handball was popular with everyone, especially during the Easter holidays. William Fitz-Stephen noted during the twelfth century that in the winter 'the ball is used by noblemen and gentlemen in tennis courts and by people of meaner sort in the open fields and streets'. Handball was mentioned several times in the twelfth century and in 1361 the scholars at Winchester School were forbidden to play ball games in chapel.

37   Tossing the ball

38   A game of bowls, near Smithfield, London

39   Bat and ball, near Smithfield

Bowls were popular in 1366 and Edward III, afraid that his men would give up practising archery, said that he considered the game 'dishonourable, useless and unprofitable'. Bowling went to America with the first settlers, but did not enter its modern phase until 1895. (In 1960 some of the 'bowling-alleys' had nurseries attached where mothers could leave their babies while they had a game.)

A boys' game played with a club in the fourteenth century was called 'bandy'. It was the forerunner of golf and was also known as 'cambue'.

40   The game of Bandy, with curved stick. England

Little Edward V amused himself by playing handball when he was 12 years old and a prisoner in the Tower of London.

Walter von der Vogelweide mentioned that ball in Germany was the first sport of summer in the Middle Ages, 'when I saw the girls on the street throwing the ball, then came to our ears the song of the birds', and in England Sir Thomas Elyot wrote that football was a game of 'beastly furie and exstreme violence' and wished it forbidden.

Trapball in the fourteenth century was played with the 'trap' slightly raised so that the player was standing upright when he struck the lever which raised the ball in such a position that it could be hit away.

Later traps were a shoe-shaped box with a wooden lever placed upon the ground and in order to strike this the player had to stoop down, the examples in the museums at Cambridge and Hertford varying slightly. Boys without this special contrivance would make a round hole in the ground and place the ball on the flat brisket bone of an ox which they used as a lever. Bats were usually short and wide but the game could be played by using a stick. The boys at Eton played trapball in 1765.

When Charles Moritz, a young Prussian clergyman, came to England in 1782, he observed when in Richmond, Surrey, 'on a large green area in the middle of the town, a number of boys . . . were enjoying themselves, and playing at trap-ball'. This is mentioned in *A Prospect of Richmond* by Janet Dunbar.

Rather similar to trapball was the game of piggy, played in Yorkshire at least until 1910. Instead of a ball, a stick was placed on a flat stone or brick. The stick, being about $\frac{3}{4}$ inch in diameter and 4–5 inches long, was sharpened at one end like a pencil, and nose, eyes and ears sometimes drawn on in ink to represent a pig. A flattened stick or bat was used to hit the snout, when it somersaulted upwards and was hit again as it fell down. The object of the game was to hit it as far as possible and count the steps from the stone to where the piggy fell. Another name for this game was 'tipcat'.

41 The game of Trapball. England

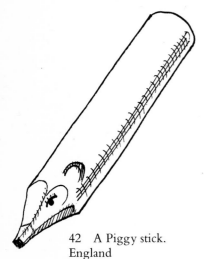

42 A Piggy stick. England

43 The game of Trapball. England

26

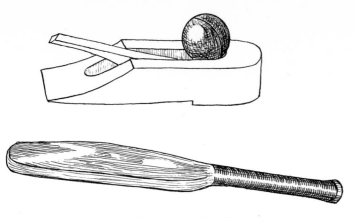

44   Bat, trap and ball.
English

45   Boys playing with
ball and mallets

A Parisian woman named Margot played hand-tennis in 1424 using the palm and the back of her hand 'better than any man'. Games must have been exciting, for Charles VIII of France died while watching a game of tennis, which was now played by royalty.

Early in the sixteenth century on the right hand of Whitehall 'be divers fair tennis courts and bowling alleys and a cockpit'. In the expenditure items for Henry VII appeared 'for the kings loss at tennis, twelvepence; for the loss of balls, threepence'.

Henry VIII in 1512 played bowls and was also good at tennis. He wore special coats when playing and he also had some tennis slippers. White goatskin tennis-balls filled with hair have been found in the roof timbers of Hampton Court and also in the Tower of London, slightly smaller than modern tennis-balls, the game being different from that of today.

By 1514 stone bullets were used in warfare and perhaps these have been mistaken for balls as they have been unearthed from time to time. By 1550 stone bullets were replaced by iron ones.

Cricket was played in Guildford about 1550.

In Shakespeare's time footballs were sometimes made of leather with a sheep's bladder inside. The game was played by the common people and again in England it was referred to, this time by Phillip Stubbes, as a 'bloody and murderous practice'. Bladders were also used, and an engraving of 1587 shows these being blown up by youths at the side of a playground. In a painting by Peter Brueghel the Elder, done in 1560, there is a child swimming in a river with a bladder tucked up under each arm like the water-wings of the early twentieth century, while another child has a long streamer to which is fastened a bladder which may have been flown as a toy balloon.

In 1561 the Arabian knights used a long mallet, and balls were hit with mallets in many games which became popular with princes at French and Italian Courts.

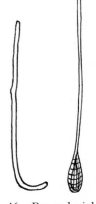

46   Bat and stick

27

Francis Drake played bowls; most people know he was doing this on Plymouth Hoe when the Spanish Armada loomed on the distant horizon in 1588. But why should a croquet-ball be the exact size of a cannon-ball? At home, we had one which was so like the black ball that when no one was looking we would swop it before the game commenced. A gentle tap with a mallet – nothing happened; a harder tap and still the ball remained stationary, then who ever had chosen black realised that all was not as it should be!

John Earle remarked that a bowling-alley 'is the place where there are three things thrown away besides bowls, to wit, time, money and curses and the last ten for one'.

Many games were played with balls both outdoors and indoors, and beautiful balls of coloured porcelain were made for rolling along the galleries of the stately homes of England in Early Jacobean times. These were sometimes known as 'carpet balls'. Henry Devigne, a French artist, may have invented the game of billiards, which in Jacobean days seems to have been played with hooped goalposts on a table and the ball hit with a kind of club.

There were a number of tennis-courts in London during the mid seventeenth century, and many of these were let out for hire. The Duke of Bedford went several times to the tennis-court in 1661.

Boys in America were not allowed to play football in the streets of Boston in 1657, in fact football seems to have been a 'bloody' game wherever it was played, though Shrove Tuesdays were days set apart for play at Chester and in the Strand, London.

Edward Phillips, a nephew of Milton, mentions cricket in 1650 in his *Mysteries of Love and Eloquence*, and Thomas Samborne remarked

48 Carpet balls or 'Woods'. English

on a 'certain healthy exercise called Fives'. By 1653 a long bat was used for sending a ball through a hoop, and handball alone seems gradually to have been left to children.

Young Henry, the son of King James, enjoyed playing tennis and also a Scots game which was said to be like mall, another forerunner of golf. It was said that none of Henry's amusements 'has any smack of childishness'.

49   Mallets and balls for Paille Maille

The French ball game of Paille Maille or Pale Maille was to hit a ball through an iron arch by means of a wooden mallet, using as few strokes as possible.

'The Mall' in St James's Park was commonly regarded as the place where the game of paille maille was first played in England. Strutt calls it the game of 'mall' but in 'the spacious street between the Haymarket, N.E. of St James Street S.W. we have preserved the entire name of the game – Pall Mall'.

Charles II caused the Mall in the Park to be made for playing the game, which was a fashionable amusement in his reign, but it was introduced into England much earlier. By Sir Robert Dallington, in a *Method of Travel*, 1598, paille maille was described as an exercise of France, and in *A French Garden for English Ladies*, 1621, it was described as a French game. King James I in his *Basilicon Doron*, recommended paille maille as a field game for the use of his eldest son, Prince Henry.

Pell Mell Close was partly planted with apple trees (Apple Tree Yard still exists), and the name of Pall Mall occurs in the rate books of St Martin-in-the-Fields under the year 1656.

Pepys mentioned the game as played in the park – '2nd April, 1661: to St James Park, where I saw the Duke of York playing at Pele-Mele, the first time I ever saw the sport.'

In 1670 Nell Gwyn lived on the east end north side, in a house on the south side with a garden towards the park, and according to Evelyn: 'it was upon a mound in this garden that the impudent comedian stood, to hold her familiar discourse with Charles II who stood on ye green walk under the wall'.

The name is derived from *palla*, a ball, and *maglia*, a mallet, and a set was described in the *Curiosities of London*.

In 1854 were found a box containing four pairs of mailles or mallets, and one ball such as were formerly used for playing the game of Pall Mall upon the side of the above house, No. 68. . . . Each Maille is four feet in length and is made of lance-wood; the head is slightly curved and measures outwardly $5\frac{1}{2}''$, the inner curve being $4\frac{1}{2}''$, the diameter of the Maille ends is $2\frac{1}{2}''$, each shod with a thin iron

29

hoop; the handle which is very elastic, is bound with white leather to the breadth of two hands, and terminated with a collar of jagged leather. The ball is of boxwood, $2\frac{1}{2}''$ in diameter. The pair of mailles and a ball have been presented to the British Museum by Mr George Vuilliamy.

This account appears in the *Illustrated London News* for 9 June 1855.

50   The game of Paille Maille

Slate billiard-tables were used in England, the players using a mace until 1826, when the cue was introduced into this country by foreigners.

Children played with hollow rubber balls about 1839, many brightly coloured and of all sizes. These balls have been made ever since, except possibly during the Second World War, when embroidered balls made in sections like those in the days of Socrates took their place.

A golf-ball of 1840 is in the Museum of Leathercraft. It is of tawed leather hide and sewn so that the stitches never come to the surface. It is filled with feathers, 'as many as would fill a top hat'. In the late nineteenth century the bladder inside a football was replaced by one of India rubber.

Shinny was played in the U.S.A. about 1840, named for the damage to the shins caused by the sticks. Toole's picture of the game being played on ice may depict the game as the forerunner of ice-hockey.

By 1850 croquet was common in England and was played by both sexes. When crinolines were fashionable, ladies discovered that they made an ideal covering for surreptitiously moving the ball into a better position. There were croquet tournaments and games in the vicarage garden, but as yet no woman played tennis in spite of the example set by Margot in the fifteenth century.

'Trock' was the U.S.A. name given to a kind of indoor croquet played on a table, and in England indoor croquet sets could be purchased during the latter end of the nineteenth century and are popular at the present day.

'La Crosse' was demonstrated at the Crystal Palace in 1867 and was said to have become the national game of the colonists in Canada. At the demonstration it was played by a team of Indians wearing smart red and white outfits, the game being declared exciting and not as dangerous as hockey or football. Baseball was essentially an American game and was played in England in 1874 by two teams from the U.S.A. It was preferred to cricket in that country and was a game much like rounders only with more rules.

When women took to playing tennis, elder brothers in 1878 were warned that the game facilitated flirting:

> the healthy and invigorating exercise calling up the exquisite rose tints to the rounded cheek, the brilliant light to the speaking eye; and the constant motion, displaying to advantage the graceful gestures and the piquant costumes of England's fair daughters of the present day – all these, together with the sparkling jest and merry laugh equally revealing the ready wit and pearly teeth of the gentle players, combine to render the games particularly dangerous to all who have not steeled themselves against such insidious and too irresistible attractions.

This extraordinary description of the game of tennis is quoted from the *Boy's Own Book* of that year.

A game peculiar to the Irish was that of road bowling, popular in the 1890s, and described by Alan Fitzpatrick. This was played on the roads, generally with one player a side, each throwing in turn a small iron ball, the object being to cover a set distance in the least number of throws. The ball, called a 'bullet' or a 'bowl', weighed about two pounds, and on summer Sundays the game is still played in the by-roads of Cork and Armagh, often followed by spectators who lay wagers as to who will be the winner.

In parts of Norfolk a game called 'knur spell' was played with a 'knur' which was a round ball of hard wood, hit with a 'kibble'.

A modern football is of 12 identical panels; it is sewn by hand, then turned inside out, and is the same as that made by Joseph Pracy in 1903 and known as the 'Locust Ball'.

Since the Second World War many balls have been made at home and stuffed. Cut from paper patterns with eight or ten sections, they are usually made up of coloured felt and embroidered – they are pretty indoor playthings and suitable for young children when sequins are omitted from the decoration.

A new toy appeared in 1968, a pear-shaped rubber ball on which a child could sit and bounce along the ground. It was called the 'Ride-a-Roo kangaroo jockey ball' and worth $3. They were made in England, the inventor refusing to be identified in spite of the U.S.A. ordering over £6,000,000 worth from Stanley Tozer of Worcester. This kind

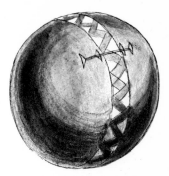

51 Cricket-ball of mangrove wood. Trobriand Islands

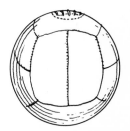

52 The 'Locust Ball' by Joseph Pracy. England

of toy was also known as 'the fantastic space hopper', the child gripping two rubber 'handles' as it bounced along.

There is no end to the size and variety of balls with which children play; from the brightly coloured ones of threaded beads from Africa, and the Chorotis where seeds or pebbles are placed inside to make them rattle like those of ancient Greece, to the square balls of Samoa woven from the leaves of the palm tree, and the round plastic balls of today. However, by June 1969 there was not a rubber ball to be found in the local toyshop, except for a few small ones of Sorbo rubber. All the other balls were of plastic in various sizes and colours, the colours having been sprayed on, leaving slightly wuzzy edges.

53   Tocoro ball containing nuts. Choroti, South American

54   Japanese girl with bouncing ball

55   Ball of plaited cane

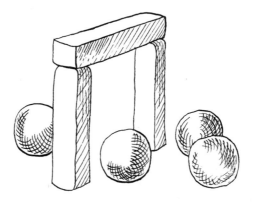

56   Stone marbles. Egyptian

MARBLES

Marbles, that is little balls, were used in play long, long ago, by grown-ups and by children. Some were found in a child's grave at Nagada, Egypt, belonging to the fourth millennium B.C., together with a set of ninepins and three rectangular bricks which could have formed an arch through which to trickle the balls.

A centre for making marbles and beads was at Chanhudaro in 2500 B.C. Here they were made of jasper and agate and were used in games, and Minoan boys played with pebbles and knucklebones in 1453 B.C. Many round pellets of clay have been found in England dating from 312 B.C. which could easily be marbles, some having designs similar to those on the stone balls from the Stone Age.

Roman children in 27 B.C. played marbles, and it is said that Caesar Augustus descended from his litter in order to join in a game with nuts and marbles when he came across a group of boys· playing. In fact nuts and the galls from the oak tree make good playthings.

Marbles seem to belong to any age from prehistoric times to the present day, played with on their own or as part of a game. Many glazed marbles belong to a period about A.D. 200, and were favourite treasures with soldiers. A game such as solitaire was said to have been invented by a prisoner in the Bastille during the seventeenth century, and is played on a round board, sometimes with marbles, sometimes with rounded pegs.

In 1788 Hoffman invented a machine for making marbles for children, and took out an English patent:

> There are stones broke to an inch and a half square or two inches square to be put into concentric circles, of which the bottom part is stone and the top part wood, which may be alternately changed, so that either the top or bottom part may perform the revolution. The forming of the marbles is done by percussion, and not turned upon the centre, as billiard balls or fossils turned into small globes, etc.

Bristol, a town well known for glass manufacture, made marbles of glass, some of which are in Pollock's Toy Museum. Another source was the Toy and Marble Warehouse in 8 Great Street, St Andrews Street, London, belonging to J. Pitts in 1813. Threaded marbles are very beautiful.

The *Boy's Own Book* in the U.S.A. for 1829, included a rating of marbles. The cheapest were of variegated clay, known as 'Dutch', the next were of yellow stone with spots or circles of black or brown, and the best were taws, large choice marbles much prized by their owners, and the pink marble ones with dark red veins were called 'blood alleys', possibly a corruption of the word 'alabaster'.

Cüno and Otto Dressel, of Sonneberg, made marbles of glass and of porcelain in 1875.

Games of marbles were played in the Orange Free State in 1892, but never by girls. Boys played 'big ring', which may have come from the Cape Malays. A ring was drawn by scratching with a stick on the dusty surface of the school playground, or market square, about ten or 15 feet across, and the surface trodden bare and flat in the hot African sunlight.

The marbles consisted of a 'vaalie', which was a common baked-clay marble, a 'lemmie', which was a green glass marble like those from lemonade bottles, and 'glassies', which had beautiful internal stripes of various colours. Players shot from the outside ring with the 'goen', the boys leant over the line but no part of their body must touch it. The marble chosen as the goen could even be a golf- or a billiard-ball.

Another game with marbles was 'fatty', played by younger boys, in which the marbles were knocked out of a tiny ellipse about 12 inches long and six inches wide. A glassie was worth about 24 vaalies.

The word 'marble' should only apply to the little balls of clay or marble. The glass ones are really the glassies or taws known to most boys as such, though early in the twentieth century round the districts of Bethnal Green some boys referred to these as 'glannies'. Incidentally, marbles are not played with in the fee-paying schools. Here, in the playgrounds boys played with model cars in the late 1940s, a pastime which would have been scorned by the ten-year-old marble-playing boys.

57 'Choice marbles or taws'. English

58 Rattle of stone. Egyptian

59 Rattle in the shape of a pig. Roman

RATTLES

The history of rattles is lost in obscurity. Hollow rattles from Chanhudaro, about 2500 B.C., had pellets within and made a noise when shaken, some were ball-shaped, some were in the shape of animals. They could have made a sound loud enough to ward off evil spirits at the time of a birth or at a death or they could simply be shaken to make a gentle tinkling sound to amuse a baby.

A child's rattle made of earthenware about 1360 B.C. was found at Tel el-Armarna, Egypt, and is now in the Horniman Museum. Here also are timeless Japanese rattles made like balls; in the centre of each is a bivalve shell containing a pebble. These balls are filled with bran and covered with silk.

The Greeks were fond of making clay rattles in the shape of pigs, a significance between childhood and the god Bacchus. Others were in the shape of birds, pigeons and owls being popular between 400 and 300 B.C. Some were dedicated to the infant Dionysus, and were surely used by babies, for there are no protuberances to hurt a child, the little pig's ears being smoothed away, and there were no legs on the pigs or on the birds which are so easily broken.

Both balls and rattles were dedicated to the infant Bacchus and

34

later, when the owners grew older, the girls' toys would be offered to Diana and those of the boys to Mercury or other gods. 'Philocles consecrated to Hermes his bouncing ball, his resounding rattle of boxwood, his knucklebones which he loved so much, his revolving top, the toys of his younger days.'

Today's children at Christmas-time take a cast-off toy to the Toy Service held in many churches, and it is a pretty sight to watch these tiny mites clutching their toys and parting from them. However, it has been said that they should take one which they really love, otherwise it is no sacrifice. What busy-bodies some of these grown-ups are! Do they send off their best clothes to the local jumble sale?

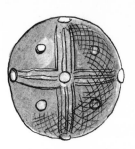

60 Pottery rattle. Mexican

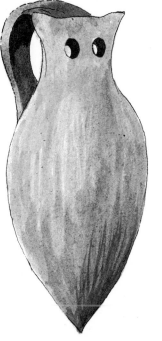

61 Striped pottery rattle. Mohenjodaro

62 Clay rattle. Cyprus

63, 64 Baked clay rattles. Greece

A beautiful little rattle found at Pompeii differs little from those of today, being a circle on a stick with beads threaded round the ring. The colour blue was regarded as a powerful prophylactic, and both in Greece and Turkey a blue bead would be fastened to a rattle or tied in the child's hair.

Cremer wrote in 1875 that 'a comica [*sic*] human head of extraordinary development was found near Nashville, Tennessee, the primitive monumental mounds of the Mississippi valley. It was made of terracotta and intended for a child's rattle and contained six balls of clay which gave forth music to the ears of some small aboriginal American.'

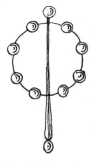

65 Crepitaculum. Roman

66   Seed rattle. West Africa

67   Seed rattle. Equatorial Africa

68   Ball rattle. Japan

69   Carved rattle. South Africa

70   Carved rattle. South-east Alaska

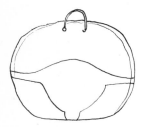

71   Rattle, shown open and closed. South America

In Africa, rattles could be mere seedpods attached to a stick or made of split cane.

Clappers are more like the castanets used in Spanish national dances, though Archyrus, mathematician and soldier, was said to have perfected those children's toys made like clappers, originally to drive away evil spirits.

There were a number of clapping toys made about 364 B.C., and the mythical Kouretes was said to guard children with clacking noises to drive away demons. In Greece, rattles imitated the noise of a rattle-snake, and in Rome the priests of Isis rattled sacred timbrels among the crowd.

Analarin, a priest, spoke of boxwood rattles, which were used to announce the clergy from the ninth century. The *crécelle*, or 'cressell', was once used in Roman Catholic churches during Passion Week instead of a bell.

In the Middle Ages rattles were used to call the faithful to prayer at a time when church bells were forbidden. They could be made of bone, horn, coral and of shell and were played with by children throughout the year. In the royal accounts of France there is mention of 'mending, nine in all, silver rattles for Madame Jehanne de France' in 1391. Sometimes a wolf's tooth was fastened to a child's rattle in order to chase away illness. Ivory was a favourite material for these baby toys, and coral was often added as a decoration, for this again was considered as a charm to chase away evil. It is like a fairy god-mother presenting a precious gift to the new baby, often its first gift, some being made with a teething-ring attached and on which later it would cut its teeth.

Early in the sixteenth century clappers were mentioned by Rabelais as being worn by lepers who carried them suspended from their waists to signal their presence, and in Italy they were used to turn away the 'evil eye'.

During the sixteenth century rattles became costly things. Little silver bells were hung on the crystal and silver rattles, some children wearing them on a chain fastened to a waistband so that they did not lose them. By the seventeenth century the stem could be made of rock-crystal, a silver whistle added, and many little silver bells for decoration and also to protect the baby from harm. More precious still were rattles of gold with crystal facets and gems given to royal children and those of the nobility.

The little girl in a portrait by Albert Cuyp painted about 1650–60 holds a rattle in her left hand. Rattles belonging to well-known children were amongst the Treasures Exhibition at Eresby House, where one of silver and coral, lent by Sir William Lawrence, had belonged to Louis XIII.

The children of George III played with an eight-inch-long rattle made of gold and coral and decorated with gold bells. The little King of Rome, Napoleon's son, had one with the face formed as a punchinello with an ivory handle and eight bells, in fact, a poupard. This punchinello had Napoleon's face, made expressly by his order for his son.

72 Clapper rattles. European

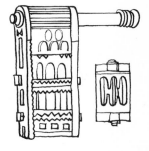

73 Rattle. France

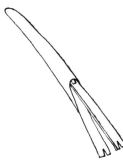

74 Hochet or clacker. Italian

75 Crécelle. France

76 Doll rattle. Bavaria

77 Bauble. Peasant jewellery for a child. Spanish

A pretty toy from Spain, in the eighteenth century, is a silver whistle and bells making an ornament to dangle on the end of a silver chain. It is a child's bauble and is a traditional piece of peasant jewellery. These little things vary somewhat, but they are similar to one another in their details and construction.

In the Museum of the City of New York is a silver rattle of 1745 with ivory teething-ring, little bells and a whistle, much like those of Spain. Two gold rattles were given to the Prince of Wales (later Edward VIII) by Queen Victoria when he was a baby.

Mention should also be made of the Victorian policeman's rattle, smaller sizes of which could be bought in toyshops in Edwardian days and which are now used as football rattles by enthusiastic spectators.

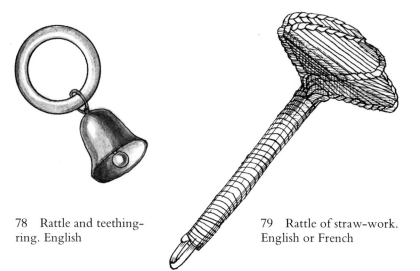

78 Rattle and teething-ring. English

79 Rattle of straw-work. English or French

POUPARDS

'Poupard' is the name given to a doll which has a stick instead of legs and is used as a rattle. Often the doll is merely the head with an elaborately dressed stuffed body, with silks and fringes edged with bells. The original poupards came from France, and although the heads were sometimes imported from Germany, by the time the finished doll appeared the result was still very French.

Poupards, however, can have legs and in this case the complete doll is fixed to a stand on the end of a turned stick which could be of wood or ivory. They still have bells amongst their elaborate clothes and some may be made to bow forwards from the waist.

Beneath the clothes a squeaker would be concealed, and more elaborate ones would have a musical-box, the music being played by twirling the doll around. The pointed collars edged with bells would splay outwards and the muslin frills would be lifted to show frilly

38

petticoats. These poupards were popular in the 1870s, and Queen Victoria added to their popularity by purchasing them as presents.

Frequently the doll heads were made by the firm of Schönau and Hoffmeister with the sign of the five-pointed star and the initials P.B. within, P.B. standing for *Porzellanfabrik-Burggrub*, the Bavarian town in which they were made. The heads were then sent from Germany to France, where they would be fixed to bodies, musical-boxes, etc., and dressed in a typically French manner with laces and tinsels.

Another poupard I saw recently was merely the head of a doll fixed above a circular musical-box on a handle. A satin collar of several points edged with gold lace hid the musical-box and fanned out as the handle was twirled, and several tinkling tunes emitted in sequence. This doll's curly white hair was topped by a wide pink hat trimmed with ostrich feather and ribbon. She was an A.M. doll, no. 3200.

In recent years poupards have returned in a simple form, and in 1963 a doll in a gay costume could be found at the John Siddeley boutique. Disabled men and women made rattles like those earlier poupards, only this time the caps and clothes were of various coloured felts, but still complete with bells.

80   Hochet de la Folie.
French

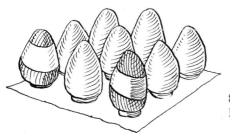

82   Stone ninepins.
Egypt

NINEPINS

The game of ninepins is usually played with balls larger than marbles and often made of turned wood about $1\frac{1}{2}$ inches in diameter. It is curious that the number nine should have been chosen from the fourth millennium B.C. to the present day.

In the Ashmolean Museum is a set of nine stone ninepins which were found in a child's grave at Nagada; these were about $\frac{3}{4}$ inch high. Stone ninepins have been found in the graves of Egyptian children buried along with other toys in 1500 B.C.

81   Poupard with
musical-box. French

39

83 Set of ninepins. England

84 Playing Kayles at Smithfield

The Romans played skittles in the days of Julius Caesar, and later the game spread to Holland and thence to Britain. Skittle-pins were sometimes made from bones, and the balls used were larger than those for ninepins. Often the kingpin in the centre was of a different shape from the others.

Manuscripts of medieval times show boys playing at ninepins placed upon the ground. Usually the pins are knocked down with a ball, but in the fourteenth century a stick could be thrown at them, the game being called 'club kayles' or simply 'keyles'.

In the reign of Edward IV in 1472, Louis, the Governor of Holland, was led to Queen Elizabeth's rooms where he found her and her ladies-in-waiting playing marteaux – a game like bowls – and throwing balls at ivory ninepins.

In 1653 Samuel Pepys had a go; 'my lord and we at ninepins this afternoon upon the quarterdeck, which was a very pretty sport'.

Ninepins could simply be pieces of wood, but usually they were turned and later coloured in stripes. Some were made like stump dolls, in fact in doll shape like Bartholomew babies, and later on as soldiers complete with captain.

85 Ninepins and balls

86 Ninepins with 'captain'

As a child, Louis XIII of France played with a miniature set, and there have been these tiny sets made in Victorian times and again during the Second World War – always nine pins and often two balls.

An unusual set of nine felt rabbits, stuffed, about five inches high, can be found in Bethnal Green Museum. Fixed to rounded wooden bases, difficult to bowl over, and made in the late nineteenth century. Again there is a captain wearing a grand coat. A set in the early twentieth century and probably made in Germany is of nine papier-mâché frogs standing on their hind legs with one 'hand' laid out across the stomach, the flat base being about one inch in diameter, and the height of each frog about eight inches.

In 1899 the ancient game of skittles crossed the Atlantic, and ninepin bowling in basements and alleys became such a craze in the U.S.A. that the game was banned in order to prevent men from neglecting their work. Later on this ban was overcome by simply adding another pin.

Thus we have ninepins, tenpins and even fivepins up to the middle of the twentieth century, carved in wood and painted.

In 1960 the game of skittles returned from America to this side of the Atlantic with tenpins and automatic pin boys. In Scotland the game was played with five pins and a lighter ball. The bowling-alleys were much frequented by teenagers, and it became such a craze that even Cecil Beaton designed special costumes in which to play.

87 Elephant ninepin of three-ply wood. England

88 Top of glazed composition. Egypt

89, 90 Tops and whip. Greece

TOPS

The first tops may have originated in Japan. Clay tops found at Ur were in levels dating from about the middle of the fourth millennium B.C., together with clay rattles containing pellets or pebbles. The Greeks had tops in 579 B.C. and 400 B.C., and the Romans in 27 B.C., in fact tops are known more or less throughout the world and at all periods.

91 Spinning-top of bone. Roman

They are shown on manuscripts as early as the thirteenth century A.D. From these drawings it might be noticed that the early whips had three ends which were sometimes knotted as in a scourge, and later two ends and later still one end as in a present-day whip. Perhaps the whips shown in the fourteenth and fifteenth centuries are scourges.

Grown-ups played with tops during the sixteenth century, and Shakespeare when he visited London in 1587 wrote about various pastimes.

92 Boy whipping a top.
English

93 Whipping a top at
Smithfield

94, 95 Whip-tops.
English

96 Medieval German top

A 'scopperel' was a child's toy formed by a stick being thrust through a button mould and spun on one end of it, and was used in 1540.

In England about 1625, tops were known as 'giges', and at the end of the seventeenth century there were humming-tops which probably came from the East.

In 1760, a little book with woodcuts was printed by Marshall: *The Adventures of a Whipping Top Illustrated with Stories of Many Bad Boys, who Themselves Deserve Whipping, and of Some Good Boys, who Deserve Plum Pudding.*

Humming-tops were large, some were left plain, others were painted with pictures, many were imported into the U.S.A. in 1774. Pegtops were of plain wood with a long iron peg and were cheap, those made of polished boxwood cost more. These were left in their natural colour, whereas whipping tops were coloured green or red.

A top my dear girl is ill chosen for you.
Go take up your doll, to your babyhouse go,
and there your attention much better bestow!
Leave the peg top behind and behave like a miss,
And I'll give you this picture, these nuts and a kiss.
And should I sit on a stool with a needle and thread,
And dress up Miss Dolly and put her to bed?
Or do you not think 'twould be pleasant to see,
Master Neddy turned fribble, and pouring out tea?
The Memories of a Peg Top by Mary Jane Kilner
published in America, in 1788.

The profile of Marie-Antoinette appeared on playing-tops in 1790; these were turned tops made in such a manner that they cast the shadow of a face. The usual whipping-tops and humming-tops were in England early in the nineteenth century, though some more unusual ones were made of glass. By 1819 there were tops and teetotums made of ivory, but it was considered unladylike for a girl to be seen whipping a top, however beautifully it had been turned.

97 'Silhouette' top. Shadow showing Louis VI

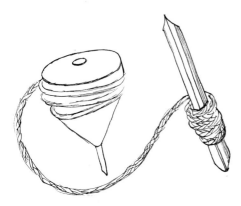

98 Wooden top. East Africa

99 Peg-top. English

Heavy tops shod with iron were specially made for whipping upon the ice of ponds and lakes. At the beginning of the eighteenth century tops had a long pointed spindle made of iron, round which the cord was wound in order to make it spin. Clever players could make this kind of top spin on a wooden bat. Acorn-shaped tops could be spun by twirling them in the hand.

A 'town top' was often kept in English villages and was whipped by the peasant people to keep them warm, a healthy exercise when frost prevented them from working. These tops were large and were whipped by several players alternately.

In the second half of the nineteenth century in England there were parachute-tops where coloured discs spun out of the hollow upper part, and in 1879, Eckhardt patented a spinning-top.

The 'choral top' was sold by A. Drukker of 22 Adison Terrace, West London. He had a stall for mechanical toys at Shop E E in the 'Orient' at Olympia, London. This top was 1s. 6d., and the Blondin gyroscopes sold at one shilling or sixpence. Many of Drukker's toys had won medals and prizes in Moscow, Paris, Belgium, etc. at the various exhibitions held during the mid and late nineteenth century. Humming-tops were played with indoors by most Victorian and Edwardian children.

In different countries tops vary, but whipping-tops are a means of exercise for both boys and men, for it seems a male pastime and mostly taking place in the open.

100 Top of polished wood. English

101 Humming-top of metal. 'The New Choral Top'

102 TOPS
i Humming-top. Japanese. ii, iii From the Solomon Islands. iv Bamboo
top. Java. v Japanese spinning-top. vi and vii Stone top with basket. Torres
Straits. viii Top from Florida

In the Torres Straits, stone tops are used by the men, who organise competitions in which the top which spins the longest is the winner. The good tops are highly valued and are kept in special baskets made for the purpose. On the upper surface of the round stone top are decorations in a whitish or a red colour.

Home-made tops could be made of cardboard and also teetotums, which were spun in lieu of dice in many board games. There are several kinds of materials used in native tops, such as a wooden peg thrust through the disc of a gourd in Zanzibar by the Wopokomo tribe, and those made from wild fruit by the Swahili people. Tops from the East are beautifully coloured and of great variety.

A spinning-top craze known as 'put and take' appeared in the 1920s, and this craze returned in 1957 for a different generation. An interesting little top known as a 'tippe top' came in 1953; this turned itself over while spinning and continued spinning on its back. It was a great commercial success for the British Indoors Pastimes Company.

Humming-tops to play tunes were popular in 1959. One played by means of records which fitted into the top and could play 'O Sole Mio' or a lullaby, or sing 'Happy Birthday'.

103   Lantern tops. Japan

104   Top spinning. Japan

105   Japanese top with whip

106   Spinning-top. Japan

107   Humming-top. English

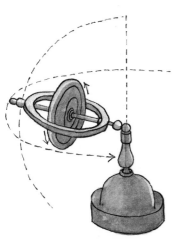

108   'La Toupie Magique'. French

109   German patent by J. H. Dreckmann

110   'Tippe Top'. English

111 Antelope.
Chanhudaro

112 Stone bull.
Mesopotamia

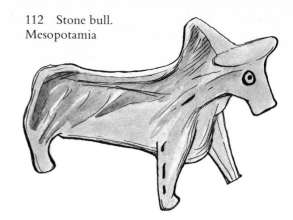

3   Animals, birds, Noah's arks, farms, horses, hobby-horses, rocking-horses

113   Clay bull. Kulli,
Western India

114   Nodding bull.
Mohenjodaro

115   Monkey. Indus
Valley

ANIMALS

Toy animals have always played an important part in the world of children, and unlike dolls, they appeal to both boys and girls alike. Often it is the child's first pet and takes the place of a live animal without all the bother.

Elephants, horses, cattle and goats were made of clay and baked during the Harappa civilisation of 2800 B.C. They were covered with a red wash or smooth polished red slip or left in the pinkish-buff colour of the natural clay, sometimes so pale that it was almost white.

Little humped cattle were painted with vertical strips and some had painted eyes, the toy animals having similar humps to the Ethiopian cattle of today. The making of the eyes was interesting; a small slit in the head was widened slightly, a round pellet was inserted into the cut, and the lashes were indicated with a pointed tool.

There were cattle with movable heads which could waggle with a string, and there were monkeys which could slide down a rope and stop by tightening a cord. A toy climbing monkey with out-of-alignment holes to check its movements on a string was carved in terracotta at Harappa between 2400 and 2000 B.C. It was $2\frac{3}{8}$ inches high and is in the Central Asian Antiquities Museum at New Delhi.

Others near the River Indus were carved in the city of Chanhudaro, which specialised in the making of toys. There may even have been professional toy-makers to make the monkey-like animals with movable arms and the bulls with nodding heads which worked by a stiff fibre.

Not all the little animals were toys, some could be ornaments, the majority may have been votive offerings for they have been found on

46

rock shelves within the household shrines. The same applies to those found in Egyptian graves, where they were placed for the use of the occupant in the life beyond.

A variety of animals came from Egypt. There were toy dogs, elephants, wooden cows and mice, but although most of the toys which have survived are of clay, there were also many wooden ones which have perished with time or have been broken or lost way back in history.

Camels were used as transport in 1491 B.C., and a toy camel from this period has been found in a grave.

116 Mouse of painted steatite

Elephants and hippopotami were of porcelain, queer dwarfs with cats' heads had a blue glaze, spotted cows were made of wood and there were movable dogs. Crocodiles and mice had moving jaws and moving tails, and models of apes driving chariots were among the curious little toys made by the Egyptians way back in 1184 B.C., that is about 300 years after the Egyptian army had been swept away by the Red Sea.

Cows, cats, fishes and hedgehogs made in clay, some of blue pottery, some of purple, came from the Ptolemaic period, 457 B.C., and there were pinkish-coloured toy tortoises, carved wooden lions and Molossian hounds.

The Greeks made pigs, rabbits, dogs, rams and fish of baked clay, and donkeys carrying loaves of bread. They made horsemen in terracotta, and many little riding toys such as a boy on a horse and a man on a swan, mostly from four to five inches high.

Children wore amulets which, apart from those in the shape of limbs, were of fishes, lions, toads and ducks, each animal signifying something different. Many were a blue colour, or had a blue bead added among the other charms.

Several little animals were made of bronze: goats, dogs, boars, geese and bulls by 75 B.C. but not in the New World, which was still unacquainted with metals and where there were no tame animals.

The Romans made toys for their children, and in 30 B.C. some lucky child had a lion with a movable jaw.

Marriage toys were given as presents to the boy-bridegroom amongst the Kutiya Kondhs, a hill tribe at Belugunta, Ganjam, in India. These were little animals, riders, carts, etc. which can now be seen in the Indian Department of the Victoria and Albert Museum.

During the Sung dynasty in China, A.D. 960–1279, beautiful toys were made; there were little rabbits of palish green porcelain and tiny animals carved in semi-precious stones.

47

117 Deer, made by a child. India

In India today, the handmade toys are much the same as those of ancient times. They are still made of clay, an ochre or reddish colour, which is sunbaked or fired, when black is added it is burnt with charcoal. In the house of a potter even a small kiln is kept apart for the womenfolk to make dolls and toys, timeless toys like those they know so well, many illustrating their folk-tales and some being turned on a native lathe.

In Korea, children have few playthings, perhaps a new toy once a year when they are sold at the children's festival. Image-lanterns, birds and beasts are some of the toys, and there are others made from story-book characters such as a tortoise with a rabbit riding on its back, a cat watching a rat in a box, and turtledoves. When riding on a horse the singing girls carry umbrellas, as they must be covered.

118 Playing at bull-fighting. Spain

In the Escorial near Madrid hangs an eighteenth-century tapestry designed by Francisco Bayen. In it children are shown playing at bull-fighting, the bull being an effigy made of plaited wickerwork rather like an upturned cradle, with a basket handle and a head and horns at one end.

Tyrolean toys were carved by hand, the craft being handed down from generation to generation:

> *Magdalena Paldauf*
> *Can carve a dog, a cat or wolf,*
> *Her mother's mother taught her*
> *And she taught her daughter's daughter,*
> *An elephant, a goat, a sheep*
> *Two sizes, choose which you will keep.*

Little horses were made of tin in Germany and were covered with goatskin, but wood was the main material used for carving animals in the countries of central Europe. Just as with dolls, the animals were carved by peasants living in wooded districts, and in other parts they were made of pottery. From here, many inhabitants emigrated to America and settled in Pennsylvania during the early part of the nineteenth century. One of these was William Schimmel, 1817–90, who carved animals and also made them of pottery in the New World.

48

1 Mouse. Egypt. 2 Pig. North Syria. 3 Horseman. Greece. 4 Dog with hare. Boeotia. 5 Monkey. Greece. 6 Monkey. Sah Dheri. 7 Goat. 8 Spotted animal. 9 Camel. 10, 11 Animals from China

Toy animals of wood or papiermâché underwent a flocking process to imitate skin in about 1856, and many dolls were treated in the same way.

Apart from animals which just stood about on their own four legs, such as the traditional wooden horses from Dalarna, there were others which were parts of toys, such as monkeys-on-sticks, and small canes with coloured animals' heads. When rubber was introduced there were woolly lambs and other animals which jumped around when a rubber ball was pressed.

The small tortoise whose legs and neck shivered in a glass-topped box came from Japan. There is a tiny example in the museum at Hertford.

Just as dolls could be bought 'in the flat', so could animals. Dean's in England and Arnold's in the U.S.A. printed parts of animals on cloth sheets ready to be cut out and joined together at home and stuffed. Cats, dogs and horses were printed in this manner, and later on were sold ready stuffed, many being stiffened with wire or cardboard.

119   Old woman with traditional horses. Dalarna

120   Tortoise with nodding head. Mexico

121   Elephant of wood. Somaliland

Naturally the smooth calico or linen soon gave way to more furry material, and animals were made from scraps of real fur, or fur fabric, and thus entered all those fluffy animals one sees in nurseries or lying back in prams, and now made of nylon fur in any colour.

One of the first toy creatures made to represent a living animal was Caesar, the pet dog of King Edward VII. White with black markings, on his collar was a disc stating 'I am Caesar, I belong to the King'. When King Edward died in 1910, the real dog Caesar walked in the funeral procession immediately behind the coffin, and toy replicas were fondled by lucky Edwardian children. For a part of the procession, Caesar was accompanied by a mongrel friend.

122   Bulldog of papier-mâché

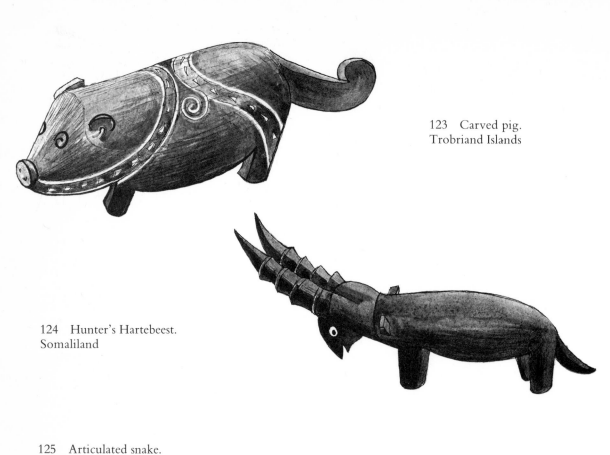

123   Carved pig.
Trobriand Islands

124   Hunter's Hartebeest.
Somaliland

125   Articulated snake.
Japan

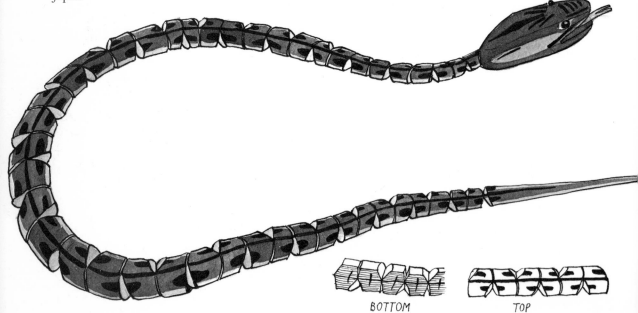

BOTTOM   TOP

In the New Forest, at Brockenhurst, animals were carved from wood by a Mr Whittington in 1925. These he made from drawings of animals at the zoo or from stuffed ones in the Natural History Museum. Ponies he could do from those in the New Forest surrounding him, their tails being clipped according to which district they belonged, either cut short on the right side, or on the left, or up the centre, thus following an ancient custom.

During the 1920s a craze started for animals with zipped tummies. Toy tigers and lions could be opened up to disclose not their stuffed inners but a nightdress or a pair of pyjamas, while smaller versions were carried around as handbags.

Lions were very popular about 1938, being made of fawn-coloured furry fabric and with kind expressions. Made in all sizes, their bodies were animal-like and not humanised as those of a Teddy bear.

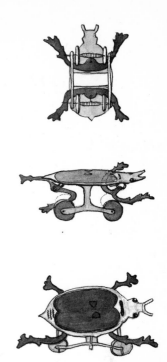

126   Tin beetle. German

127   Cow of knitted wool. English

When the Second World War came in 1939, animals became quite grotesque – because of clothing coupons they were made from scraps of material – they could have striped bodies, odd-coloured legs, knitted bodies and features. Even glass eyes gradually became unobtainable, so buttons were used instead, or the eyes were merely worked in with black wool, and were incidentally far safer for babies.

There have always been cheap clockwork animals in toyshops since clockwork was utilised for making moving toys. In 1959 there were frogs in bright green tin which hopped along on yellow feet, and there was a performing seal which could balance an umbrella on its nose as it ambled along on its flippers.

A battery-operated toy in 1959 was an elephant which could blow bubbles. This was $7\frac{1}{2}$ inches high and could nod his head and flap his ears. He came to Selfridges complete with bubble-mixture.

128   Tin frog. Probably German

In 1960, Lines Brothers, Britain's biggest toy firm, put on sale a white pom-pom poodle with a French accent to fascinate the Christmas shoppers. Also, in this year, came a large grey donkey with bells on his bridle, and a two-foot-high pink elephant called Bessie with three-inch eyelashes and a posy in her furled trunk. These two animals were the emblems of the political parties of the U.S.A.

51

129 Folk toy.
Czechoslovakia

There was supposed to be a modern trend towards things which were sharp and hard as opposed to comfortable and soft, so wrote a *Times* correspondent, who said that a Teddy bear would look out of place in a modern house. However, he was proved wrong by several small boys and girls.

Chinese children collected little handmade clay animals which were made by the people in the communes during their spare time in the winter months.

Every year saw some new gimmick in the toy world; in 1961 came full-size grizzly bears for £250 in the U.S.A. and in England luxurious cats of real fur lay about in Fortnum and Mason's and also a kangaroo with a baby in her pouch.

In 1962, the most popular toy for the children of millionaires was a mechanical basset hound with a profoundly gloomy expression. He was called Gaylord and could walk forwards and backwards, could climb shallow stairs, bark, and even pick up a magnetic bone.

130, 131   A bull and a
tiger. China

132   Plastic pig. Probably
Hong Kong

There were swan rockers made of rubber over a steel frame, very strong and solid, on which a child could sit and rock, instead of on the more usual horse. Glove puppets were made by Anna Marita and these represented cats with rubber heads and fur paws. However, puppets form a study in themselves and have been omitted from this survey.

Celluloid ducks and swans have gradually been replaced by plastic ones, and there are many varieties of rubber toys for use in the sea or in garden pools, many in the shapes of animals, fish or birds. Rather nice basset hounds, big enough for a child to sit on, were made of foam rubber by the English firm of Bendy Toys, in 1969. A steel frame inside strengthened the back of the dog. The body was coloured white and brown, the ears were firm yet pliable, and the hound was realistic enough to stroke.

ANIMAL PATENTS
133 Pig, German patent by Franz Steiff.   134 Dog, German patent by
C. Wilhelm Meyer.   135 Goat, German patent by Casimer Bru, junior

136   Wooden bird. Egypt

137   Wooden pigeon

138   Bronze hawk.
Greece

139   Tomb pottery.
China

Birds are as popular as animals in the toy kingdom, especially pigeons, owls and domestic hens.

Pigeons were moulded at Kurdistan (Assyria) in 4750 B.C. from pink clay, just a smooth body, head and beak, with perhaps the eyes indicated and a line along where the folded wings would be.

In Mesopotamia, about 2800 B.C., pigeons were made in much the same shape, but here they were hollow, with a hole at the tail end. When blown into a loud hooting noise was produced. At Chanhudaro, about 2500 B.C., bird whistles were made which imitated the call of a bird. Other bird toys could have sticks for legs, open beaks and many of them were coloured.

Toy birds found in miniature cages suggest that real birds may have been housed as pets. Since 1000 B.C. the jungle fowls of India had been turned into domesticated hens, and down through the ages cocks and hens, not to mention chicks, have been favourite toys with children and made from all manner of materials.

Earthenware rattles in the shape of birds, usually doves and some-times owls, were made in Greece and were popular about 400 B.C., which was the year Archytas made a flying dove. A pretty toy in the British Museum shows two doves cooing on a branch, and by means of holes in the sides of their bodies they are able to sway gently up and down.

About A.D. 9 there is the legend of the boy Jesus making some little birds in clay. The story is told by Thomas:

this little child Jesus when he was five years old was playing at the ford of a brook: and he gathered together the waters that flowed there into pools and made them straightway clean and commanded them by his word alone. And having made soft clay, he fashioned there of twelve sparrows. And it was the Sabbath when he did these things, or made them. And there were also many other little children playing with him.

And a certain Jew when he saw what Jesus did, playing upon the Sabbath day, departed straightway and told his father Joseph, 'Lo, thy child is at the brook and he hath taken clay and fashioned twelve little birds and hath polluted the Sabbath day.' And Joseph came to the place and saw, and cried out to him 'Wherefore doest thou these things on the Sabbath, which is not lawful to do?' But Jesus clapped his hands together and cried out to the sparrows 'Go', and the sparrows took their flight and went away chirping.

One cannot help thinking of the old nursery rhyme:

> *Tale, tale tit, your tongue shall be slit,*
> *and every dog in the town, shall have a little bit.*

In 1834, Edward Bingham, of Gestingthorpe, made clay bird whistles which cried 'cuckoo' when one blew into their tails, and in Switzerland many cuckoos have been carved which give most realistic bird sounds when one blows into their tails.

Fluttering clay and feather birds on pieces of wire came in 1870.

Early in the twentieth century little wooden hen-coops were made. When the door was opened, out would step a hen or a cock on a wooden hinge, and at the same time would cluck or crow as the case may be. The little birds were carved in wood, mostly left uncoloured, but with a brightly dyed feather for a tail.

Real coops such as these were still used in everyday country life in the 1930s. Usually the centre strip of wood could be lifted up to let loose the broody hen, but they have gradually disappeared and wire-netting is fixed to the fronts. The toy coops have gone, but thank goodness, no battery hen sheds have taken their place.

Wooden toys from Russia, left in the natural light-coloured wood, were and still are most attractive. Here again, birds feature as much as animals. They were carved by peasants mostly in the winter, but later instead of peddling their own wares they were handled by agents and sold in the bigger towns and exported to other parts of Europe.

There were birds on perches bobbing up and down, much the same as those of Greece, 2,200 years ago, two birds pecking at a piece of wood each bobbing up in turn. There were hens fixed to a circular piece of wood who moved their necks up and down by means of string fixed to a ball, below the board, which could rotate, and there were owls who could flap their wings and lift their ears by gently pulling at a string. The prices were anything from sixpence upwards according to size or if they were coloured. Some of the Chinese shops in London now have these pecking chicks coloured in their own manner, the result being more oriental than traditional Russian.

So many duckling chicks were caught and stuffed for export from China during the first quarter of the twentieth century that by the thirties the practice was banned for the species was vanishing – fluffy yellow ducklings with webbed feet and a suggestion of fluffy wings, with beady brown eyes, they were beautiful to look at, and much loved by small girls.

Plastic bird shapes vary little from those of ancient days. Many were made in China or Japan and about 1932 a pea would be placed in the hollow body in order to make a whistle. Others could be filled with water and would make a chirrupy noise when blown into at the tail end.

140   Clay birds with feathers. Czechoslovakia

141   Swan of solid lead. English

142 Clockwork parrot and goose. Probably German

Woolly birds made on the principle of a woollen ball hung from pram hoods and canopies during the thirties. Made over two pieces of cardboard with a hole in the centre, the wool was wound round and round until no more would pass through the hole. It was then cut with scissors between the two cardboard circles and tied firmly before being pulled away. A bird would consist of one large and one small ball with eyes and beak added later.

Clockwork geese and parrots which moved backwards and forwards when wound up and nodded their heads disappeared from shops early in the Second World War. The Japanese birds on sticks also vanished until the war was over. The birds were made of coloured cotton wool with feathers and two strips of wood for a tail. A tiny metal disc made whirling noises as they whizzed through the air on the end of a piece of twine fastened to a bamboo stick.

143 'Flying bird'. Japan

144 'Chirpy, the Clockwork Chick'

56

In 1961, Liberty's in London had metal starlings for their Christmas shoppers. These were well coloured and worked by clockwork, by which means they could crow, hop and flap their wings, a toy to delight tourists, for London city is full of starlings.

Little Ookpik was the name chosen for the official mascot of Canadian exhibitions abroad in 1964. It was a native interpretation of an Arctic owl and was about six inches tall. The Fort Chimo Eskimos worked steadily on piecework to make enough Ookpiks for the expected demand. This little bird was made of sealskin, and in Ottawa there were requests for Ookpik colouring books, Ookpik comic books, and Ookpik story-books, for he was to be a symbol of success.

145 'Little Ookpik', made by Fort Chimo Eskimos

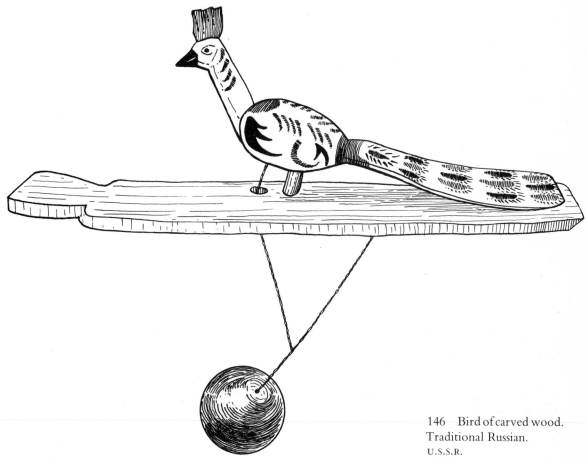

146 Bird of carved wood. Traditional Russian. U.S.S.R.

147   Noah's ark.
Scandinavia

In 2349 B.C., Noah's Ark was supposed to have rested on Mount Ararat, a mountain in Armenia. This summit has been described as 'a little plain of snow, silent and desolate, with a bright green sky above'. This piece of ancient history has led to many toys being made in the shape of arks, filled with toy animals and the close relations of Mr Noah.

Because the story came from the Bible, it has been said that toy arks were played with on Sundays and that the rest of the week they were put away, this being the reason for their good state of preservation.

An early seventeenth-century ark made in Scandinavia from a solid piece of wood was lent to the Treasures of Famous Children Exhibition by Sir William Lawrence in 1934, but most arks belong to the nineteenth century, one in 1812 being made by Cacheleux.

The shape of an ark was usually a house resting on a sturdy boat with bow and stern. Sometimes they were painted to represent two storeys, some had doors at one end with porches, but whatever the details the ark itself was a kind of box with one of the walls made to slide, or the roof being the lid, and when this was lifted off, all the animals were within. Possibly the dove is missing for he may be painted on the roof with the olive branch in his beak, denoting that the flood was abating.

Over the sign outside Hamley's shop in Regent Street may be seen the toy Noah's ark brought from their earlier shop in Holborn.

Early in the nineteenth century, many arks were made in Saxony, though the originator of the ark as a toy has been forgotten. One particular family made nothing but Noah's arks between the years 1825 and 1875.

In the London Museum, a painted ark has a porch at one end, painted windows and a frieze under the eaves; this frieze varies in detail on similar arks. The ark at Blaise Castle is a house with a front door and windows upstairs and down. Other arks are made of pine-wood decorated with straw-work, usually the work of French prisoners-of-war. There is one at Peterborough made in Huntington about 1810 and another in Bethnal Green.

A silhouette of a Noah's ark, dated June 1830, by August Edouart shows an early ark belonging to the Misses Todd, and another in the Treasures of Famous Children Exhibition was made by the diamond-cutters of Antwerp who were refugees in Yorkshire during the First World War.

Dickens's character Calib Plummer remarks that most of the Noah's arks had knockers on the doors, and 'that there were many in which the Birds and Beasts were an uncommonly tight fit I assure you'.

Sometimes there were as many as 150 pairs of animals together with Mr and Mrs Noah, their three sons Shem, Ham and Japhet. Often the sons were accompanied by their wives, thus making eight figures in all and 300 animals. When piled neatly away they all pack into the ark, but when laid out in a line with a small space between each pair they can stretch out in a line of 30 feet or more.

The hand-carving of the wooden animals took a very long time, and eventually the ingenious method of the circular ring was employed. An example of this can be seen in the hot-house at Kew Gardens devoted to different kinds of woods near the main entrance. The head end was usually towards the centre of the circle because this is narrower than the tail end on most animals. In the tiger family it is the reverse, therefore the wide head points towards the circumference.

After the ring was sawn into sections, the legs were separated, horns and ears added and many details still done by hand, thus the animals varied one from another and sometimes male from female. Various sized rings were used, the deer family, cattle, sheep, etc. coming out particularly well.

Elephants, giraffes, spiders, grasshoppers and ladybirds went in pairs into the arks, but when Cremer, the toyman, visited Saxony in 1875, he noted that many of them were the same size.

'We see in the Noah's ark', he said, 'the boar as large as the elephant, the mouse as big as the cat, but it may have happened that the Saxon toymen wished thus to impress on the infantine mind that in the antediluvian epoch Nature now and then indulged in a wild freak . . . four hundred animals from the elephant to the glow worm, with Noah, his sons, and his wife and sons' wives.'

After this observation by Cremer on the scale of animals, these workers in Saxony, in 1875, said that 'a just proportion shall be maintained in future'.

Not only in Europe were these arks and animals made, they were also carved in Pennsylvania, where again there were many varieties. Japan and China also produced Noah's arks, where Noah was known as Fohi. They were of wood and beautifully decorated, the animals being especially bright in colour and usually flat in section and fixed to flat stands.

148　The ring, from which slices are carved as in a cake. Saxony·

149　Elephant of plywood. England

150   Ark. Central Europe

151   Ark. Japan

In 1964 we returned again to the unpainted ark. John Spence, a furniture-maker by trade, produced an ark with animals carved from different kinds of wood. A set of 22 animals and the very modern ark, almost 'Henry Moore', cost 15 guineas when new.

A German Biedermeyer's Noah's ark of painted wood, containing numerous pairs of carved and painted animals, sold for 24 guineas in a 1967 sale. The ark was 23 inches long. Another ark, 22 inches long, also from Germany and of painted wood containing over 130 pairs of animals, well carved and painted in colours, went for 50 guineas. The average length of the animals was 3½ inches, and the whole affair dated from the middle of the nineteenth century.

Today we have animals from the zoo, complete with ponds, railings and houses mostly made from metal alloys. However, even these are becoming difficult to obtain as the more modern species are made of plastic.

152   Zoo animals, tapir, ibex, orang-utang and walrus. England

153   Zoo animals and fences. England

154 A homestead of
pottery. China

155 Back views of
figures on colour plate,
facing page 192

FARMS

In Cremer's tiny book *The Toys of the Little Folk* he mentions
'pasturages', which are homesteads or farms with many animals. He
draws attention to the European peasants making complete animals
whereas later on there was division of labour, those who did the
initial rough work living at Fridenbach, Neustadt and Schalkau.
They carved domestic animals for the toy farmyards and wild animals
for the menageries, scale seemingly unimportant. The circular ring
was used later, each ring being used to make one kind of animal.

Towards the end of the eighteenth century the Hilperts in Germany
made many kinds of zoo animals in tin, with their Latin names on
stands and arranged in groups. These were 'in the flat' and the small
stands were usually painted green, again scale being of little concern.

They also made gardens with trimmed hedges and fountains,
peopled with ladies and their gardeners, dotted around with groups
of gods and goddesses, fashionable at this period. A bed of flowers
could be taller than a man, a man could come half-way up a cyprus
tree, so it was quite a task to arrange these tin objects in such a manner
that the perspective of a group would appear correct.

However, about the middle of the nineteenth century two large
firms decided to conform to a certain size. Heinrichsen of Nuremberg
and Allgeyer of Fürth made their grown men not more than $1\frac{1}{3}$ inches
high, and from then on their little objects in the religious processions
and harvest festivals were made to scale. The two half moulds were
cut out of slate and engraved, then put together and filled with the
melted tin.

In 1916 Henri Roidot made a model farm for his own children, and from this disabled Belgian soldiers produced toys under their name 'Le Jouet Belge'. These were well-built farms and sturdy animals, farm carts, etc. as realistic as time permitted. Carved in wood, they lasted for a generation, and after the Second World War the little farm things were made in metal.

Farmyards and sets of animals were sold in chip-boxes usually oval in shape and from two to 14 inches across. Later, cardboard took the place of the thin wood, and later still the animals were laid out on cards with rubber bands and protected by a sheet of cellophane, or sold in a plastic bag.

156   Tree of lead.
England

157   Farm figures.
Austria

In 1948, farmyard animals came in sets, minute cats in baskets, dogs in kennels, and plenty of fences and gates. Set up on a green cloth and with home-made farm buildings, these looked most attractive as this time the animals were more or less to the same scale. The firm making Dinky Toys modelled their animals from actual beasts such as the Devon Red amongst their cows. Today the same moulds are used for their plastic animals.

Apart from miniature articles, there were those toys which children use when they pretend to be grown-up such as the toy-size farm and garden implements made for the children of the English Royal Family. Theirs have been handed down in an oak box containing tools in miniature for several generations.

Scenes with cribs are hardly toys but many an animal from the Ark must have wandered into one now and again. The real crib animals had their heads bowed in a reverent attitude and the figures were carved especially to take their place at the Christmas crib. A famous collection is in the Bavarian National Museum at Munich.

158   Dog from a
Schoenhut circus.
Pennsylvania, U.S.A.

J. Hill & Co. was a firm started by a former employee of Britain's, his toys going under the name of 'Johillco'. He made figures and animals in the same fine tradition. Another firm is Timpo who make the Buffalo Bill series, soldiers, cowboys, Red Indians, and many circus figures, beautifully coloured with all the accessories.

No mention of circus toys is complete without including those of Albert Schoenhut, who arrived in the U.S.A. in the mid nineteenth century. He came from Germany and gradually built up his toy business. In 1903, he announced his Humpty Dumpty circus, with over 20 figures and animals, each with six joints enabling them to be put into endless positions. The hands and feet of the clowns had slots so that they could balance on chairs or climb ladders. Later, more figures were added and the sets became the most popular toys of the early twentieth century.

159   Farm animals of
lead. England

160   Rabbits and hutch
of lead. England

64

1 Noah's ark containing 'flat' animals. 2 Noah's ark with animals in the round'. 3 Set of frog ninepins

161 Terracotta
horseman. Cyprus

HORSES

Of all the animals taken as a model for toys, the horse is the most
popular, almost throughout the world, and down through the
centuries it reigns supreme in the hearts of many children. Between
the clay horses of the ancients and the sophisticated horses of today
come many varieties: little clay horses, pull-along horses, hobby-
horses, ride-on horses, and rocking-horses, the latter probably being
the largest toy in the nursery.

A beautiful little bronze horse, intact, was discovered during
excavations in a broad valley where the Olympic Games were held
from 776 B.C. every four years. Maybe it was a toy dropped by a
child, or it could have been a talisman for one of the athletes.

The Egyptians, in 500 B.C., made wooden horses about $8\frac{1}{2}$ inches
high on strong wheels without stands, the axle passing through the
solid legs of the horse. In 400 B.C. the Greeks made terracotta horsemen
about the same size.

The early horses may be dated by the harnesses which are sometimes indicated with paint. Real horses had saddles made of leather in
A.D. 304, but stirrups were not in use until A.D. 400 and then rarely in
England. Possibly the first hollow, wooden toy horses were those sold
to travellers in the city of Troy in A.D. 425.

By the year A.D. 700, horses were shod only in time of frost and
later, William the Conqueror was said to have introduced the shoeing
of horses into England. Saddles were more common, and in the year
A.D. 886 horses began to wear collars. Stirrups were not in general use
in England until after 1100. Small toy horses about $5\frac{3}{4}$ inches high
made of clay, and those during the thirteenth century in Germany,
show saddles and the figure of a knight riding one of them.

162 Horse and rider.
Greece

163 Horse and rider.
China

164 Horse and rider.
Roman

65

A French thirteenth-century toy shows a knight on horseback, one of the earliest tin toys in existence and only 2¾ inches high. Reins, collar and saddle were indicated, and also stirrups for the knight.

Horses were made at Sieburg in the fifteenth century, sometimes with the use of moulds, many being complete with rider.

By 1520, there were bronze knights made in Germany, riding on horses which were fixed to stands with four wheels. The toys were small, being about five inches high. These were probably playthings for the sons of lords, for it was considered necessary for the nobility to be familiar with horses. The little models show various horse-trappings and details of the knights' armour.

Large wooden horses on wheels came at the end of the sixteenth century and were big enough for a child to sit on, and more popular than the hobby-horse with its one wheel at the back or two wheels with a crosspiece. For one thing, a young child could be given rides on these large horses whereas the hobby-horse was for older children who could career around indoors and out, waving a whip at the same time.

'The honourablest and most commendable games that ye can use are games on horseback, for it becometh a Prince best of any man to be a fair and good horseman.' In these words King James urged his son in addition to practise running, jumping, wrestling, fencing and dancing in 1603.

In the eighteenth century there were many expensive horses made on frames with four wheels, as an aid to walking. They had beautifully carved bodies, manes and tails of horsehair, and leather harnesses. The child could also ride on these, using his legs to move along.

Early in the nineteenth century the little town of Sonneberg conducted a flourishing trade in papiermâché horses. These horses were made in a mould to give them the correct form and were then sent round to peasant families who would paint them in primitive

165 Wooden horse. France

166 Wooden horse. England

167 Horse with 'barrel' body. England

168 Horse covered with real skin. European

66

colours. The details were carefully added and each horse varied slightly, one from another.

The Hon. Leopold Cust had a present of a wooden toy horse from Queen Victoria in 1839, for this queen like others before her was fond of giving toys to her friends' children.

In 1871, some of Queen Victoria's grandchildren had the whooping cough and they were confined to the old nurseries on the top floors of Buckingham Palace. Here they had great fun for they found strange sorts of bicycles which had formerly belonged to their uncles. These bicycles were adorned with horses' heads and tails and had saddles. Among these uncles would have been our Edward VII, born in 1841, Arthur born in 1850 and Leopold born in 1853. Assuming the boys to have been round about nine years old when they played on these things, the dates would be between 1850 and 1862, which ties in well with the toy horse-bicycle which belonged to the Prince Imperial who was born in 1856. The child sat on the body of the horse and steered by two handles which came up through the horse's head.

About 1878, children rode toy horses which were on a tricycle frame, that is, there were two wheels at the back and one in front with which to steer. The future Dean of Canterbury, born in 1874, had one of these before graduating to a penny-farthing bicycle with a 36-inch-diameter wheel.

This kind of toy was patented by Ayres in England in 1887.

Many contrivances for making model horses move up and down as on roundabouts were patented in 1887, and toy horses pulling toy carts were made to imitate galloping by means of clockwork. Other toys were horse-drawn dogcarts with a small wheel placed centrally under the horse.

The cheaper mass-produced wooden horses of the late nineteenth century had round barrel-shaped bodies, a head and neck fitted into a slot like an early rocking-horse and a real tail at the rear end. Four legs like hoop-sticks were fixed to the barrel and splayed out slightly to fit into a wooden stand which had four solid wooden wheels, and later on a handle to push. These horses stood about two feet high and most Victorian nurseries had at least one. Some had leather harnesses, sometimes studded with metal discs and other much cheaper ones had red-painted reins and blue paper saddles. Rows of such horses in varying sizes hung from the ceilings of toyshops or village stores until the beginning of the Second World War.

About 1939 the barrel horses were replaced by horses with metal legs but with a flat seat of stuffed imitation leather as the body, and a traditional head dappled grey, a horsy tail and a handle at the back.

169   Horse on stand. France

170   Horse with 'barrel' body. Austria

171   Edwardian boy with wooden horse. England

67

RIDERS
172, 173, 174 Horses of painted wood. Erz Mountains,
Saxony. 175 From Northern Nigeria

GWEN
WHITE

176 Playing at tilting.
England

177 Tournament game
with hobby-horses.
Flanders

HOBBY-HORSES

It is well known that the children of Socrates had a hobby-horse, and since that time these toys have come and gone down through the ages, both in the West and in the East.

The fourteenth-century manuscripts show boys riding on sticks, the forerunners of the hobby-horse. Woodcuts from Nuremberg show boys on these toys in which the horse's head was fastened to a long stick and held up by reins. In a fifteenth-century manuscript, the child Jesus is shown on such a one, and later in an eighteenth-century engraving the horse still has a plain stick at the back even though the head end has reins and legs, and a cross-bar to hold.

However crude, the hobby-horse was a favourite toy all through the Middle Ages. One day when Henry IV was riding round on his son's hobby-horse, the Spanish Ambassador called unexpectedly. 'Are you a father?' asked the King, and when the reply was 'Yes', Henry said, 'Then in that case, I will go round again.'

Chinese children played with hobby-horses during the Ming dynasty. A painting from 'The Hundred Children' shows them at play, one horse having two wheels at the back.

In 1821 the hobby-horse could have a real mane and a pretty topknot of wire, pennons and bells but with no wheels at the back. In the U.S.A., Charles T. Crandall covered his hobby-horses with real hide.

In *A Chinese Childhood*, written in 1909, Chiang Yee says of hobby-horses in China:

In China, children rode on bamboo horses made from a bamboo stick of about 3 cms diameter, and 2 or 3 metres long. I would put the stick between my legs holding the upper part of it with my right hand as if wielding a whip, and I made a sound to urge my steed forward. Our elders could have bought paper heads for us to fasten on our bamboo sticks, but my father asked a carpenter to make ten wooden ones instead.

Gradually the hobby-horse went out of fashion, but in recent years they have staged a comeback. Some modern examples have soft heads and woollen manes, while others have the traditional painted wooden heads.

178 Boy with hobby-horse. Japan

Gee up, gee up, gee whoah,
On a stick we ride just so,
With a head and a tail, ho, ho, ho, ho,
It's our legs which make him go.

Two wheels at the back or one
It matters not which, 'tis fun,
With a crack of a whip away we go
Gee up, gee up, gee whoa, gee whoa.

A ride on a rocking-horse now
Forward and backward we go
With a hand on the mane, a grip on the rein,
A frightening speed to and fro again

Gee up, gee up, gee whoaooh
Gee up, gee up, gee whoa.

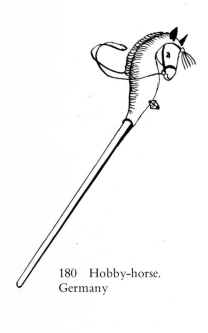

179   Boy with lantern
horse. China

181   Hobby-horse.
England

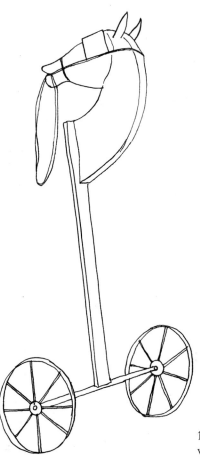

182   Hobby-horse.
Japan

180   Hobby-horse.
Germany

183   Hobby-horse with
wheels. France

The Great House, Cheshunt, has a rocking-horse from the royal nurseries of Charles I, about 1628, and another early one is that belonging to Lord Grantley, said to have been made about 1650. This is a complete carved trotting horse, with carved mane and tail, standing on rockers, and formerly belonging to the last male child of the Chapple family at Wonersh Park, Surrey. The first Lady Grantley was a Miss Chapple.

Other kinds, also rare, are those which are made to lift off and to place on a stand with wheels. Later examples of the seventeenth century were two pieces of wood carved almost into a semicircle and placed side by side. A block of wood between the straight edges formed the seat, sometimes covered with leather, and in the front was a carved wooden head with arched neck. Often a horsy tail was added and later a pillion seat.

The two thick pieces curved away giving a suggestion of outstretched legs, and there were two little blocks on which to rest one's feet, reins, and even a place for a holster. The semicircular pieces gradually assumed a different appearance, the curves appeared lower down, and the body of the horse was more apparent.

184   Rocking-horse. England

Sometimes the legs were painted on the boards, and eventually the gap between the legs was cut away, the carved horse was almost complete, and towards the end of the eighteenth century it was placed on rockers, thick in the centre and tapering to curved ends with the horse's legs outstretched upon them.

At the turn of the century the rockers protruded far beyond the horse's legs for safety, whose outstretched limbs were fixed to the outside of the rockers at the hooves.

William Long, cabinet-maker and carver from London, arrived in the U.S.A. in 1785 and put an advertisement in the *Pennsylvania Packet*, in which he 'respectfully informs the Ladies and Gentlemen of this city that he makes Rocking Horses in the neatest and best manner to teach children to ride, and give them a wholesome and pleasing exercise'.

185   Rocking-horse by William Long. Pennsylvania, U.S.A.

There were stirrups on either side of the leather saddle, and the horse on the playing-cards issued by Wallis in 1788, in England, was such a one as these. As usual, there was a moral:

> *The Rocking-Horse pursues its course*
> *Directed by your hand.*
> *Children should thus their friends obey*
> *And do what they command.*

These noble horses from the palaces and stately homes of England were beautifully carved, much loved, and worth preserving. Some were made on the estates and most of them had leather saddles and reins, horses' manes, horses' tails, and either painted eyes or inset eyes of glass. Thus the horses varied, and gradually the heavy rockers were succeeded by two long curved strips put together with a platform in

186   A Wallis playing-card. England

187 ROCKING-HORSES

i, ii English, 17th century. iii French, 18th century. iv Danish, early 19th century. v U.S.A., *c.* 1800. vi German, early 19th century. vii English, *c.* 1788. viii English, late 18th century. ix English, early 19th century. x English, 1800. xi English, 19th century. xii English, early 20th century. xiii English, 1915. xiv English, 1961. xv Danish, 1966

GWEN
WHITE

Hatfield Horses, Spring 1929.

the centre, and a turned piece at either end, the two long curved pieces getting closer together at the ends and less like a rocking-chair.

The little Duke's rocking-horse at Knole was made for the fourth Duke of Dorset in 1799, and the one at Hatfield House is possibly of the same date. The seventh Earl was created Marquess of Salisbury in 1789, and this beautiful rocking-horse wears a leather medallion decorated with the coronet of a marquess. The body shows the early method of dappling black on white with uneven strokes, current about 1800. Later horses were painted with a more conventional dapple, which eventually developed into the 'wire-netting stipple'.

In France, wooden horses on rockers came early in the nineteenth century and were soon the fashion, for the little King of Rome had one of these new model toys. By the Second Empire, 1852, horses were mounted on iron rockers and their bodies covered with hide. French patents for toy horses came in 1822, one by Gourdoux in November and another by Coube, in June. The patent secured by M. Klein in 1869 was for a child's horse stamped in metal.

Patents were also taken out in England and the U.S.A. A British toy horse patent came in 1858, and in 1861 William Kennedy took out one for a rocking-horse. Shortly afterwards, George Burrows took out a rocking-horse patent for a horse on a wire frame stand, and

189 Badge worn by the Hatfield House rocking-horse

190 Rocking-horse by William Kennedy. English patent

191 Horse by Brown
and Eggleston. New York,
U.S.A.

192 Horse by
Montgomery Ward.
U.S.A.

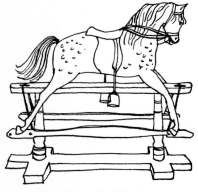

193 Horse by W. A.
Marqua. Cincinnati, U.S.A.

Richard Brooman for a 'hobby-horse' on a very complicated frame with four wheels.

A small polished wooden rocking-horse, of about 1830, in the American Museum at Bath, wears a fly-net over its back. Other small horses may have this idea carried out in brush strokes.

Benjamin Potter Crandall was born on Rhode Island in the early nineteenth century. He and his four sons made a name for the family and themselves with their toys, velocipedes, rocking-horses, hobby-horses, doll carriages, blocks, etc., many of which have become collectors' pieces. These four brothers, Benjamin junior, Jesse A., Charles T., and William E. helped in the firm of Crandall & Co., or set up for themselves in Brooklyn and New York. The McClintocks in *Toys in America* have much to say about this large family, which made toys between the 1840s and the 1890s.

Soon after Benjamin Potter Crandall went to New York he improved on the German rocking-horse. The flat board sides were cut away so that they looked more like the legs of a trotting horse, and fixing these to rockers, he made a model which was known as the 'cricket'. He also made rocking-horses, covering some with hide, but later he returned to those of painted wood as these were much stronger. Another model was known as a 'spring horse' and one of these was sent to the Prince of Wales, later Edward VII.

A kind of double rocking-horse with a wide seat was also made by Crandalls and was known as a 'shoo-fly'.

In London, by 1877, there were 11 different makers of rocking-horses and spring horses, and at the end of the nineteenth century rockers were replaced by a frame with a system of rollers and pulleys. The horses, usually dapple-grey, had arched necks, flashing glass eyes, manes and tails of real horsehair, and legs stretched out at a jump.

There were many ideas for rocking-horses, some with springs on which the children were encouraged to take exercise, such as that of Purchese in England, but the most successful was that of W. Marqua in the U.S.A., a maker of hobby-horses. In 1880, his firm in Cincinnati, Ohio, patented a horse in which a stand replaced the rockers, and the motion was to and fro in addition to up and down. These heavy stands continued through Edwardian days and well into the twentieth century.

76

About 1880, the expensive rocking-horses made in the U.S.A. by Morton Converse had real hide and tails, and manes of horsehair, whereas the cheaper ones were painted, their manes and tails being made of cow hair.

Walter Lines, our famous English toy-maker, remembers carving rocking-horses in the family factory about 1896 when he was 14.

The rocking-horses made at the end of the nineteenth century were handed on to the children of the twentieth century. They were dappled grey with open jaws showing rather frightening teeth, real horse manes and tails, perhaps leather reins, saddles and stirrups, and the whole mounted on rockers.

In 1908 the rollers wore grooves in the nursery floors and 'chars' complained of getting splinters in their hands when scrubbing. These horses with fearsome looks in their eyes could move gradually forward with their young riders, who were emulating the pictures of John Gilpin with his wig flying, repeated over and over again on the nursery wallpaper.

By now the rocking-horse was not so heavy because the body was hollow, and pennies and other treasures were posted in its inside. With more houses, more nurseries, rocking-horses began to be scarce, and wooden horses carved in the Black Forest for roundabouts at fairs could be altered for the purpose.

Dobbin was a favourite name for horses. Hamley's had a rocking-horse with this name in 1934; it was dappled and had a detachable saddle.

Now they have undergone many changes; in 1961 the beautiful London shop of Fortnum and Mason had one on a steel frame, and in the U.S.A. rocking-horses, again covered with real skin, were on sale at Christmas-time for £50. Heals in 1963 had some with box-shaped bodies, these being easier to mass produce, the other parts being traditional. But horses in stores with not such good taste as Heals have lost their proud disdainful look and have a knowing wink about the eye à la Walt Disney.

The I.C.I. company in 1964 produced a special paint which with one application could paint a rocking-horse, spots and all.

A modern Danish rocking-horse was so simple that it was not far removed from those of seventeenth-century Europe. However, hand-carved specimens are becoming things of the past and like dolls their monetary value is increasing. A Georgian one carved about 1800 fetched £100 in 1966. This was painted a soft dappled-grey and stood about four feet six inches on its rockers. Another carved wooden rocking-horse, 'expertly restored', was advertised in *The Times* in 1967, for £75, and their price is still rising.

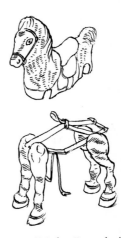

194 'Mobo Broncho' England

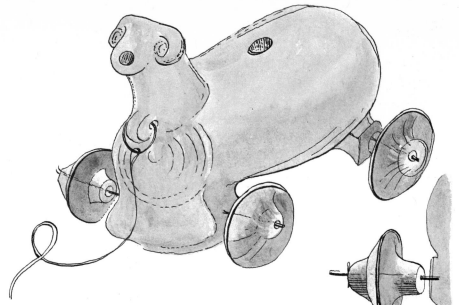

195 Animal on wheels.
Mesopotamia

4 Wheels, pull-alongs, carriages, cars, engines, doll-carriages

WHEELS, PULL-ALONGS

Which came first, the real cart or the toy cart? the real boat or the toy boat? When watching a log float downstream that would surely give one the idea of carving out the centre so that there was room to sit in it. Maybe when a father was dragging home a bundle of wood, what would be more natural than to put a tired child on the pile and pull him home.

A sledge seems to be the forerunner of the cart, and it would be from gazing at the heavily laden sledge that the idea of a wheel might come, at first a solid wheel, a kind of roller, and later one more open to make it less heavy.

Thick wheels, solid and with no spokes, were made by the Sūmerians about 3000–2750 B.C. when they were living in the valley of the River Euphrates. These were used on their carts, with sometimes two wheels, sometimes four. Asses and oxen were trained to pull these along, and many little model carts have been unearthed from this district, Mesopotamia, Egypt and later on in India.

A model chariot from Tell Agrab had solid wheels with studded rims, and was pulled by four white asses. Made of cast bronze, this

78

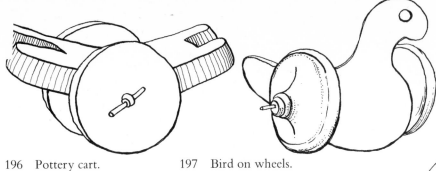

196 Pottery cart.
Chanhudaro

197 Bird on wheels.
Mohenjodaro

198 Mouse on wheels.
Egypt

199 Chariot of wood.
Egypt

200 Horse with rider.
Cyprus

201 Horse of wood.
Egypt

little object demonstrates an early example of casting by the *cire perdue* technique.

At Mem Damb, a toy bull was found which had its stumpy legs pierced for wheel axles, and a hole through the hump on its back was to take a string. Children could pull along such toys as these and also other little animals on stands with solid wheels.

In 2600 B.C. sledges were still used at funerals, it probably being an honour to be pulled along by men, just as today when a coffin may be placed on a gun-carriage and taken through the streets by two lines of men with ropes.

Sculptures from Mohenjodaro and Tell Asmar in 2400 B.C. show wheels consisting of three pieces of wood mortised together, and bound with leather tyres which were attached with copper nails. These wheels turned in one piece with the axle, which was secured to the body of the sledge with leather thongs.

In Sūmer, two or more persons could ride in their high, forked, two-wheeled chariots. The wheels were solid, two half discs dowelled together against the hub, and the chariots were pulled along by oxen or asses. The Indo-Europeans on the north fringes of Sūmer and Akkad kept carts with solid wheels for farm work and introduced spoked wheels for sport and warfare, horses pulling these lighter vehicles, some wearing little bells made of metal. By the end of the second millennium the spoked wheel had reached places as far apart as China and Sweden.

Just to give an idea of numbers, Solomon alone had 40,000 stalls for his horses and chariots, and 12,000 horsemen.

Athens had its first chariots in 1486 B.C., and by 1400 B.C. iron was in use. Farmers could purchase their own tools, and ploughs were used in Greece, Asia and Egypt. Rameses III is shown riding in a chariot which had wheels with six spokes.

The bodies of the Egyptian chariots were of leather, the Celtic and Aegean chariots were of wicker, which was imitated by lines of paint on their toys. The axles were attached to the wooden floors with leather straps, the floor projecting on each side to take the wheels which were secured by linchpins to their outer faces. This same method was used in the toys.

79

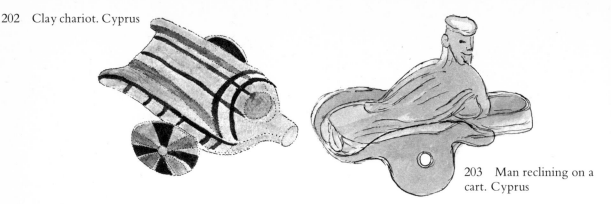

202 Clay chariot. Cyprus

203 Man reclining on a cart. Cyprus

In 1100 B.C. when the foundations for a temple were laid at Susa, in Persia, the onlookers placed all manner of things into the excavation, as was their wont, and among these pious offerings two little toy animals were found. One was a pig, the other a lion, and both were made of white limestone and could be pulled along by means of a string. There is an illustration of these in Karl Gröber's *Children's Toys of Bygone Days*. Many supposed toys from graves are now known to have been funeral offerings put there to serve the person in the world beyond.

The chariot axle was centre to the floor during the Iron Age, but later on, the Assyrian coach-builders moved the axle towards the back of the body. Early Hittite, Egyptian and Mycenaean wheels had four spokes, Homeric wheels eight and metal tyres.

Iron Age Celtic wheels had four to ten or 12 spokes, and later Hittite and Assyrian wheels had from six to eight spokes. Rims of wheels known as 'felloes' were a single piece bent into shape.

204 Bronze chariot. Sūmeria

205 Clay cart with imitation wickerwork. Roman

207   Clay chariot pulled
by cocks. North Africa

Horses were harnessed by means of a yoke and a single central pole during the Eighteenth dynasty of Egypt and in Celtic Britain. Toy horses were usually made of wood, and in 657 B.C. many could be pulled along with a cord. About 600 B.C. the Celtic horse-races were held at Carmen Fair in Ireland, and Aryans raced along in their u-shaped chariots across a set course to a certain mark and back again.

Apart from clay models, wooden toys, etc., there were lead chariots and horses made in Greece about 400 B.C., and also little warriors on horseback. Many were funeral offerings found in the tombs of children from Melos and Athos. A lead wagon, height $1\frac{1}{2}$ inches, came from Smyrna in 200 B.C., and ivory chariots with wheels which could turn came from Rome in 27 B.C. Sometimes the names of the winners of the chariot-races would be carved on the toys, forerunners of the James Bond motor-cars, which incidentally have disc wheels in place of open ones with spokes.

The Little Clay Cart was a well-known Indian play written about A.D. 700, in which some jewels were hidden belonging to a small boy. These dates 27 B.C.–A.D. 700 denote a gap in history owing to the Dark Ages, the fires, and the wooden toys being destroyed.

The ancient Mexicans knew of the wheel and used it before the coming of Christopher Columbus. Huge stone wheels have been found at Tiahuanaco, and many specimens of wheeled toys. Actually, wheels would not be used much before A.D. 700 until animals were trained to pull vehicles. About this time, clay animals resting on rollers were made from tubes of clay. These may have been connected with wooden axles socketed to the holes in the legs.

Away in China, in the T'ang dynasty A.D. 618–905, a toy buffalo cart with a height of four inches shows that wheeled toys were made in the Orient.

208   Horse on wheels.
Lower Egypt

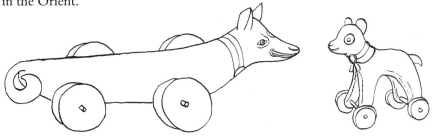

209, 210   Clay animals on
wheels. Valley of Mexico

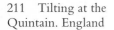
211 Tilting at the Quintain. England

Toy knights on wheels were made of bronze in Germany, early in the sixteenth century, at the time of our Henry VIII. They were about five inches high, and were made to pull along by a string. These wheels had six spokes and thick rims, but wooden toys still had wheels of solid wood. Towards the end of the sixteenth century, wooden horses made in Nuremberg were large enough for a child to sit on the carved wooden saddle, and were nearly two feet high.

An automatic coach and horses was made for Louis XIV when he was a child in 1649. This 'moved naturally and variously' and there was a footman and page, and a lady riding within. Real carriages, heavy affairs, were let out for hire in 1650 in Paris.

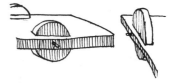
212 Inset wheels on wooden toys

213 Man riding on hobby-horse bicycle. England

Many wooden toys came from Thuringia during the eighteenth century, pull-toys on wheels and little carts. On one cart was a woman and some geese which wobbled about on springs when the cart was pulled along, and most had solid wooden wheels inset into the solid wooden stands.

The children of George III had a pretty wooden cart, about eight inches long and painted with flowers and scrolls. It was pulled by two wooden horses. An idea for a toy horse at the end of the eighteenth century was to conceal the wheels under the hooves instead of having a stand. There is an example of this in the museum at Bethnal Green, where the horse is 15 inches high.

The Essex Institute, Salem, U.S.A., has a proud horse on a stand belonging to the nineteenth century on which the wooden wheels are solid, whereas those on the little carts had spoked wheels.

By the 1870s in England, toy dappled-grey horses were much in favour, some pulled bright yellow carts with tip-up backs, some pulled coal-trucks, others pulled haywains and dust-carts, all of these being a convenient size for a child to pull along on a string. Large toys were popular at this time, and by the end of the nineteenth century the wheeled toys were numerous. There were brewer's drays, trains, toy fire-engines which pumped real water, and model milk-floats complete with churns and workable taps.

214 Man on hobby-horse bicycle. England

215 Pull toy. German
patent by Gustav Schwabe

216 Carriage and four.
Belgium

218 Animated frog.
German patent by Joh
and Issmayer

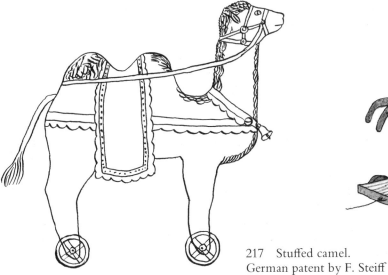

217 Stuffed camel.
German patent by F. Steiff

Nicholas Bentley, born in Edwardian days, in his book *A Choice of Ornaments* recalls in his youth an American fire-engine 'which ran about by some mysterious means that I never understood, making a very satisfactory and authentic sound of wailing as it did so'.

Apart from horses, some made as an aid to walking, there were large dogs provided with handles for children to push along. Big shaggy brown dogs or smooth Dalmatians with black spots were available in the 1930s. These had chromium-plated stands and four bright red metal wheels. Such toys were fairly expensive and large enough for a child to sit on, but most of them disappeared from the shops during the war.

219 Wooden toys made
by children. Austria

220 Hay Wain by
Britains Ltd. England

A 'buzzy bee' was one of the few insect toys, and came in 1950.
It was made by Fisher Price, U.S.A., and had springing antennae,
plastic whirling wings and a wooden body.

In a pull–along wooden hen toy, the legs were fixed to the wheels,
and as the legs went round, the hen flapped its wings and could also
cluck and lay eggs.

Another wheel toy was a baker's barrow on wheels, 14 inches high;
it was filled with buns, loaves and crumpets and came from Hamley's.
This toy in 1959 was a peep into the past, for wheeled barrows such
as this one, had not been in use for a number of years.

Today, one can meet all kinds of animals being pulled along,
families of ducks going 'Quack, quack, quack', ponies with real skin
bodies, and wooden toys not so far removed from those of the
Romans in days gone by.

Scooters have not entirely vanished. In 1968, we saw one on the
Edgware Road, a home–made looking affair, but with two wheels at
the back and a lamp on the front.

Many Victorian toys have now reached the salerooms and fetch
far higher sums than their original prices.

A large clockwork trotting cart, with the horse running on a wheel
and the rider moving up and down, was sold recently for 40 guineas.
This was 13 inches long and possibly American.

A lady sitting in a Bath chair pushed by a uniformed attendant with
walking mechanism was made by Fernand Martin about 1890. Known
as 'Le Fauteuil Roulant', it was a fly–wheel–driven model in the
original box, and this sold for 17 guineas in the same sale.

A carved horse on wheels went for 11 guineas, and 38 guineas was
paid for a clockwork model of an ostrich pulling a wickerwork
governess-cart; the cart had a rear driver's seat which was decorated
with poker-work. The ostrich toy was 18 inches long and the horse
and cart eight inches.

221　Wooden elephant
with cart. England

222　'Buzzy Bee' by
Fisher Price. East Aurora,
New York, U.S.A.

223　'The Cackling Hen'
by Fisher Price. U.S.A.

Hackney coaches appeared on the London streets at the beginning of the reign of Charles I. They were lumbering leather-covered carriages, and Samuel Pepys preferred to travel up and down the city by water.

The Queen's State coach was built in 1761 and the coach for the Lord Mayor of London in 1757. A 'flying coach' which went between Manchester and London in 1754 made the journey in $4\frac{1}{2}$ days. Since then there have been many little toys representing either the Lord Mayor's or the Queen's State coach.

At the back of the eighteenth-century vehicles, before the arrival of 'the boot', were huge wickerwork carriers known as 'baskets'. Any old luggage was placed in this, together with less-favoured children and servants. Palmer of Bath designed coaches which were adopted by the Post Office, and the mail-coaches became the cream of coaching with limited passengers exempt from paying tolls. In Regency England, coaching became a pleasant pastime on roads improved by McAdam and Telford, and beautiful examples of private carriages have survived.

Shillibeer's bus came in 1829 drawn by three horses. Later two horses were found sufficient to pull these closed wagonettes, which eventually had outside seats, and later on the substitution of a motor for horsepower.

The omnibus or horsebus was first seen in London early in the nineteenth century, the first omnibus going from Paddington to the Bank of England in 1829.

Cabs, short for cabriolets, were introduced into the streets of London early in the nineteenth century, and by 1823 there were 12 which plied for hire. At the 1844 Paris Exhibition, M. Saint-Hormayères of Paris was mentioned for his toy mechanical horses and carriages (he lived in the rue du Faubourg), and M. Guérin, of the passage Brady, was mentioned for the great care which he took in making his little carriages and horses with simple mechanism, and also for his beautifully made model of a carriage.

At the Great Exhibition of 1851, a clockwork stage-carriage cost £2 8s.

In 1860 the interior of the omnibus had the inside of the roof raised along the centre lengthwise, and this made a seat on the top for outside passengers and, was named a 'knifeboard'. At first it was reached by a vertical ladder up the back of the body, and the people sat on two long seats, back to back.

This year also came the tram, in Birkenhead and in 1861 in London at Bayswater. 'Garden seat' buses came in the 1890s. The driver's box, high up, was a direct survival from coaching practice. When reasonable curved stairways arrived, ladies and girls ventured on top, displaying limbs and underclothes which was considered very daring, but it was unavoidable.

Reversible flapseats were introduced in 1895 on the upper decks of the Bristol tramways. The dry side was turned up in rainy weather,

224   Pull-along tram of wickerwork. Probably France or Spain

225   Wooden cab. England

and this idea was still in use on the London buses in the late 1920s, with also a mackintosh apron attached to the seat in front, making almost a little house for a child to sit under. Later the inside staircase appeared which led to a closed saloon at the top.

A charabanc on a bus chassis became a motor-coach, and by 1914 it had spoked wheels and solid tyres. Parties were taken to the seaside, to the races, or on a tour of beauty-spots. From these grew the modern motor-coach with pneumatic tyres and roofs to replace the old folding hoods à la perambulator, and wood was no longer used in the construction.

From the foregoing it may be possible to date the numerous toys representing vehicles on the roads many of which came from Germany. Cremer in 1875 said, 'from Hilberghausen come the velocipede riders', but many of the velocipedes and automatic toys came from Paris, where they were made by Jules Steiner in 1869.

Most of the cars which we call 'veterans' today were on view at the Motor Show of 1911, and many of these can be obtained in what is known as the Matchbox series, though they certainly would not fit into a matchbox. The Lesney Rolls Royce, one of the veteran cars in this series was given the Queen's Award for exporting in April 1968.

Early in the twentieth century there were tin vehicles of about ten inches high and smaller ones about six inches high to go along the ground either by clockwork or by pulling. Many of these have reached museums, there are some fine specimens in the Luton Museum, but, as with boats, one must try to distinguish between a toy and a model.

227   'Genevieve' by Charbens. England

226   Tank by Benbros. England

228 Pedal car for a child to ride in. England

Bigger cars worked with pedals came in the late 1920s and are much the same today, except that the chassis has altered slightly. Our eldest son, born in 1938, spent hours in his, either riding about or camouflaging it with a mixture of mud in a toy bucket, wearing dungarees and a tin helmet. There are American jeeps about today with a white star on the front and there are more elaborate versions known as 'generals' jeeps' with three white stars.

There are also various kinds of tricycles, some made with animals' bodies, or bicycles with what are known as 'stabilisers' on which a child may learn to ride a real bicycle.

Meccano Ltd. started to produce model cars in 1933, known at first as Modelled Miniatures and by April 1934 as Dinky Toys. Each model was die-cast and was based on an actual vehicle. The French Dinky Toys were made at a factory in Bobigny, just outside Paris.

In 1934, the little cars had a 'criss-cross' chassis and metal wheels with detachable rubber tyres. At first these tyres were white, but after the war black ones were used.

During the 'blackout', many real cars and lorries had their front wings painted white, in order to avoid accidents. A Dinky Toy known as a 'Pool' petrol tanker was also painted in this way.

There were dust-wagons with opening lids, vans and petrol tanks, many carrying advertisements of products which have since dis-

229 Steam-roller, a Tri-ang Mini toy. England

230 'Silver Cloud' by
Lesney. England

appeared. The delivery-vans of the four great railway companies were painted in their individual colours before they were taken over by British Railways.

Dinky Supertoys came in 1948 and there were many accessories such as petrol pumps with rubber hose-pipes which later on were replaced by plastic.

The little cars were painted in one colour, but in 1956 two colours were used and the first Dinky cars to be fitted with windows came in 1958, and also plastic wheels made in one piece. Corgi cars already had windows in 1956, and in 1962 their model cars, apart from side windows which went up and down, and a boot which opened, had also a bonnet which could be lifted up.

Die-cast wheels were replaced by plastic wheels about 1962. Previously the alloy consisted of zinc, aluminium and magnesium, and the very early models contained lead. In 1964, Dinky Toys were bought up by Lines Brothers.

Lesney Toys had marketed a small gilded coach in 1952 for 2s. 11d., which was very successful, and a few years later they packed their toys in 'matchboxes'. The engineering skill was that of Jack Odell and the marketing flair was by Leslie Smith. The third man was Rodney Smith, hence the name Lesney.

The sales of toy motor-cars were enormous, and not only are there cars, there are all the accessories to go with them. In 1960 there were road sections with flyovers and banked corners on which sports cars and saloons could whizz along at a speed of 250 m.p.h., which apparently was a real speed of from six to seven miles per hour. Car race tracks had layouts with electric remote driving controls and, like the train sets, they could be added to and expanded.

Children have always been observant and keen on having their toys realistic when they reach the age of nine or thereabouts, so much so that one toy car maker received more than 50 letters from children in which they complained that the filler-cap on a sports model car was on the wrong side. Apparently the makers of the real car had changed their design but had not told the toy-makers!

This craze for realism now led the toy manufacturers to try to make their models from still secret plans for new cars. Should a car firm scrap its plans and jigs, then the toy firm had to follow suit. It is a far cry from the days when grown-ups knew best and children 'were seen and not heard'.

In 1962 toy police cars which used to be black were now in bright colours also, just as the real ones seen on the roads today.

'Mr Kelly's Car Wash' was a toy made by Remco where a toy car could be automatically wetted, scrubbed and dried in 1963.

For keeping youngsters occupied on long journeys there was a dashboard which could be fixed behind the front seat of a car. This was fitted with gears, brakes and traffic signals and a small boy could play in the car or practise with this gadget at home by having it fixed to the back of a chair.

To return to yesterday, in 1963 there were veteran cars which were worked with pedals and also penny-farthing bicycles.

'One of the most interesting novelties of 1964 was the Motor Roarer, the real Grand Prix sound', said Triang (not the neighbours). These were little motors that gave the authentic 'brmm . . . brmm' noise and could be fixed to any child's pedal-car or scooter. 'They could rev up to a real high-speed noise for only 49s. 6d.'

For £97 17s. 6d., there was a real B.S.A. model-type sports car in green fibreglass with a real single-stroke engine, but these were to be driven on private estates only.

In 1966 a battery-driven Aston Martin D.B.5 had 'mystery evasive action'. This silver-grey car, with an $8\frac{1}{2}$-inch body, travelled at speed, changing direction as it glided along to put pursuers off its track. The Aston Martin Lagonda factory gave Prince Andrew a scaled-down model of the famous James Bond car, with electronic machine-guns concealed in the sidelights and a bullet-proof screen. When a control was operated, smoke billowed from the rear of the car, and there was also a water-squirter.

231   A jeep with pedals. England

In 1967 in the grounds of the Summer Palace of Saadebad, the Crown Prince Reza was seen playing with his electric runabout car, watched by his sister the Princess Farahnaz.

Pedal-along racing-cars with battery-operated hooters had their racing number painted on the bonnet.

Less realistic were plastic buses on which the child sat in order to move along, and like most toys some cars are large playthings while others are small enough to hold in the hand.

At a sale in 1967, a large model, that is 12 inches long, of a Renault car sold for 42 guineas. It was painted white and gold, the red wheels with solid rubber tyres, and with working brake and adjustable steering. It was accompanied by a chauffeur and two female passengers – probably made in England, it was complete in a glazed case.

A model of the London, Bath and Bristol coach, 13 inches long, and painted in colours was also in a glazed case – this together with a toy water-cart and wooden horse on wheels went for 48 guineas. The cart, by Gamages, was painted red and green, and the white horse could tow the watering-cart, the total length being 30 inches.

Beaties of London in 1967 offered to buy model trains and Dinky Toys in exchange for Scalextric racing car sets. Also Tootsietoys, and large tin-plate car models, pre 1948 were wanted privately.

ENGINES

The first public passenger railway in the world was the Oystermouth between Swansea and the Mumbles in 1807. Stevenson invented his locomotive in 1814, and the first public steam railway was the Stockton and Darlington in 1825, the passengers riding in what looked like the front portions of two ordinary stage-coaches spliced together at the door. In 1830, the Liverpool and Manchester Railway was opened, carrying both passengers and goods behind locomotives.

The carriages were made to resemble mail-coaches as closely as possible, so as to allay passengers' fears of the unfamiliar. Each 'body' or compartment contained six well-padded seats with elbow-rests and head-rests in between, and as on the roads, the luggage went on the roof, even as late as 1860.

Extra-special passengers, the v.i.p.s, could ride with the mail, with two seats on each side instead of three, but the 'common people' stood and swayed about in what were little more than open trucks, perhaps with an awning, perhaps not. Holes bored in the floors let out the rain. In 1844, Gladstone insisted that the people should be protected from the weather.

Coaches were usually four-wheeled, though the Great Western had six-wheelers from the first. In 1852 they put on the celebrated 'Long Charleys' which were eight-wheel carriages, still with curved windows dating back to the coach-building of the Renaissance.

Bogie trucks were seen only in America or areas under American influence such as Russia and south Germany.

232 Panama railway train. U.S.A.

Although railways came early in the nineteenth century, no toy trains seem to exist before the 1840s, though there must have been a few home-made examples. Mr Charles P. Wade lent the 'earliest known toy train' to the Treasures of Famous Children Exhibition in 1934. Here also was the Manchester fire-engine of 1840 complete with ladders and helmets, all in miniature.

In 1835 the first German railway was between Nuremberg and Fürth; later, toys would be based on this. In the Victoria and Albert Museum Exhibition of 1958, a German clockwork train was displayed, possibly the earliest surviving toy of its kind, and still working perfectly, complete with engine, tender and passenger coach.

There is a toy train of 1840 in the Gunnersbury Museum, and another in the London Museum which was made about 1845. This is of wood and runs along a sloped wooden track. The wheels are solid discs, and the whole toy was made in Germany. A Berlin firm, G. Söhlke, manufactured trains in the very early days of railways.

A toy railway station made in wood in 1850 was for the children of Viscount Alford, and consisted of carriage, horsebox, passengers and luggage.

RIDGES ON TREAD

233　Tin railway engine and tender. Probably German

By 1860 toy steam-engines had whistles, but miniature gas-lamps on stations would not appear until after 1863.

Metal trains manufactured in Germany about 1873 had metal wheels with four spokes, and the engine had a tall funnel. Toy engines and their carriages seem to be about ten years behind the times, and for a long while these toy metal engines made in Germany had long funnels serrated at the top.

In Japan the first railway was opened in 1872 by the Mikado. It ran from Yokohama to Shinagawa.

Returning to England, the real dining-cars came in 1879, with meals being cooked on board, and in 1875, the Midland Railway abolished its second-class carriages.

The clerestory type of roof was popular from the late 1890s to about 1917. Side corridors leading to a lavatory came in 1881 on the Great Northern Railway on six-wheeled first-class coaches and in 1889 on the Midland for their third class, a 12-wheel coach winning the Grand Prix that year in the Paris Exhibition. A complete gang-wayed corridor train came in 1891 on the Great Western Railway.

The first electric tube railway came in 1890, the Waterloo and City line in 1898 and the Central London line in 1900. Before this steam had been used. When my father and mother spent part of their honeymoon at the Arundel Hotel near the Temple Station the smoke and fumes reached them from the vents, for the Metropolitan Railway was not electrified until 1903, four years later.

Large toy trains were of wood, whereas smaller ones were of metal. Many of these were made in Germany and after 1890 most of them were stamped with the letters D.R.G.M., *Deutsches-Reichs Gebrauchs Muster*, and indeed other toys and dolls had either the initials or the words 'Made in Germany' to agree with the Act passed in that year.

Many engines still resembled Stephenson's original engine, and MacQueen Pope, who has written much about his Victorian childhood days says: 'wooden railway engines were equally primitive, resembling puffing billies and are still about today [1948] only slightly modified in form'.

Märklin became the name most associated with toy trains in Germany, while in England it was that of Basset-Lowke. A toy steam locomotive of the first quality came in 1901, it was built to scale by Basset-Lowke, and it ran on standard gauges.

234   Train. German

Escher used a toy engine for his sign in 1881, which was registered in Germany, and both engines and boats appeared in the sign used by the Globe Supply Company in 1902, in England. The firm of Gebruder Bing of Nuremberg registered their mark in England in 1906, on which the initials G.B.N. appeared, and the well-known firm of Lines registered their thistle mark in 1910.

The Hornby clockwork trains became very popular after the First World War. Before this the clockwork train market had been dominated by German firms, notably Märklin, and Bing. Electric trains arrived later, also in the 'o' gauge for young children, whereas the more sophisticated boys went in for electric trains in the 'oo', which were called 'Dublo', for 'Double O'. This is the only electric gauge now made.

Frank Hornby died in 1936. His firm had been responsible for Hornby Modelled Miniatures, which added realism to the lines and stations with their station staffs and porters' trucks, etc., apart from the well-known Hornby trains.

Clockwork trains with lines to fit together on the floor or on a large table have always been favourites, some nurseries being fitted to

235   Edwardian engine.
Probably German

take the track on a shelf round the walls. Actually the fun was in laying out the lines and deciding where they should go, especially the points. Everything was made to scale and could be added to without limit. These were popular from 1910 to 1950 and even then were not entirely ousted by electrical sets.

236 'Looky Chug-Chug', by Fisher Price. East Aurora, U.S.A.

A 1949 engine for a young child to pull along was the Fisher Price 'Looky Chug-chug' with tender. It had a face painted on the front and a bell to ring, and also a patented locomotive sound. It is interesting to note in the drawing the return to solid wooden wheels. These pull-along toys were made at East Aurora, New York. The toys are of ponderosa wood, the pictures on them are lithographed on paper, rather in a Walt Disney style, and as the toys are pulled along funny animal noises are heard.

In 1961 engines had smoke coming out of the funnels and existing engines could have this idea fitted when taken back to the factory.

Small boys in 1963 could have traction engines with real steam coming out of the funnel, and Old Western locos had flashing lights, hooters and cow-pushers. Self-propelling metal trains with a red glowing funnel and noisy hooter, battery-operated, were another attraction.

Pull-along engines designed by John Gould were at Abbatt's in 1963 and were said to be strong enough to bear an adult on top. Electric train sets, in 1966, consisted of a Pacific-type engine, car transporter wagons complete with cars, scenic trees and track-lights, and a full set of straight and curved rails.

An early small wooden train set, complete with engine, coaches, three sections of a sloping grooved track and two trees in the original box, together with a small painted model of a carriage and horses also in a box, were sold recently for 12 guineas – both had probably been made in Sonneberg.

The 11 August 1968, saw the last of the real steam locomotives on British Rail. Since then, we have had diesels.

237 'The Pioneer', a Marx toy. England

In 1870 perambulators were newfangled things and were very heavy affairs built on the principle of a carriage.

In 1874 dolls' prams or doll-carriages as they were known, had wooden wheels with wooden spokes, usually eight on the larger back wheel and six on the front. The 'hood' was a kind of canopy or umbrella fixed to a single wire from the back as in a cradle or it could have a support on either side. The handle was at the back, that is the doll faced the way it was going as in a push-chair.

In 1886, there was a three-wheeler with the small wheel in front, and about this time came a collapsible hood. About 1889 wire spokes appeared on some of the better prams, arranged alternately, 16 in number on the real prams and less on those built for dolls.

In 1890 dolls in France could ride in wickerwork prams with wickerwork hoods and delicately trimmed with muslin, similar to the dolls' cradles of the period. The wheels also were of cane.

'Mail-carts' appeared in the late nineteenth century and wickerwork push-chairs. Some had imitation leather and iron wheels, and others were known as 'Victorias'.

An early mail-cart for a doll was of canework and made in England about 1840. There were two large iron wheels and two small ones – almost a 'double penny-farthing'. There was a little 'well' for the feet and two prongs to prevent it from tipping. The one in Bethnal Green Museum is 21 inches high.

Until about 1886, the doll-carriages in the U.S.A. had wooden wheels, the two back ones being larger than the two at the front, and there was a single handle at the back. Another version was a three-wheeler with the small single wheel at the front.

A German doll's pram of about 1880 was a wicker cradle on an iron stand with four iron wheels of equal size. The hood at the back, near the handle, was fitted with curtains which were tied back with ribbons.

In 1909 dolls were pushed about in well-made prams fairly high from the ground and finished with painted lines and imitation wickerwork as were the carriages of the period. Some had cream-coloured canopies lined with dark green, and wicker stands to take a doll-size umbrella. The 'babies' tucked up inside would have feeding-bottles and dummies which were known as 'comforters', their little wax or bisque faces surrounded by swansdown, and protected with a veil to keep away the dust and smells from horse traffic.

Prams were usually made to take a doll at either end, though the collapsible hood was at the end opposite the handle. There was a 'well' in the centre to take the feet of the doll and a little lid which was placed over this when the pram was occupied by a long-clothes baby doll. The large wheels had thin rubber strips for tyres, the seats were of padded leather and edged with braid.

In 1961 many dolls' prams cost as much as one for a real baby. Nearly 15 guineas seems a tremendous price to pay, but Gamages had these which were made of fibreglass in two colours and were called

238 Doll's push-chair by Shrives of Cambridge. England

239 DOLL CARRIAGES

i, ii U.S.A., c. 1870. iii English, c. 1880. iv English, c. 1884. v U.S.A., 1888.
vi U.S.A., 1890. vii English. viii English. ix English, 1890. x English, 1908.
xi English, early 20th century. xii English, c. 1890. xiii English, 1908.
xiv U.S.A., 1910. xv English, 1911. xvi English, c. 1890

'Fonteyn'. A Silver Cross dolls' pram was known as the Rolls Royce of prams and cost £14 7s. 6d. and yet back in 1938 a real baby's pram cost only £8 10s. 0d.

Push-chairs for dolls are now made of vinyl, and strangely enough a small sunshade is gradually taking the place of a hood.

240 Pram with thin rubber tyres. England

5   Boats, darts, arrows, boomerangs, windmills, swings, kites, aeroplanes

BOATS

The fertile soil and mild climate of Egypt produced the necessaries and comforts of life in such profusion that the inhabitants were content to stay in their own district, therefore it is rare to have model or toy boats from here before the year 2000 B.C.

The Phoenicians who lived near Palestine excelled in boat-building, and as their ships became larger they were manned by slaves. Paintings on the New Kingdom tombs depict the Phoenicians in their barges on the River Nile, bartering trinkets with the peasants from the neighbouring villages. They plied the Mediterranean, even reached Cornwall to obtain tin, and traded with Arabia and India, thus being ahead of the Greeks who still kept within sight of their own land when they went aboard.

'Myrmecides made a ship, with all the tackling to it, no bigger than a small bee might hide it with her wings', so wrote Pliny when describing this tiny miniature of long ago.

241   Model boat. Egypt

The term 'galley-slave' arose from the galleys built by the Corinthians about 907 B.C., in which the boats had 25–30 benches on each side, manned with about four or five slaves to each bench.

Alexander in 332 B.C. built ships in Egypt which sailed up the mouth of the River Indus, where he met elephants for the first time. Pytheas, a Greek, who knew that the world was round, built a merchant ship which was propelled by a square sail and 100 oarsmen, and he is said to have reached Iceland.

In 262 B.C. the Romans built ships based on those they had seen used by the Phoenicians. North Americans made their canoes from the barks of trees, and the Eskimos made theirs from whalebones covered with sealskins.

With the coming of boats more countries were explored, and by A.D. 300 the Vikings were the seamen of the North venturing eastwards towards the Baltic and southwards towards the British Isles. However, it was not until the magnet was discovered by Flavio Gioia that sailors could venture far afield and steer when the sky was cloudy or on the darkest night.

In 1350 five canoes reached New Zealand manned by Maori voyagers carrying the dog on purpose and the rat by mistake. They introduced the gourd, taro and kumara from the Polynesian Islands to the New Zealanders.

About the same time as Drake sailed round the world, Captain Yorke explored the 'Icie Seas'.

Phineas Pett was first master of the Shipwrights' Company in 1612. He made a model ship which was for a toy for Prince Charles. It is now in the Tradescant Collection in the Ashmolean Museum.

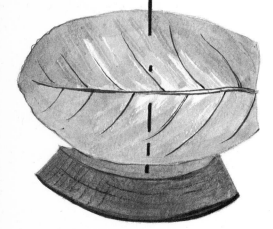

242　Coconut husk boat with leaf sail. Trobriand Islands

243　Wooden warship. Jura mountains, Switzerland

In America, the first steamship, the *Phoenix*, put to sea and went from New York to Philadelphia, and in 1819 the *Savannah*, a steamship with sails, was the first American boat to cross the Atlantic.

Toy steam engines and ships were made by Maltête and Parent in France.

In 1869, Ives made clockwork boats at Bridgeport, Connecticut, and one of their first was a rowing-boat in which a man rowed with two oars. It was patented by them in 1869, and there is one of these, about 12 inches long, in the museum at Bethnal Green. Reeds were famous for their wooden toys during the last quarter of the nineteenth century, and in 1877 they made some pretty ferry-boats.

In 1899 toy steamboats were scarce but yachts, luggers, fishing-boats and lifeboats floated at the edge of the waves, for by now it was the thing to go to the seaside with the children for a summer holiday, where some of them were allowed to paddle or even venture into the sea itself.

245   Boat to float. U.S.A.

246   Pull-along boat. German patent by Gustave Schwabe

In the early part of the twentieth century most boys possessed a sailing-boat. It was the fashion to dress children, both boys and girls, in sailor suits with straw hats on the band of which would be the name of some ship in gold letters, such as H.M.S. *Victory*, and children might paint the same name on their toys.

A boat which was easy to float was a 'finbat'. These never became popular because they were unreal in appearance. However, there is a dearth of toy boats in museums, where many are models. Most toy boats have either sunk or sailed away beyond the horizon. Once I watched the dredging of the Round Pond in Kensington Gardens and there were many, many boats lying in a sea of mud.

Models of famous liners and of ships of the Royal Navy were made by Meccano Dinky Toys, the first ones appearing in 1934/35, and then reappearing when the Second World War was over. They were waterline models made of metal alloy with much detail, and were eagerly sought after by schoolboys.

A musical French showboat in pale colours cost about £3 in 1960. It could play a gay little tune when wound up, and had imitation smoke coming out of the funnel made of fluffy white feathers – obviously for a very young child.

Then in 1963 came a return to the Roman galleys. One named Big Caesar had banks of oars, an army with a land fort and catapults and opposing soldiers to complete the battle scene, the whole outfit costing about ten guineas.

247   Model of the Queen Mary, by Dinky Toys. England

248   Child with dart. Greece

DARTS, ARROWS

Away in Egypt in 1500 B.C. boys and men threw knives at blocks of wood, similar to the more modern game of darts.

Arrows were used against an enemy in warfare or when hunting wild animals. In 1491 B.C., when Saul was chosen to lead the Hebrews into battle, he was overcome by the bows and arrows of the Philistines.

Darts with feathers attached were used in ancient Greece and Rome, and bows were used in 745 B.C. in Aryan India and in the Orient. These arrows were tipped with metal and the bows had a cowhide thong. Africa already exported wooden bows, and they were much the same throughout Siberia, Turkey, Persia and India, though those used by the North American Eskimos were shorter and were made from horns and sinews. In most places a smaller size was made for children to use.

The bows of the Eskimo were made from three pieces of fir or larch, each making part of the same arch. The back was braced with a thread of linen made of deer sinews and also the bowstring. For greater strength they were dipped in water, as this made them contract and gave them more force. Eskimos can shoot with great dexterity, as they practise from their youth.

Bows and arrows were universal in America, but in the countries of Chile and Patagonia slings were used. Stones about the size of a fist were fastened to each end of a leather thong of about eight inches in length. These were swung round their heads, and were thrown with such accuracy that they seldom missed the target at which they were aimed.

Every American warrior besides his arms, carried a mat and a small bag of pounded maize, and he was then considered to be equipped ready for any service. The great idea was to surprise the enemy and destroy him. If his enemy was prepared, it was better to retire than have a victory stained with the blood of his own countrymen, and this was their belief which was not held through lack of courage.

On the Trobriand Islands, the toys used by the children are copies of the things used by the adults. The Massim children play with bows and arrows but these are only made as toys and are not used by the men for hunting.

Baby boys in Japan were sent a bow and arrow in the December of the year in which they were born.

When the Greek Dionysius grew up he invented a catapult, a huge affair which could send darts and arrows, and it was also used for throwing large stones.

Manuscripts in A.D. 400 show that archery was common in England, and by A.D. 449 the long-bow was six feet in length and the arrows three feet. The best-known character who used bows and arrows was our Robin Hood, dressed in green and surrounded by his Merry Men, in Sherwood Forest.

Among the instructions to parents of boys in 1570 at St Albans School, Hertfordshire, were the following: 'ye shall find your child ink, paper, pens, wax candles for winter . . . and ye shall allow your child at all times a bow, three arrows, bow strings, a shooting glove, and a bracer to exercise [sic] shooting.' A bracer was used in archery as a protective covering for the forearm, and the regulations were drawn up by Sir Nicholas Bacon.

In the U.S.A., a Massachusetts law of about 1630 required all boys from ten to 16 to be trained in shooting with bows and arrows.

In the Victorian era many places had archery-grounds, women also had their games. Targets made of straw ropes bound round and round formed a large circular board which was placed on a kind of easel. During the early part of the twentieth century children could be seen peering through the dusty flowering hedges to watch both men and women shooting with large bows and using feathered arrows, the women wearing long, flowing, thick skirts left over from the last century.

And so the game goes on. The children emulated their elders, and many a small girl was hit by blunt brass-tipped shafts at this time, but in June 1960, in Hungary, the manufacture of toy bows and arrows was officially halted.

The reason was that children had seen in an English version on television, the story and feats of William Tell, a Swiss, famous for shooting an apple off his son's head in the fourteenth century. There were so many eye accidents that the eye hospitals became over-burdened and in England also there were many casualties to trusting little sisters with elder brothers.

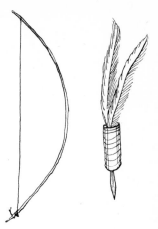

249 Dart and bow.
Trobriand Islands

250 Boy with bow and arrow

251 Toy boomerang.
Australia

BOOMERANGS

In Australia, from the time a young aborigine boy can walk, he is trained to use a toy boomerang made by his father. One arm of a boomerang is slightly longer than the other, though both weigh the same – one side is flat, the other rounded or cambered. At first the boy practises on his own, later he joins the other lads and an eight-year-old boy could kill a cockatoo on a branch at 30 yards.

When he becomes a man, he is permitted to have a real boomerang, made from the bend or elbow of a native tree, such as an acacia. In the twentieth century some aborigines have been killing surfacing fish with galvanised iron boomerangs, according to Dal Stivens.

In the 1950s toy boomerangs made of plastic were included as a free gift in packets of cereals.

252 Boys with windmills. Holland

WINDMILLS

Windmill toys were usually those with the sails of a windmill fixed to a long stick, and not models of little windmills. They are medieval toys and appear on manuscripts and early woodcuts and engravings, showing both girls and boys at play. The 'sails' are usually two cross-pieces of wood loosely nailed to the end of a stick.

The little girl Isabel, of Bavaria, mentioned in so many books on dolls, had also a windmill made of gold and studded with pearls. This toy appears in the household accounts for 1390.

Windmills are played with outdoors in the winter months and on a French calendar of the fourteenth century they appear on the first page. In a collection showing the play of children in 1587, the windmills are for the younger ones, and in an early Flemish calendar of the sixteenth century, again it is the younger ones who have these toys which most probably originated from the Low Countries.

During the sixteenth century Rabelais told of the education of Gargantua, how he was given a windmill in his fifth year. The making of windmill toys was a small Parisian industry and in the series the *Cries of Paris* there are merchants holding long sticks with a windmill fixed to one end.

There is an engraving by Poisson made in 1774 of an old woman selling all kinds of windmills; many of these have a little mill at the

253 Windmill.
Netherlands

254 Windmill. France

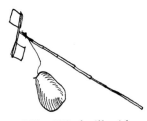

255 Windmill with bladder attached.
Netherlands

end of a stick on which the sails are fixed. An engraving of 1807 also shows this kind of toy windmill.

In France during the nineteenth century, the ancient windmill toys were made into genuine playthings at Notre-Dame de Liesse, and went under the name of a *moulin tapage*, meaning a noisy windmill. This was a toy far removed from those which had been used for announcing the arrival of lepers in years gone by.

During the 1880s wooden windmills were made in the U.S.A. in the old traditional manner, but in 1882 a self-regulating windmill appeared which was made entirely of iron. It was patented by C. J. Hamilton, a clock- and watch-repairer.

Simple paper windmills were on sale at fairs in England or at the gates to a park when perhaps a circus was to appear. These toys costing about one penny or a sixpence were very popular with their bright colours. Sometimes a piece of metal was fixed to the pin between the paper and the stick, so that when the sails revolved a whirring sound was heard.

Now the paper has been replaced by plastic, but paper ones can still be made at home quite easily, all that is needed is a headed pin, an eight-inch square of paper, a bead and a stick. The bead is to keep the paper from touching the stick as it whirls around.

Chinese windmills make a buzzing sound, for there is a little piece of bamboo striking a tiny drum below as they whizz round.

256 Windmill. France

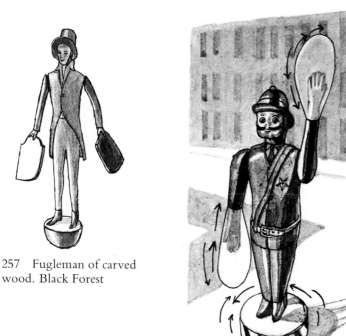

257 Fugleman of carved wood. Black Forest

258 'Oskar', a metal policeman. Italian OSKAR

259 Parachute. France

103

Swings at first were hung from the branches of trees, and later became well known in paintings by Boucher in which maidens swung precariously in the green glades of the countryside.

See-saws were merely a long stout branch placed across a log, the bigger the better. A hammock is hardly a toy, and neither is a rocking-chair, nor a rocking-cradle, and yet much amusement is derived from all three, and replicas have been made for dolls and dolls' houses.

A child's playground of today always has a swing and a see-saw, the latter often rotating in addition to going up and down, but the Victorian fandango has become a huge, dangerous contraption only to be found at fun fairs.

KITES

Kites were employed in China for military signalling in 206 B.C. and from here the practice of flying kites spread to India and eventually to Europe. Since then, the Chinese have always been fond of kite-flying, the aim being to see how high the kites could go. Some were made of thin tough paper, usually rice paper, others of fine silk, and the frame-work was of split bamboo. The shapes were of all kinds, some simple, some like butterflies, and some in the shapes of curious birds or fishes.

The raising of a kite in the sky was considered by some to be a symbol of the Resurrection of Christ. However that may be, the kite season begins in the spring, in the few weeks before Easter. The cry 'Look, there's a kite' is a signal for everyone to look up, and the first to see it shouts, 'There it is, there it is, over there.'

As long ago as A.D. 1160 there were kites which could make a humming noise by means of round holes and vibrating cords. A stork or a tortoise was a favourite decoration.

The colour prints from China or Japan show boys flying kites, and in medieval times there are woodcuts showing children at play, sometimes one with a kite and another with a windmill.

Kite-flying is a national sport in the East, and bets are laid. A favourite game is where the string of one kite may cut the string of another when the lines are crossed, in fact the cord of a kite usually costs more than the kite itself.

In the spring festivals in China, there were many kites for sale at booths which sold toys and food. Kites were shaped like eagles, geese, other birds, animals, insects and butterflies. A favourite kite was in the shape of Sun Wu-kung, the Monkey King, who was a famous character in a Chinese story.

There is a curious kite in one of the colour prints of Hokusai, and in a picture by George Romney (1734–1802) called *The Charteris Children* there is a boy about to fly a kite. An engraving of 1807 shows a French boy flying a kite with a tail, and a younger boy playing with a windmill.

260   An early kite. English

261 Kite-flying. China

In all the Victorian ABCs, K is usually for Kite.

Just like the Kite, the giddy Youth
Soars upon pleasure's wing,
Forgetting that some skilful guide
Should regulate the string.

from cards by Wallis, 1788

In British Guiana, the kite season came during the weeks before Easter Monday. In 1820 the kites were of all shapes and sizes, many were home-made, others were bought in shops. As Easter approached, everyone seemed to be out with a kite, kites like the local butterflies, and kites so large that they were safe only in the hands of a grown-up.

Kites could be made at home, or sold complete both here and abroad, and Oriental cut-outs were sold for the children to make up. Two patents for kites were taken out in France in the nineteenth century. In 1867, M. Charrier had one for 'des perfectionnements aux jouets dits cerf-volants', and another in 1869 by M. Hilst 'pour un cerf-volant'.

Traditional Japanese kites are still flown, and many are exported to England. Those bought at Heals include a hollow fish filled with air, small ones were 1 foot 5 inches across and the large ones were over 13 feet. Other popular ones were painted butterflies on bamboo frames. There are several in the Chinese shop near the British Museum.

These enormous kites show that grown-ups as well as children indulged in the sport of kite-flying, and any visitor to Kensington Gardens sees as many old men as children holding a taut string with a kite on the other end. One enthusiast had a large black one which swooped round the children like a great bird of prey, while other too successful kites may be caught high up in the trees for ever.

During wartime the flying of kites was forbidden, so by the time the Second World War was over, kite-flying was a complete novelty to most children, like the eating of a banana. It was on 25 June 1940 that the flying of kites and balloons was forbidden throughout the United Kingdom by an Emergency Powers Order.

262 Kite-flying. Korea

Cut-out kites were still obtainable in 1967, the Tako Japanese kite book had several designs, and a large book was published, *The Historical Survey of Kites*, written by Clive Hart which showed what a tremendous subject the art of kite-flying could be.

263   Butterfly kite.
China

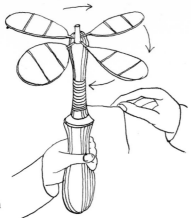

264 Aerial Screw
Propeller by Joseph
Myers. England

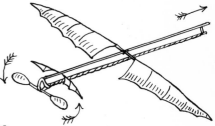

265 Flying model by
Penaud. France

AEROPLANES

Early in the twentieth century, Count von Zeppelin developed the
first practical rigid airship and models of stamped tin were made.
The little airships were about eight inches long, the propellers were
driven by clockwork, and the models performed endless circles when
suspended from a gas-bracket in the centre of a room, by means of a
length of black thread.

In 1909 a similar stamped tin toy became the rage. This was the
Blériot monoplane and it commemorated Blériot's crossing of the
Channel.

The first model aeroplane to fly under its own power was made by
a designer of machinery for making lace. This was Stringfellow who,
in 1848, made a model which flew inside the length of the lace factory,
a distance of 22 yards, in the little town of Chard in Somerset. It was
the first model in the world to fly on its own.

The early models were largely based on the work of Sir George
Cayley, 1774–1857, and were made to test the theory of stability. They
can hardly be considered as toys, for they needed much adjustment
and were not made for children.

The first models approaching toys were sold in Paris after 1874,
when Alphonse Penaud had designed and made a fairly simple one
driven by twisted elastic. Later M. Daudieux powered models by
using India rubber bands.

Many of the famous pioneers of aircraft began by designing and
building flying models. Before the First World War the models were
either of the 'A' type or the 'stick'. The 'A' framed model had the apex
of the A at the front and two propellers at the back, whereas the single
'stick' usually had the propeller at the front. The wings with frames
of wood or piano-wire were covered with paper or oiled silk.

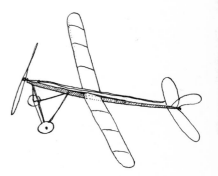

266 'Stick' model.
England

267 Tractor model.
England

107

268 'A' frame model by Grimmer. England

These 'A' frames which at first were hand-launched were on sale complete and ready to fly inasmuch as father probably did most of the flying. The 'stick' models and the Bragg Smith biplane could also be purchased at Gamages and other stores, together with those of Mann and Grimmer, who claimed to be the first to mass produce models just before the First World War. Thousands of these were sold and exported to every country in the world by 1913.

Complete 'stick' models were on sale in the early 1920s in which the wings had to be fixed by the purchaser and carefully adjusted.

A true toy aeroplane came about 1932, a model which could be flown by a child. This was the little F.R.O.G. aeroplane of metal and celluloid, costing 10s. 6d. It was advertised as having 'a quick take-off and climb, 650 feet per second air speed', and a certificate of airworthiness was signed by Hamley's head ground engineer. The model came in a box which was fitted with a patent starter which eliminated inaccurate hand-winding. Should there be a collision in the air, the little aeroplane was so constructed that it fell to pieces unharmed.

By 1934, these little 'Frog' planes appeared with the international markings of the British R.A.F., France, Belgium, Holland, Italy, the U.S.A. and the Argentine. There were none with German markings, for at this date Germany had no air force owing to the Treaty of Versailles. These models had a wing-span of $11\frac{1}{2}$ inches, they could fly 300 feet, and were marketed by Lines Brothers, at their famous Triang Works near London. The letters F.R.O.G. stand for 'Flies right off ground'.

Aeroplanes of die-cast metal appeared in the Meccano catalogue for 1934/35. The first five were the D.H. 'Leopard Moth', the Percival 'Gull', Low Wing Monoplane, General 'Monospar' and the Cierva 'Autogiro'. These cost sixpence each, and another, the Armstrong Whitworth 'Atalanta', cost ninepence. The complete set of six aeroplanes cost three shillings.

During the war these disappeared, but they came again in 1946, and the 'Shetland' flying-boat was made as a Supertoy in 1947. However, these little aeroplanes were difficult to obtain until about 1955.

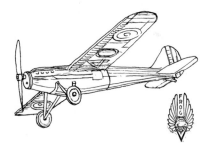

269 Frog aeroplane. England

270 Gaming pieces from an Israelite city

271 Bone dice. India

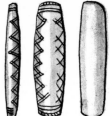

272 Choroti dominoes. South America

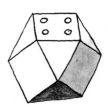

273 Nine ivory pieces. Alaska

274 Stone die. Indus Valley

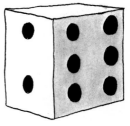

275 Wooden die marked with clay

6 Dice, counters, teetotums

DICE

Men have played games of chance with whatever has been at hand, and pebbles, nuts and shells have been used all over the world. Depressions or holes in the ground were made and the nuts thrown towards the hole and bets laid.

Palamedes of Greece was said to have invented dice about 1400 B.C. and advice was given to the men at Knossos to prevent them from wasting their time: 'Play not with dice, go cultivate thy cornland.'

It is strange how interesting even a little thing such as a die may be. How many persons will have noticed that in modern dice the sum of each pair of opposite numbers is seven?

A die with two ones was used by cheats towards the end of the twelfth century. To make it easier to detect these, the opposite numbers were made to add up to seven. This was said by Eustanthius, Archbishop of Thessalonica, who died in 1193, and was mentioned by G. Cardano, in his *Liber de ludo aleæ* in 1663.

At Mohenjodaro, stone and pottery dice belonging to the period 1500 B.C. were cubical with the numbers pitted or inlaid. Number one was opposite two, three was opposite four and five was opposite six.

276 Ivory die

277 Two dice

278   Die

279   Ivory die

280   Terracotta die. Lydia

281   Ivory counter

282   Long ivory die. Akhim·

283   Die. Ochyrynichus

They have not always been cubic in shape. Tabular dice made of ivory had the numbers one, two, three on three sides and the remaining side ornamented with lines. Others had hieroglyphics and incised patterns, but the precise use of these has not been ascertained.

A blue faience Egyptian die, of about 600 B.C., was found in Greece, in the shape of a ¾-inch cube. Each side was decorated with symbols – amphora, head of Harpocrates, a hand holding a branch, Aphrodite, head of Bes, and a twisted rope. Again one wonders to what purpose this die was put.

Dice were of many materials, ebony, ivory and glass, the last being particularly beautiful.

Stone dice used in Egypt about 250 B.C. were ten-sided, cut out and decorated with triangles – others were six-sided with incised holes or marks of a circle with a dot in the centre almost appearing to have been marked with spring-bows. There are some in the Metropolitan Museum of Art at New York and also in the British Museum, London.

During the reign of Augustus, Rome imported marble from Egypt and Africa, and games of tali and tessera were played, *tesserae* being the Latin name for dice.

284   Die, made of steatite. Greek or Roman

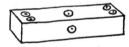

285   Three bone or ivory dice. China

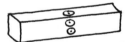

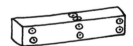

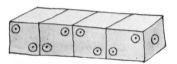

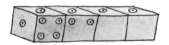

286   Two counters or four-sided dice. China

287   Long die, showing the four sides

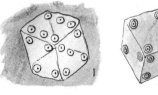

288   Three dice. Greek and Roman

289   Die in the shape of a figure. Roman

290 Bone die. Roman

291 Die. From an Israelite city

292 Die, found in Germany

293 Dice box with bone die, found in England

294 Bone die, found in England

In the Middle Ages there was much boredom between wars. Games of chance were played, sometimes between prisoners taken during battle, and thus new games were introduced.

There are accounts of travellers falling into evil hands and drinking and playing themselves destitute at the game of hazard. In an early fourteenth-century manuscript there is a picture of two men who, being deprived of their money, have played for their clothing. The younger man is reduced to his shirt, and the older man is stark naked.

The King of Cyprus in 1357 played dice and hazard with Henry Picard, the Mayor of London. The King won 50 marks and as the Mayor paid up he said, 'My lord and king, be not aggrieved, for I covet not your gold but your play.' Henry Picard was a vintner in his private life and 'he kept his hall against all comers that were willing to play at dice and hazard, and the lady Margaret, his wife, did keep her chamber to the same intent'.

There were many games in which dice were used, and consequently false dice were made, for these games encouraged gamblers and cheats. In 1532 there were loaded dice known as 'contraries', and 'bristle dice' in which bristles were fixed to influence the throw.

295 Playing with dice at Smithfield

Other dice were made to turn up or not to turn up certain numbers and had special names. Those which never turned up the three or four were called 'barred cater-treys', never the five or two were 'barred cinque-deuces', and never the six or one were called 'barred six-aces', the names seemingly derived from the French, in fact almost phonetic spelling, and note it was the opposite numbers which did not turn up, the ones adding up to seven.

On the other hand, some dice always turned up certain numbers, the flat cater-treys always turned up the three or the four, the flat cinque-deuces the five and two, and the flat six-aces the six or the one.

In 1542 false dice were still in use, and in England cheats were severely punished. They could be imprisoned, fined or put in the pillory or both.

Dice seem to have been marked by having the dots hollowed out and filled with coloured wax, but in 1692 Thomas Neale invented a new kind of die known by the name of 'mathematicks'. These were 'cutt perfectly square by a mold with spotts stained on them to prevent deceipts at play'.

By 1827 there was much gambling and an Act was passed in England to regulate the licence of the makers of dice, and for the sale of the same.

Today, the dice in toyshops are mainly made of plastic and sold in little plastic jars. Most board games are played by either tossing dice or twirling a teetotum or using counters or both.

296 Gambling or divining dice. India

The American Indians used nuts or fruit pips as counters, black on one side and white on the other, and down through the centuries counters have been made of the same materials as dice though with more variety. Many hand-painted counters came from the East.

Ivory was a favourite material, sometimes beautifully carved, and mother-of-pearl was delicately cut into various shapes, fishes, etc. and decorated with fine incised patterns. The Victorians were fond of shells and large cowrie shells were collected and used as counters, gradually acquiring a high polish and being quite indestructible.

Early eighteenth-century boxes to contain counters and tallies were very beautiful, some of the French ones having a revolving disc on the lid for scoring. A French box in the Victoria and Albert Museum opens to reveal four smaller boxes of this type, all beautifully decorated with raised patterns and discs for scoring.

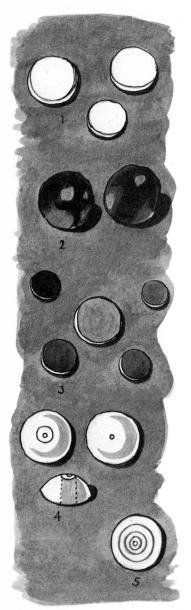

297　Counters found in England
1　Pottery counters
2　Two clay pellets
3　Five roundels
4　Three counters
5　Bone counter

298　Tallies. Malest, meaning 'Bad Luck', Victor, for the winner, Nvgator, meaning 'Trifler'. Roman

299　Bone counters in a little box. English

112

300   Teetotum. English

301   Teetotum or
Trendle. Probably
German

302   Teetotum with
letters. English

303   Teetotum with
numerals. English

TEETOTUMS

The spinning of a teetotum was regarded as harmless, but dice were
'wicked things' and encouraged gambling. Therefore parents were
advised not to introduce them into their Early Victorian homes.

There were various ways of making these little spinners. In *A
Voyage of Discovery* or the *Five Wayfarers* the teetotum is made in the
form of a compass.

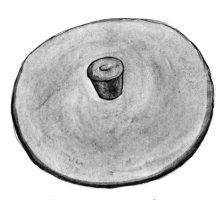

305   Dobeli spinning-top
from a nut

306   Teetotum from wild
fruit. Swahili

304   Teetotum made
from a gourd. Zanzibar

307   Fruit top from
Florida

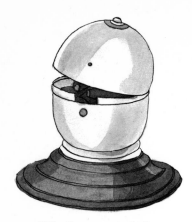

308 Lottery set. Italian

309 Stick with holders.
Italian

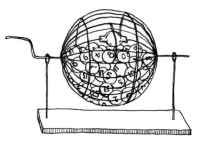

310 'Gadget for
Lotteries'. Denmark

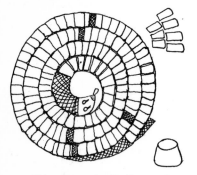

311 Game in the form of
a coiled snake. Egyptian

7 Board games, chess and draughts

BOARD GAMES

Game boards were used at Ur in 2400 B.C., but sometimes the pavements were marked out instead. In India a marked brick was used, being divided up in much the same manner as in the Egyptian game of 'Senet'. Some had shallow depressions, others had compartments to take the forfeited pieces and were similar to games played by various tribes in Africa.

Various board games were known to the ancient Egyptians. An interesting one is that in the form of a coiled snake with a red tongue, belonging to the Third dynasty or earlier, that is before 2423 B.C. The 'board' was about 16 inches across and one inch thick, and stood on an alabaster base about half the length across.

312   Board game, with onlookers. Egypt

313   Senet. Egypt

314   Tau or Robbers. Egypt

315   The Bowl. Egypt

316   Detail showing complete circles with dice

Many board games are pictured on Egyptian frescoes with the plan placed vertically or in elevation as is usual in their paintings, and not drawn in perspective.

Two men are shown playing the game of Senet, and also the game of Tau, or Robbers. Note the dainty manner in which the finger and thumb of the right hand take the pieces in order to move them.

The game of the Bowl has a circular board marked out in concentric circles. It was played with dice, each player gradually moving his pieces towards the centre. The shape above is a vase to indicate that they are competing for a prize, and in the painting the players are watched by spectators.

Mancala was a board game played in the East by women and children. Cowries are used as counters, and are moved from one depression to another by spinning a teetotum.

The Saxon game of Hnefatafl came from Denmark, a game which was played there about A.D. 400 and brought by them to Iceland and Britain. An English manuscript written during the reign of King Athelstan, 925–40, contains a diagram of this game. It is reproduced in *Board and Table Games* by R. C. Bell. According to Murray's *History of Board Games other than Chess*, the pieces were known as 'hnefi' and 'hunns'. A hunn found at Woodperry in Oxfordshire is similar to one found in Tokenhouse Yard, London.

317   'Hunn' from the game of Hnefatafl. Saxon

318   Probably a Hnefatafl piece

319   Cribbage board.
Alaska

320   Gaming piece of
ivory from 'hounds
chasing jackals'. Egypt

Cribbage, Crib for short, was mentioned by Sir John Suckling in the mid seventeenth century and was said to be an improvement on an older game called 'Noddy'. Although the game is played with ordinary packs of playing-cards, a special board with holes is a necessity and also the little pegs, some white and some scarlet.

Boards are usually of inlaid wood, ivory or ebony, but some in 1829 were made of brass. There is one of these in Salisbury Museum. Sometimes they are box-shaped and part of another game, the lid being the crib board and the box below containing dominoes. The more usual way was to have the lid opening back with a space below to take a pack of cards.

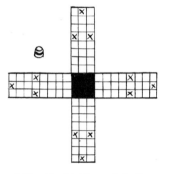

321   Pachisi board. India

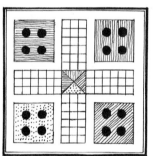

322   Ludo board.
England

Pachisi was the national game of India. The Emperor Akbar in the late sixteenth century played on courts inlaid with marble. The game, also known as 'Twenty-five', is still played today and appeared about 1896 in the Western world as Ludo. It was in a slightly different form, Pachisi being played with dome-like pieces and Ludo with flat counters in four different colours.

Even and Odd, a game of chance, was mentioned as a child's game by the poet Cleveland in 1660, and is known as 'E.O.' It was played on a round wooden board with inset ivory letters, and the board constructed to spin. Examples shown in the Victoria and Albert Museum were made about 1810.

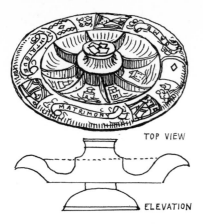

TOP VIEW

ELEVATION

323   Pope Joan board.
European

The name Pope Joan comes from a legendary figure of the ninth century who was supposed to have died giving birth to a child while walking in a procession. The game of Pope Joan is played on a special circular board with divisions, and often lacquered in red and gold upon a black background. It was played early in the nineteenth century and several boards exist, many in museums and also in some of the stately homes of England.

It was a popular game with the Prince of Wales, later William IV. In 1828 Lord Errol wrote that the 'favourite amusement of our future sovereign being Pope Joan, at which he plays every night, but will never trust himself beyond the stake of one shilling. The Duchess is a great worker and carries on that occupation by the band table, whilst Billy and the young ones go on with their Pope.' 'Billy' was born in 1765, so at this time he would be 63.

During the early part of the nineteenth century gaming boards were popular especially at watering-places like Tunbridge Wells and Bath, and at places where races were likely, such as Newmarket.

Backgammon boards are divided into eight equal parts by transverse lines; the pieces number 16 on each side, and are moved according to the throw of a die. These boards with their crossing lines lend themselves to decoration. Late sixteenth- and early seventeenth-

324   Counters from the game of Squails. Indian

325   The game of Squails. German

117

326 Peg Solitaire board.
English

327 Solitaire board with
ivory inlay. English

328 Modern board of
plastic. Probably Hong
Kong

century German examples were engraved and inlaid with ebony and ivory or even the horns of a stag. Turkish boards of the seventeenth and eighteenth centuries could be engraved with mother-of-pearl, tortoiseshell and ivory. In Japan, children play a kind of backgammon known as 'Sugoroku', usually at the New Year.

Peg Solitaire was played at the end of the nineteenth century using a wooden circular board with a handle, and wooden pegs. There were 33 holes in the board. The wood or plastic boards of today have depressions in which marbles are moved instead of pegs. The French game of Taquin was played in 1880, in which 15 pieces had to be moved into 16 compartments in as few moves as possible; the word *taquin* means 'a teaser'.

The actual boards for games have been made of many materials and shapes all over the world, the patterns varying according to the game. Wood was inlaid with other woods, with precious metals, ivory, ebony, glass or mother-of-pearl. Many native boards are marked out with poker-work, the Aztecs painted their patterns on mats, while in parts of Africa and in the Orient, leather was used, the 'boards' being inlaid with different colours.

The American Indians marked out animal hide with coloured dyes and added beads or porcupine quills to make the pattern. Embroidery was skilfully used in India, and other boards were made of beaten metal. In China, paper was used and in Japan also.

In Europe many games were played on boards made of paper which was backed with linen as in a folding map, in order to open out flat on a table. The games were played with dice, or teetotums, and counters.

The Georgian and Early Victorian boards were often marked out in some kind of numbered route which was followed by the players according to the number which they tossed. The dates of boards cannot always be ascertained by the method in which they were printed, for this varies. However, they could mostly be bought plain or coloured, some children preferring to colour them at home.

The forerunner of these numbered boards was the Game of Goose, a game said to have been played by the ancient Greeks. It was a game of chance needing 'a Paire of Dyce', and became popular in France in 1725. The board was painted with the representation of a goose, each feather being numbered. Players went forwards or backwards according to the feather on which they landed. There were 63 'squares' and a goose was marked on every fifth space. The game was played throughout France in the eighteenth and nineteenth centuries, and is still played today, with variations, in many parts of Europe.

In England 'A Journey through Europe' or 'The Play of Geography' was printed by Carrington Bowles, and was played the same as 'The Royall and Most Pleasant Game of Goose' which here was printed by H. Overton. Later on this game was replaced by that of Lotto.

Carrington Bowles were the printers who produced the first known dated race game which came in 1759.

A board game printed by Wallis and Newbery in 1790, 'The New Game of Human Life', advised the players to use a teetotum 'as this would avoid introducing a Dice box into private Families'. The 'Overland Route to India', Sallis's teetotum game, came in England in the mid nineteenth century, and also 'Grandma's new game of Natural History' which was coloured by hand. Wallis's 'Game of Genius' came in 1825.

Between 1840 and 1850 board games swept the U.S.A. and Europe, and were played by both grown-ups and children. Wallis's 'Locomotive Game of Railroad Adventures' was published about 1840, and an interesting game was produced by William Spooner in 1843. This was called 'An Eccentric Excursion to the Chinese Empire', the four players travelling by different routes. S was for steamboat, W for walker, R for railway and A for the aerial or flying-machine.

In 1855 Jaques, wholesale toy-sellers of Hatton Garden, produced two new games. 'The Imperial Contest or the Allied Armies New Game of Skill, founded on a scientific basis, highly amusing, price with men complete 8/6 and 10/6 or with ivory men 21/–.' The other was 'Cannonade or Castle Bagatelle, the most amusing game yet brought out, 31/6. Sold at all Fancy Repositories throughout the kingdom.' These were advertised in the *Illustrated London News* for that year,

The 'Royal game of Steeplechase', price one penny, coloured twopence was a sheet of paper published by Bishops of Houndsditch, with directions printed in the centre, and played with lead horses and jockeys.

E. C. Spurins of Bond Street had what was known as a manu-factory and repository. In 1867 they advertised their English and French toys and dolls. Also in their announcement were included dissected puzzles, scripture and geographical maps, together with 'All the New Games of the Season'.

Many games were educational or moral, even the early Snakes and Ladders had a moral significance. The little pictures depicted good and bad deeds. A child who carried a load for an old woman would go up the ladder, but one who was greedy and over-ate would go back down the body of the snake, virtue being rewarded and vice punished.

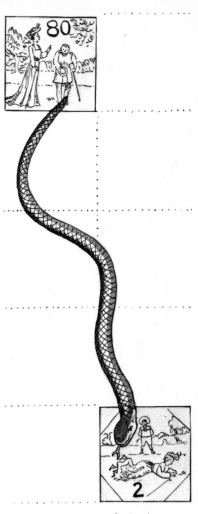

329   Portion of a Snakes and Ladders game

330   Board game with pieces. Probably English or German

331   Hoop-la. English

Early in the twentieth century, a pretty board depicted a fairy-tale, in which good dwarfs and good fairies helped one along a perilous path beset with caves, goblins and witches, in order to seek for treasure in a casket or to rescue a princess.

Some games brought history up to date, such as the board game in the First World War, played with little lead boats and submarines which were moved about on a blue and green sea with the coastlines round England and the Channel marked in. 'The merchantman often escapes from a perilous position early in the game, only to meet with disaster later.'

Many modern games are more in the nature of greed and speculation. Monopoly in 1938 and 1939 was merely buying and selling. Careers in 1957 was a game in which the goal was to reach the top first and make the most money.

332   Game pieces of porcelain

333   Game pieces

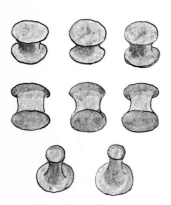

334   Draughtsman

CHESS AND DRAUGHTS

Much has been written on the game of chess, which is one of the oldest board games to survive to the present day. King Merenptah was painted playing a game of chess and Queen Nefertiti was painted on a tomb playing draughts.

The pieces used by the Egyptians were of various shapes. Some were carved to represent human heads, some resembled ninepins, and most of those made about 1453 B.C. were of ivory or wood. Others were of clay, agate or chalcedony. Many were coloured red, dark grey or yellowish pink. Some were conical, some tetrahedral, some more like those used in our Victorian game of Halma.

Chessmen for Muslims scrupulously obeyed the ban against the making of images, as a true believer would not play with pieces which represented a human being in any form.

The Persians played chess in the sixth century A.D., the Chinese in the seventh and the Merovingians in the eighth before Pippin became King of the Franks, and many chess pieces belong to this last period. The kings and ministers are mounted on elephants, there are knights on horseback, castles and foot-soldiers, the games being played in lulls between real battles.

120

335 EARLY CHESS PIECES
i, ii Whalebone, English. iii Walrus ivory, English.
iv, v, viii Bone, English. vi Walrus ivory, Isle of Lewis.
vii Merovingian. ix, x Ivory, French

336 Draughtsman made from a horse's tooth. Anglo-Saxon

Charlemagne was typical – in the summer he made wars and in the winter he played chess with ivory pieces. In England, life was dull in the castles, feasting being the chief amusement, interspersed with music and song from jesters. Chess became the hobby of the wise, and draughts the hobby of the knights.

The 'Book of Chess' was produced by Ad-Adli during the ninth century and draughtsmen used by Anglo-Saxon England were made from horse's teeth, and in the Isle of Lewis from walrus ivory. Other carved pieces came from Moravia and Bohemia.

337 Bone piece 338 Ivory piece 339 Bone piece 340 Piece or counter 341 Piece

342 Chessman of walrus ivory. Isle of Lewis

The set of chessmen in the British Museum found on the Isle of Lewis consists of perfect specimens carved in ivory. When out digging in the parish of Uig, a peasant came across these little objects and he thought they were elves or gnomes. He flung down his spade and fled home frightened and dismayed.

His wife induced him to return partly from curiosity and he brought away these little ivory figures which he had mistaken for the pigmy sprites of Celtic folklore. This apparently happened in 1831 but the little chessmen were found to belong to the eleventh or twelfth century.

During the Norman conquest of England, checked boards were used for counting coins for tax purposes; many inns are known as 'The Chequer Board', and in St Albans there is a Chequer Street near the old market-place. Later on, when the early settlers took the English game of draughts to North America, it was known as 'checkers'.

In the thirteenth century a French bishop had forbidden the clergy to possess either chessmen or chess boards, and apprentices in London were forbidden to play chess in the year 1457.

Edward IV played chess and in 1474 William Caxton printed *The Game and Playe of Ye Chesse.*

343 Board with players. England

344 Chess pieces at the time of Caxton

A sixteenth-century Venetian board for draughts was made of coloured woods inlaid with silver and ebony, a German one of 1660 was also of coloured inlaid woods and one of 1704 had the draughts engraved showing important personages and events.

The French aristocrats played chess while travelling round in the lumbering coaches of the eighteenth century. Because they jogged from side to side along the rough roads, their chess boards were made like cushions with embroidered squares, and the chess pieces were formed on tapered spikes which could be speared into the correct place.

In Victorian days some boards were made to fold over and to look like a book when placed with others on a shelf. Played with by clerks in dusty offices, they could quickly be hidden when steps were heard on the stairs.

Some sets caricature politicians, and materials used today can be wood, bone, ivory, pottery or perspex, and occasionally metals. Many are made of plastic and come from Russia and cheap sets coming from Hong Kong fit easily into a schoolboy's satchel, for nowadays children are encouraged to play the game.

The Russians are chess addicts, and a modern set in porcelain shows the pawns as happy women harvesters under the Communists, whereas the pawns of the capitalists are shown miserable and bound with chains.

Halma, a popular Victorian pastime, seems hardly to be mentioned nowadays. The checks are smaller than in draughts, being 16 each side, i.e. 256 squares altogether. The game was issued by Ayres in England, in 1888.

345   Miniature chessman. Mexico

346   Wooden pieces used by Hausa Emigrates. Nigeria

8 Knucklebones, atep, dominoes, spillikins, tiddly-winks

KNUCKLEBONES

The game of Knucklebones was played by the ancients and there are examples in the British Museum. The knucklebones are tossed in the air and caught on the back of the hand. In a picture by Brueghel the Elder, dated 1560, the game is played by two girls.

It is still played today by both boys and girls, the modern sets being of plastic and much lighter in weight. It is known as 'Osselets' in France, 'Jackstones' or 'Knucklestones' in the U.S.A.

347 Two girls playing knucklebones

349 The game of Atep. Egypt

348 The game of Mora shown on a counter. Italy

ATEP

Atep was a Greek game where the players held up their hands and did finger changing. The drawing shown is interesting and was found in the tomb of Ak-Hor. The players are standing on a vase and the checks show that it is a game of pleasure as in Tau and Senet. The whole is surrounded by a purse with an outside pouch in which to carry off the prize. Atep was played in Italy under the name of 'Mora'.

Edward Falkener in his book *Games Ancient and Oriental* describes exactly how these were played.

124

DOMINOES

Dominoes are played without a die and without a board. Long ago they were played with by the ancients, the better ones being made of ivory and ebony, and the cheaper ones of wood. The boxes containing them could be carved, inlaid, lacquered or painted. In 1850, John Phyfe in the U.S.A. advertised his dominoes and dice-boxes as being 'richly carved and plain'. The *American Girls' Book* in 1831 gave a description of how to play.

During the nineteenth century, dominoes were popular in England and France. In the U.S.A., the Embossing Company turned out 64,000 sets in 1872, and still the demand grew. The wood was sawn into smooth blocks by a special machine which left a high polish and eliminated sand-papering.

Pretty dominoes with letters and pictures as an aid to reading came in 1887, and were patented in England in that year.

Dominoes for children with black dots on one half and half an animal on the other half, which had to be matched together were known as 'Noah's Dominoes'. These came towards the end of the nineteenth century, about 1889. Usually dominoes are white with black dots, but in 1914 black dominoes with white dots were made in the U.S.A. which apparently were quicker to produce.

Today, as with so many things, dominoes can be made of plastic.

SPILLIKINS

At Windsor Castle, the Court played 'spillikins and puzzling with alphabets' about 1845, and spillikins became a popular Victorian game in the mid nineteenth century and in the U.S.A., where it was known as 'Jackstraws'.

It was played with ivory or bone pieces about five inches long with assorted ends. These were tumbled out of a box into a pile on the table and each player, using a specially designed tool, would try in turn to remove a spillikin without upsetting the others in the pile. Victorian ladies, proud of their long white fingers, would daintily retrieve the spillikins by hand, where no tool was given.

Sets were made up of different things. There were those made with carved ends in the shape of lances, swords, daggers and crosses, and there were others consisting of curved ends, hooks, blades, clubs and arrowheads. Some sets were made as miniature garden implements or as totem-poles, usually containing a tool with which to extract the spills from the pile.

A typical nineteenth-century set might consist of 30 spillikins, two ivory hooks and a specially carved ivory box to contain them.

About 1874 Crandalls in the U.S.A. made jackstraws about five inches long with letters of the alphabet printed on the flat round heads of the straws, and English sets had the letters carved out on the ends of the spillikins, both countries using ivory or bone.

350 Domino box of carved bone. French

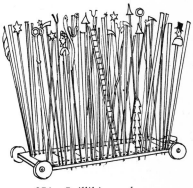

351 Spillikins and cribbage board. French

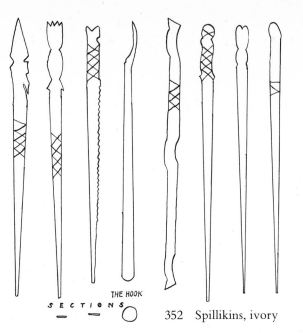

THE HOOK

SECTIONS

352 Spillikins, ivory

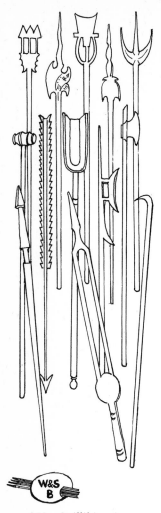

353 Spillikins, ivory

In 1921 an idea was to put matches head downwards into an egg-cup. Each player took it in turn to pull one out and lay it back on top of the others, any which were spilt he kept and they counted against him. This was played until all the matches were used (about two boxfuls), and the egg-cup was empty, the one spilling the least was the winner.

Spills, spilling, spillikins, then spellicans, this was probably how the name originated.

TIDDLY-WINKS

Tiddly-winks was a popular game of the nineteenth century. Counters were flipped into a cup placed in the centre of a table. Early counters were of bone or ivory, later ones of plastic, usually coloured. They were of two sizes, the larger ones about the size of a penny being used as flippers. They were unknown in the U.S.A. about 1883, and were a fairly new thing in England in 1892.

Lady Emily Lytton in her book *A Blessed Girl* gives a long description of the game as it was played at Terling Place in 1892, calling it the most exciting game that was ever invented.

In 1957 the Goons, with permission, called themselves 'Prince Philip's Royal Tiddly-winks Champions' and played against the Cambridge University Tiddly-winks Club (four years old) in aid of the National Playing Fields Association.

A writer in *The Times* says: 'the subtle art of Tiddleywinks . . . here all depends upon the steady hand, the strong nerve, the experienced eye . . . etc., etc.' It reminds one of the saying

> *Do not make tragedies of trifles,*
> *Do not shoot butterflies with rifles.*

126

9 Hoops, yo-yo, diabolo, bilboquet or cup and ball, battledore and shuttlecock

354 Rod and hoop game. Egypt

HOOPS

Hoops are among the ancient toys known to the Egyptians and to the Greeks. Since then they have been playthings on and off from medieval times to the present, sometimes taking a back seat and at other times a front place in the top of a shop window or hanging up by the door of a village store.

The Greek children had hoops fitted with spokes on which were discs of metal which jingled about as the hoops went round. A similar idea was that of the hoops with spokes covered with beads, bowled along by Victorian children and shown in my *Book of Toys*.

'Les Grâces' was a game played with a leather-bound hoop and two sticks rather like walking-sticks, the hoop being fairly small, only about ten inches in diameter.

The South American hoops were simply a piece of cane bound into a circle with a cord to join the ends together. In New Guinea, a similar hoop was thrown into the air, and pointed sticks hurled at it by native boys, the aim being to pass the stick through the centre of the hoop. This game was called 'Killing the Hoop'.

Hoops were for winter months, and a sixteenth-century Flemish calendar shows them for the month of February, the hoops being very thick and of two sizes, the boys hitting them with stout sticks.

355 Playing hoops. Flanders

In England hoops were bowled along in late autumn, girls with wooden hoops and sticks. Boys had iron hoops with iron hooks attached, known as 'cleets' or 'skimmers', which needed a knack to get them going, in fact it was almost a game of skill. It was not a little gentleman's game but was played by boys in heavy boots making a terrific noise as they clattered along on the pavements at quite a speed. The idea of attaching the iron skimmer to the iron hoop came in 1885 and was patented by R. Jaques in that year.

As usual, the Victorians pointed a moral. The hoop was said to represent the Wheel of Fortune and that 'its roundness instructs us that there is no end to man's care and toil'.

356 Primitive hoop. South America

Iron hoops were black, wooden hoops were left their natural colour, and could be anything from one foot to three or four feet in diameter. Often higher than the child itself, a little girl could run through her hoop while it was in motion. Others used them as skipping-ropes, or twisted them round and round their waists until the hoop fell to the ground. Boys without real hoops made do with the iron rings from beer-barrels, and hit them with wooden sticks about $\frac{3}{4}$ inch round and one foot long.

Smaller children would push a kind of wheel with spokes, on which were coloured wooden beads which moved down the spoke loosely as the wheel was turned. More intricate toys would have a shining bicycle bell attached which rang as the child pushed the stick forward. Others would have a musical appliance fastened to the centre of a hoop which, in addition, had coloured spokes. The turning of the hoop made strips of metal sound like musical notes. This was in 1887.

A curious home-made toy was made about 1913 with a tin lid and a piece of string. The tin lid about four inches in diameter was pierced in the centre to make a hole – this was usually done with a metal skewer. A piece of string about a yard long was passed through the hole and a knot tied. All it needed now was a child on the other end to run and make the tin lid revolve along the pavement making a clattering noise as it went.

Gradually the hoop fell out of favour. Possibly with the increase in traffic, it was no longer safe to bowl one's hoop along the pavement and it had to be taken to the park. Perhaps it was the coming of the scooter which made it *infra dig.* to carry a hoop.

About the time of the First World War, a scooter was the thing, with smallish wooden wheels about five inches in diameter. The wheels gradually were made larger until a scooter became what was known later as a 'fairy cycle', with wheels similar to those on contemporary dolls' prams.

Home-made scooters could be special affairs made in carpenters' shops, or they could be made by boys with two rough-hewn pieces of wood put together with ball-races for the wheels. In London in the late twenties and early thirties, the Fulham Road had many of these crude scooters careering along the pavements with the fronts decorated in a peculiar manner. This was achieved by nailing brilliant metal 'crown corks' to the front board, reds, blues and greens in luminous colours, thus making the toy into an elegant affair and unique to each proud owner, who was often dressed as a Red Indian.

But the hoop returned in a different guise, and in 1958 swept the U.S.A. and Britain with what could be considered as the craziest craze of all.

This was the hula hoop, a hoop of plastic and in bright colours but without a stick. For the game was played as the Edwardian children had done before by placing the hoop round one's waist and rotating it by wriggling forwards and backwards, reminiscent of the hula skirts on tropical islands.

357 Hula hoops, one for beauty, one for fun. England

The craze began in the U.S.A., and in October the boom crossed the Atlantic and 40 firms sprang into being, some being overnight mushrooms.

All that was needed was a bag of high-density polythene dust, a handful of two-inch wooden plugs, half a pound of wire staples, and the help of a man with an extrusion machine, which simply meant anyone who could make a length of plastic hose.

The craze spread rapidly all over Britain; the station platforms were piled high with these contraptions and hoops were seen in all the big towns. In five weeks two men sold over 100,000, and one firm dispatched 20,000 hoops a day.

By November, a daily paper stated 'Stocks of hula hoops have run out of many Windsor shops, Eton college boys have bought hundreds during the last fortnight'. Women found the exercise ideal for slimming, and by January the hula hoops had reached the villages.

However, all was not as it should be. Many children and teenagers complained of a pain in the neck and round the waist. One Liverpool child did 44,000 turns in six hours before her father took it away, and a 68-year-old lady went to her doctor on account of such pains because 'she had had a go yesterday at young Willie's birthday party'.

Some children were suspected of having poliomyelitis and a 17-year-old Japanese actually died from excessive hula-hooping.

The whole idea apparently came from watching some children in Queensland, Australia, who were having a gay time swinging rusty beer-barrel hoops round their hips.

In 1960, Tony Westop, aged 7½, wrote 'the world hula hoop record does not belong to Gordon Boyd who has done 3,000. I have done 3,527 and my friend Billy has done 3,216.' By 1963 there was not a single child to be seen playing with one of the coloured hoops. Where can they have all gone?

However, in 1968, we read that the inhabitants of Easter Island are learning the sau-sau, the local version of the hula hoop.

358 'Prince of Wales toy'. England

YO-YO

These toys originated in China and consisted of two wheels made of ivory or wood put together, with a silken cord around the groove between.

Cheap examples could be purchased at fairs. They were about 2½ inches in diameter and about ¾ inch thick. The size has varied little since.

In 1789, the game was known as 'Quiz', and the grooved wheel and the thread made exactly what we call a 'yo-yo'. They were popular during the nineteenth century, and in France, where a quiz was known as a 'Bandalore'. One of 1805 was carved in boxwood and decorated with a cherry-picking scene inscribed 'Les Friands de Cérises'. On the reverse side was a representation of a battle scene, probably intended for Austerlitz.

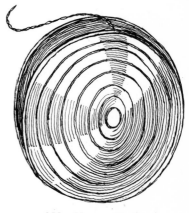

359 Yo-yo. England

In 1932, Louis Marx, an American toy millionaire, held the sole right of a toy called a 'yo-yo'. It was made of two flattened circular pieces of wood joined and with a piece of string wound round the 'waist'. It was quite a knack to make the yo-yo spin up and down the string, and children and grown-ups vied with one another to see how long the yo-yo could be kept in motion. Marx sold 100,000,000 of them, and in Britain alone he sold 35,000 in a day.

In 1967 came the Eleyo from Japan. Inside both halves of the plastic shells – for yo-yos were no longer made of wood – was concealed a battery, the shells being both hollow and transparent. As the yo-yo spun up and down on the thread it was illuminated from within.

But alas, a plastic yo-yo has a life of about two months and is outlived by those ivory ones of so long ago.

360   Eleyo yo-yo. Japan

361   Diabolo. England

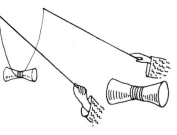

362   Diabolo. China

363   'Le Diable'. France

DIABOLO

Claretie says that the forerunner of diabolo was the game called 'L'Émigrette' and that it came to England from China. It had been known as the 'Flying Cone', and was played at the French and English Courts during the latter part of the fifteenth century. During the French Revolution, begun in 1789, the game again became popular, this time being known as 'The Devil on two sticks'.

A similar game had been played in China for centuries. It was known as 'Kouen-gen' and was played with a 'reel'. This was a kind of top made of two cones joined together at the pointed ends rather like an early cotton-reel. It was sometimes made of metal such as gold or silver and even studded with jewels, or it could be of ivory and later on of wood. (The Edwardian and Georgian cotton-reels are gradually being replaced by straighter ones made of plastic.)

Diabolo was played by fashionable ladies and gentlemen in 1796, and Napoleon himself enjoyed the game. In 1820, it was called 'Le Diable', and the craze gradually spread through Europe. The wooden reels were cheap, but soon the game lost its popularity.

Early in the twentieth century the craze gradually returned to

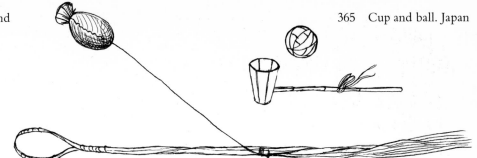

364 Primitive cup and
ball. Hawaii

365 Cup and ball. Japan

England and the U.S.A. The reel, the two sticks and the thread were the
same as before, and once again it was the thing to play diabolo, but
this time it was known as 'Topsy Twirl'. Clubs were founded and
students vied with one another to see how long the reels could be kept
spinning and how high they could be tossed before being caught again
on the string.

BILBOQUET OR CUP AND BALL

The origin of this game may have been in Italy, though a similar game
was said to have been played in Greece.

In the summer of 1585, it is mentioned by Pierre de l'Estoile:
'le roi commença de porter un bilboquet dont il se jouit par les rues'.

The game was played by royalty and the upper classes and the toys
which were turned by a turner were expensive to buy.

A beautifully engraved ivory bilboquet belonged to the little
daughter of Marie-Antoinette. The intricate design included the
royal arms of France, and the ball also was incised with fine lines.

A French engraving of the eighteenth century shows both men and
women intent on the game, in fact it pictures a well-dressed crowd
each with a bilboquet, playing in a courtyard, sometimes singly and
sometimes in pairs. It was popular all through the nineteenth century
and gradually the game spread.

When Captain Cook visited the Sandwich Islands during the
eighteenth century, he found the game of Cup and Ball already there.
In 1826 it was mentioned in the U.S.A. and in Mexico, and it was also
played by the American Indians.

The game, indoors or out, consisted of a kind of cup into which the
ball fitted. The cup was on the end of a handle and was of turned wood
or of ivory.

Handles were from about six inches long to as much as 20 inches.
Wooden handles were sometimes decorated with lacquer, and some
instead of having a cup at the end would have a spike, in which case
the ball had a hole into which the spike went. Shuttlecocks also could
have a hole up the middle and were caught in the same manner as the
balls.

The size of the latter varied, being made to fit into the cup. A
handle of five inches long could have a cup of one-inch diameter, a

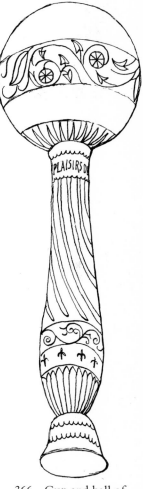

366 Cup and ball of
turned and engraved
ivory. France

368 BILBOQUET OR CUP AND BALL
i Lacquer cup and knitted ball. ii Ivory spike and ball. iii Wood spike and
shuttlecock. iv Wood cup and ball. v Rice paper

longer handle might have a two-inch-diameter cup. Balls were of ivory or wood, some were covered with crochet and all had a cord about two feet long threaded through the handle of the cup.

In the *Handbook of Fashionable Games*, 1859, bilboquet is described thus:

a ball of ivory or of hardwood is attached to a stem of the same substance, having a shallow cup at one end and a point at the other. The player holds the stem in his right hand, and having caused the ball to revolve, by twirling it between the finger and thumb of his left hand, he jerks it up and catches it, either in the cup or upon the spike, to receive which a hole is made in the ball. We need scarcely say that the latter feat can only be performed by a skilful player.

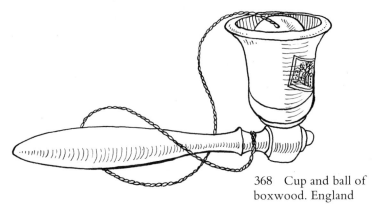

368   Cup and ball of boxwood. England

BATTLEDORE AND SHUTTLECOCK

Battledores and shuttlecocks were used in the fourteenth century in England and are illustrated in manuscripts of that period. The battledores appear to be shaped flat pieces of wood and the name is the same as that of the paddle used by Japanese women for washing clothes, and is also the same shape.

It was a game favoured by both boys and girls in the seventeenth century and played with a feather shuttlecock. The battledores were made of a piece of bent wood curved round so that both ends fitted on to a wooden handle which was then bound around to keep both ends in place.

Paintings by Chardin, 1699–1779, picture bats which are rather square at the end and are threaded with strings to form a net. In 1751 he painted a little girl playing with a feather shuttlecock and these seem to have stayed much the same shape, except that later examples have dyed feathers.

By now, boys rarely played the game, and in 1818, in Japan, the game of battledore and shuttlecock was played entirely by girls at the beginning of the New Year. It was the custom to send this toy to a baby girl in the December of the year in which she was born.

369   Battledores and shuttlecock. England

A threaded bat is shown in an engraving from the *Girl's Own Book* of 1839, but somewhere about the middle of the century the threads were replaced by stretched parchment. The Leathercraft Museum in London has a battledore with a wooden handle, the bat made of 'Warranted best vellum' and bound round with dark red leather embossed with gold. Another in the Folk Museum at Cambridge has written on the parchment 'from Grandma Withins, Aug. 21st 1865'.

In 1878, 'Badminton or Scientific Shuttlecock' was considered a ladies' game and was sometimes called 'Ladies Rackets'. It was popular in India because of the climate, where it was played outdoors, but in England the stiff breezes made it impossible to play without heavily loaded shuttlecocks.

When celluloid balls replaced the feathered shuttlecocks and were hit with the parchment bats a delightful ping-pong noise was made as the balls went to and fro. From this came the word 'Ping-Pong', which actually was a trade name for the game in the U.S.A.; all others should be referred to as 'table tennis'. Jaques, the English makers, called the game by the name of 'Gossima'.

Gradually battledores have been replaced by round wooden bats with stems which have become shorter and shorter until some are merely a circular piece of wood with or without a short handle.

370 Battledore with stretched parchment. English

371 Ping Pong bat. U.S.A.

372 Battledore and shuttlecock. Japan

Customs

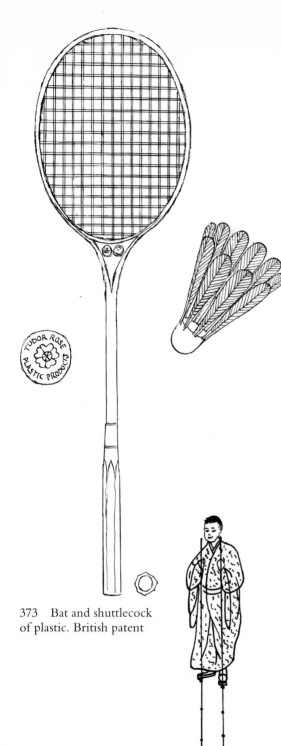

373   Bat and shuttlecock
of plastic. British patent

374   Boy on stilts. Japan

In 1724, the unrated toys for Children in England
amounted to £150, the Duty paid being £35 10s. 7½d.

Inwards

Babies or Puppets for Children, the Groce, cont 12 Dozen
Babies Heads, of Earth, the Dozen
All other toys for Children to pay 16 pence in every 20s.
of their value upon oath
Tennis Balls, the Thousand
Beads, of Amber, Bone, Box, Crystal, Coral, Glass,
Jasper, Wood
Brass Trumpets, the Dozen
Bells. Clapper bells, Dog bells, Hawksbells, French,
and Hawksbells, Nuremberg, Horse bells, Morrice bells.
Playing cards.
Dice, the pair.
Fiddles for Children
Masks of Sattin, Masks of Velvet.
Playing tables of Wall-nutt Tree, the Pair
Rackets, the Piece
Rattles for Children, the Groce. With Bells, the dozen
Whistles, Cocks, or bellows or Birds of stone

1747. *Outwards and Inwards*

Duty. Alphabets, the set of 24.
Babies or Puppets for Children, the Groce
containing 12 dozen
Babies, heads of earth, the dozen
All other toys for children to pay 16 pence in every 20s.
of their value upon oath
But if painted prohibited to be imported
Babies jointed the doz. (Toys)
Balls. tennis balls the 1000, prohibited to be imported
for Children, the small groce
Clapper bells, the pound
Dog bells, the pound

In Japan stilts are known as bamboo horses.

135

10 ABCs and toy books, building bricks, kit sets

ABCS AND TOY BOOKS

Picture-writing and learning to read through pictures is a very old pastime, and today our road signs are gradually dropping the words and resorting to pictures, in fact a picture language for all nations.

In the past much learning was handed on by word of mouth, but by 2700 B.C. and 2600 B.C. records were already being kept by the Chinese, and the Egyptians were using an alphabet of 24 letters.

Pens and ink were used in Mesopotamia about 2200 B.C. Some wrote on natural rocks, the Assyrians wrote on clay tablets. During the twentieth century some clay tablets were found at Ur, which had on one side the 'fair copy' written by the teacher, and on the other the pupil's attempt at copying it.

Papyrus was made from the stems of the bulrushes growing on the banks of the Nile, and permanent writing was done on long rolls. Parchment was discovered round about 230 BC, but many of the writings on this, or on bark, were devoured by white ants.

The Brahmins considered that their holy words were too holy to be written by hand and therefore their teachings were passed down by word of mouth. As late as 55 B.C. when Julius Caesar crossed the Straits of Dover he noted that the Druids did not commit their doctrines to writing.

By 30 B.C. school-children used bone and metal pens or points rather like ballpoint pens. The marks were pressed out on wax-coated wooden tablets and the tablets could be used over and over again.

Acrostics were invented early in the fourth century A.D. These were poems in which the first and last letters of each line made a word when read downwards.

In the fifth century, quill pens were used on parchment and little drawings made round the writings; one of these showed a Punch and Judy show. By the seventh century, the Chinese were already using wooden blocks for printing, and at Novgorod, the school-children in A.D. 900 drew funny faces as well as letters on their birchbark 'slates'.

Before the ninth century an o was used in the calendars of the Maya civilisation, but in the West no zero sign was used before A.D. 1138. At this time the Roman numerals were put aside for the Arabic figures, and by the end of the thirteenth century arithmetic symbols were in use in Europe as we use them today.

At the end of the fourteenth century boys and girls attended little schools where they learned to repeat prayers and to say grace before and after meals. The small daughters of the future Henry IV of England had two ABC books bought for them in February 1398 at the cost of 20 pence. Blanche was not quite seven and was married when she was eight years old, taking a governess with her. Philippa, her sister, was younger and had a cradle-rocker.

When paper began to be made from rags, school-books and Bibles were not so expensive.

Hornbooks seem to have arrived about the same time as printing, dating as far back as 1450. Some were oblong with a handle extension at one narrow end like a brush, but others were curved at the corners like a battledore.

Some had a cross at the top of the tablet to remind a child to cross himself before beginning his lesson; these were sometimes known as 'criss-cross books'. Others might have the alphabet arranged in the shape of a cross, and some letters were then in the 'criss-cross row' as in some primers.

A silver hornbook of about 1550 was engraved with a design of a bird perched on a branch, and others would bear the crest of some company, or the arms of the family to which it belonged.

In 1587 John Wolfe was granted a licence for a 'Horne ABC', according to Mrs Field in *The Child and his Book*. Hornbooks are also mentioned in *Love's Labour's Lost*, written in 1589.

The hornbook was usually of wood on which was pasted paper or parchment, and this was protected by a thin sheet of horn secured by a metal frame or strips of wood. Some were made from two pieces of stiff leather, the back and the handle being in one piece which was stitched to the front frame of leather leaving the parchment and horn between as in a picture. A luxury hornbook of Queen Elizabeth's day was ornamented with silver filigree and the handle and back covered with red silk.

Stronger hornbooks were of pewter with letters cast or moulded and more expensive ones were of ivory with engraved letters. One of bronze was made in 1729 with a width of $2\frac{1}{2}$ inches and a length of five inches. Many hornbooks had a hole in the handle through which a cord or ribbon was threaded, so that the child might wear it round his neck or hang it on a peg.

Early seventeenth-century examples had the alphabets written in an Elizabethan hand, those of the eighteenth had printed upper- and lower-case italic alphabets, while others might have Roman lettering or Gothic. Those of the nineteenth century had the upper-case Roman alphabet and numerals engraved in bone.

In addition to the alphabet there could be the numerals one to ten, though often the letter J was omitted, and on some the Lord's Prayer was added, sometimes in its entirety, sometimes just in part. Vowel combinations have been included in some eighteenth-century specimens.

Unfortunately, there are many faked hornbooks about, but those faked in the nineteenth century have also become collectors' pieces. Leather ones have been made from pieces of old harness, metal ones from the old moulds, and wooden ones faked to resemble old wood.

When Andrew Tuer wrote his two enormous volumes *The Horn*

375   Battledore and doll combined. English

137

Book in 1896, he had reproductions made to illustrate his point, and these were included in the pockets let into the covers of the volumes, the books being dedicated to Queen Victoria. Now some of these have been innocently included in collections as genuine specimens of the period they represent.

Apart from hornbooks, children could learn to spell by using ivory counters and learning became less parrot-like. These counters were either square or round, fitting into decorated boxes. Some were of wood with letters painted black, the ivory ones were engraved with the letters filled, with black or red. Instead of just the 26 counters with letters of the alphabet more were included, especially those with the vowels.

Numerals also were popular both here and in America, where Charles Shipman had emigrated in 1767. He was an ivory- and wood-turner from Birmingham and made both alphabets and counters in either material.

General C. C. Pinckney was given alphabet blocks when he was very young: 'You perceive we begin betimes for he is not yet four months old' wrote Mrs Pinckney from South Carolina.

In 1770 India rubbers were used. This was a substance 'excellently adapted to the wiping from paper, the marks made by an ordinary black-lead pencil'. The price for one was three shillings per cubic half inch.

In 1780 a child's writing-case made in France had minute sheets of paper together with envelopes and sealing-wax of several colours. The little sheets were decorated by hand, and as blotting paper was fairly unknown, in the case was included blue and silver dusting-powder for drying the ink.

Dr Henry Stephens began to make and sell ink in 1832, and blotting paper became common, although its use had already been recorded in the fifteenth century.

By 1844 adhesive envelopes were in use and minute ones were included in the miniature writing-compendiums for children.

During the early part of the nineteenth century alphabet rods were used, chiefly in the Balkan countries. These could be made specially for a certain child, for sometimes the child's name was engraved in addition to the alphabet and the numerals. The rods were from 18 inches long to about 24 inches, and could be rectangular or triangular in section.

In the East the sun and moon appeared as decoration, while in Holland tulips ornamented the rods which could be inlaid with ivory, brass and pewter.

Between 1818 and 1820 revolving alphabets appeared made by J. and E. Wallis of Snow Hill, London. Each letter was shown in turn on a square picture of a Regency interior mounted on wood. The 'Yankee Schoolmaster' patented by Lake in 1886 worked on the same principle. This is pictured in *European and American Dolls*.

Books with flaps which lifted up and down and known as 'turn-ups' came in 1795 and were listed in Laurie and Whittle's catalogue.

S. and J. Fuller had the Temple of Fancy in Rathbone Place, and about 1810 they issued cut-out figures in books with interchangeable heads. These originated with them and were very successful for at least 20 years. However, they were soon copied in France and Germany and some English stories were translated for this purpose. They were the forerunners of the doll-dressing cards. Rathbone Place is where the Montanaris' son Richard lived in 1875.

One of the Fuller books with cut-outs was *The History and Adventures of Little Henry*, published in 1810, and later used by the little Princess Victoria. *Ellen or the Naughty Girl Reclaimed* came in 1811, with various hats for the small figures, and also *The History of Little Fanny*. *Cinderella* in 1814 was another pretty book with elaborate cut-outs.

Ackermann in 1819 had *Fables in Action* where the figures in an envelope at the back of the book fitted into slots on the background.

Newbery in England and Isaiah Thomas in the U.S.A. insisted that their books for children were of a high moral tone. Children had to be good in order to escape from hell, and most bad children came to a very sticky end.

Nursery rhymes and fairy-stories were a great relief to those frightening tales at the end of the seventeenth century, but along came Maria Edgeworth and Thomas Day who condemned all these tales as foolish nonsense. They said that tales of exact literal truth should take their place, thus infuriating Charles Lamb. In 1834, the *Child's Annual*, published in Boston, gave a 'Lament for the Fairies'.

Indestructible books, where linen-cloth was combined with paper, came about 1830 and were popular in the 1850s. At first the colours were on paper mounted on linen, and later the printing was actually on the linen. *Bertie's Treasury* and an ABC in 1853 were two such books.

Lear made an alphabet in 1846 and in 1860 he made one especially for the children of the poet Alfred Tennyson. The most well-known illustrators were Kate Greenaway, Caldicott and Crane, while the illustrators of the frightening books seem to have been forgotten. *Little Black Sambo* was a popular book written by Helen Bannerman at the end of the nineteenth century. Now in the 1960s this book and her others about the little Negro children are banned in certain parts of Africa.

In Chepstow Museum are toys and dolls and an interesting Victorian book with pull-tags at the side. When opened to show a picture of an animal, the tag can be pulled to imitate its voice. Known as 'speaking books' they came about 1880, and were manufactured in Germany.

The famous Meggendorfers, also in Germany, produced books about this time. These designers included elaborate movements in their pictures by a complicated arrangement of strips of thin cardboard joined to operating tabs, and were extremely interesting.

Revolving pictures were published by Nister about 1900 in a book called *In Wonderland*. Later on came the 'pop-up' books which

376 'Cut-out' by Lothar Meggendorfer. Germany

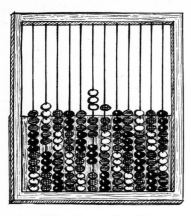

377 Abacus. English

378 Cash register by Casdon

379 'The New Alphabet Game'. English

appeared again during the Second World War when toys were difficult to come by.

Early in the twentieth century came the game Word-Making and Word-Taking. These were one-inch squares of card, black on one side, white on the other on which was printed a letter of the alphabet, there being many more vowels than other letters. The letters were placed downwards on a table and each player took it in turns to turn one up. If a word could be made with the letters on the table then the player took that word.

Word-making sets are still available, though the game of Scrabble is popular. Played on a board, this is something between the word-making game and a crossword puzzle. Other toys which are a help to spelling are the John Bull printing outfits, and the typewriters made by the firm of Mettoy about 1955.

The abacus was known in Roman times, and it is interesting to note that the beads along the wires were in groups of fives and tens according to their colour, and were not in dozens or half-dozens as in the Victorian examples. In 1969 an abacus on a toy booth at Paddington Station had the groups of beads in tens and fives, perhaps looking forward to decimal currency.

There were arithmetic books illustrated by wood engravings. 'Eight times ten are eighty, I think she's pretty weighty' had a picture of a fat woman in a sedan-chair. This comes from *Marmaduke Multiply's Merry Method of Making Minor Multiplications*.

A little book published in 1863 was accompanied by Larkin's Crystal Cube for demonstrating geometric forms.

Whether a toy cash register teaches one to add up is a debatable point, and possibly the old abacus was a better way and surely more amusing.

BUILDING BRICKS

The Victorian bricks were often of the improving kind with letters as an aid to reading, others were made to construct buildings such as the Mansion House or the Royal Exchange, the latter made in Germany about 1845. These taught children to be careful with their fingers or the whole construction would topple over, incidentally adding to the fun.

A set of building bricks produced in Germany in 1845 had a picture of Buckingham Palace, and the bricks were cleverly cut in a wedge shape to give the idea of perspective. These were lithographs coloured by hand, and were very effective. A set of these can be seen at Bethnal Green Museum.

When Princess Victoria was about six years old she played with interesting bricks made in the shape of houses. There were little wooden houses with sloping roofs, round towers with domes, circular castles, and trees made from wood shavings. Many of these are in the State Apartments at Kensington Palace, and others are pictured in Bestelmeier's catalogues.

Wedge-shaped blocks for building a circular cottage were made in England in the mid nineteenth century and were called the 'New Alphabet Game'.

An interesting label on a building kit is that of 'Austin's Toy and Doll Counter, Pantheon Bazaar'. The kit was of plain wooden parts forming a stable, together with a painted figure of a farmer and four houses. Other plain wooden bricks were a kit for a church, 1830–40, and for building a bridge.

When building cubes had pictures on them, it meant that there were six different pictures to be put together, only one being able to be seen at once. In a way these bricks were the forerunners of jigsaw puzzles and were made about 1844. A painting by the American, Thomas Eakins, 1844–1916, shows a baby at play with cubes on which are letters and numerals.

In England in 1852 there was a set of 49 pieces, the toy blocks illustrating the 'Funeral of the Duke of Wellington'.

Alphabet picture-making blocks were printed by chromo-litho in the second half of the nineteenth century in the U.S.A.

The views of the Rhine on cubes were Baxter process prints made in England, about 1860. The wooden blocks and pictures, in a box, are very pretty and have a matt finish.

Charles M. Crandall's famous building blocks were invented and manufactured by him at Montrose, Pennsylvania, and also in New York in 1867. Later on, in England, there were wooden bricks which were thin and flat with dovetailed edges so that they could be fitted together for building walls. Rather interesting this, as at the time quite small back gardens would have high walls built round them for 'an Englishman's home is his castle'.

Bricks also had a moral significance in 1870, one set being 'The Importance of Punctuality'.

Richters of Rudolstadt made building bricks of cast cement. There were various size blocks, cubes and rectangles, and some for building arches with the wedge-shaped stones incised in the cement. In 1888,

The original cover for the building slabs

380   ABC building slabs by Crandall. U.S.A.

381 Dr Richter's
'Anchor' box. Germany

the bricks were cast in three colours, natural, reddish and dull blue, the sets selling for between five shillings and five guineas.

A popular model to build was that of the Tower Bridge, which was opened in 1894. The Richter's *Anker-Steinbaukasten* won medals at the Paris Exhibition of 1900, and at St Louis in 1904, an anchor always appearing in their trademarks. Bing, of Nuremberg, also made *Steinbaukasten*, that is stone building bricks, his sign being a B and a W between the words Bing-Werke.

Lott's bricks in England were made from Italian marble at a factory in Watford. E. A. Lott had bought up the entire Richter plant and with the advice of an architect, Arnold Mitchell, the bricks were cut in various shapes suitable for assembling models of buildings such as cathedrals and colleges.

Smaller sets were made for building cottages containing bricks of black and of white, but the public did not approve of these and therefore red bricks were added. When the architect lost interest, Lott continued with various coloured blocks and other shapes, including a chimney brick. For lightness, the Lott's bricks were squares and rectangles of half a square thick, whereas the Richter blocks had been cubes and the rectangular shapes the thickness of the cube.

As the Watford factory grew, the boxes included embossed bricks, mullioned windows and a 'Tudor style' set. At the British Industries Fair, held at the Imperial Institute in 1918, Queen Mary bought the first box of Lott's bricks, and from then on they became famous, the son continuing in the family firm. Arches and bridges could be built over the railway lines on the nursery floors, and in 1920, a set was sent to H. G. Wells. He had written his book on floor games in 1913, and he noted his approval of these English bricks.

Fathers working in the city would do their shopping in their lunch hours, and such places as Gamage's and Benetfinks would sell them the Lott's bricks of 'artificial stone'. The original A. E. Lott died very

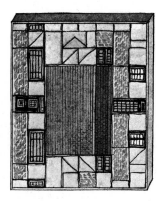

382   A box of Lott's bricks.
English

382   Cottage built with Lott's
bricks

recently at the age of 94, and the bricks were discontinued, but the name of Lott lives on in the chemistry sets now produced by another firm.

Wooden bricks gradually disappeared when war came again in 1939, but there were interesting cubes made of bakelite. Little hollow cubes, stoutly made and fitting one on to another by means of slightly raised discs.

As war continued, cardboard and paper cubes took the place of these, and with care could be piled one on another. A custard firm put out cubes in the form of little boxes, within which was custard powder or jelly crystals. As these were purchased with food coupons, they therefore took some time to collect.

KIT SETS

From brick-building it is only a short step to what are known as 'construction sets'.

Paper toys assembled from cutting out printed sheets were the first 'kit' sets. These sheets were printed in black and white and originated in Strasbourg. They could be hand-coloured and later on could be bought printed in colours on single sheets or in book form. The paper doll with various sets of clothes was a cut-out figure often arranged so that tabs held the various articles of clothing in place. Europe and America were the chief sources for these kits, whereas the folding paper toys came from Japan.

'The Newly Invented Musical Game' of 1801 was in a way a construction set, for the little pegs had to be arranged in the correct order, but a true construction toy for building a log cabin came in 1850, and consisted of 94 pieces of wood, and is now in the Museum of the City of New York.

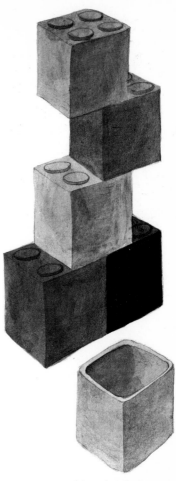

383   Building bricks by Hilary Page. England

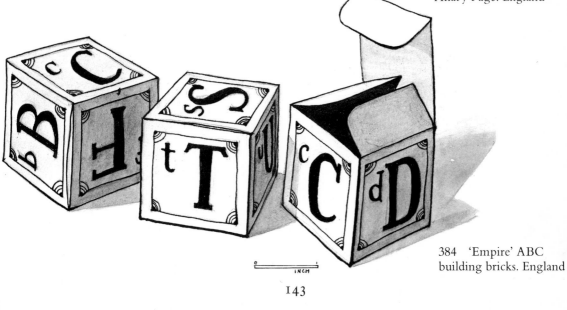

384   'Empire' ABC building bricks. England

Between 1820 and 1849, wooden toys were made in Pennsylvania by Asa Crandall, the father of Charles M. Crandall who made games, picture blocks and puzzles such as 'Pigs in Clover'. It was Charles M. Crandall who made the constructional game of acrobats, the limbs fitting together with grooves and the parts painted. In 1967, one of these sets was sold for 20 guineas in a London sale.

These Crandalls were no relation to the 'rocking-horse' Crandalls. The easiest way to remember them is that the large family with four sons made the large toys, and that Charles M. Crandall made menageries and puzzles which came from Pennsylvania.

William Rose of New York seems to have been an agent between this Crandall and Henry Jewitt of Kentish Town in England, and it is for this reason both names appear on the boxes of some of their toys and the letter R appears inside two interlacing triangles.

In 1901, a Frank Hornby in England took out a patent for a toy called 'Mechanics made Easy'. This was renamed Meccano and became one of the most popular toys for boys. They had fun joining together the strips of metal pierced with evenly spaced holes, with small nuts and bolts provided in the boxes in 1907. Wheels and handles were included in the outfit, and many things could be built, but the fun was in the building, for the results were far from realistic.

The Meccano of today has gradually assumed a new look, though pieces can still be bought separately and kit sets added to.

An American, A. C. Gilbert, marketed the Erector sets in 1913 which were similar to Meccano. In 1920 Gilbert purchased the branch of the Meccano factory in the U.S.A. He became famous for his educational toys such as chemistry sets, microscope sets and sound experiment sets and suchlike.

The descendant of a toy sold over a century before came in 1959. For 11s. 6d. from Harrods could be bought American logs with which to build a miniature pioneer's cabin. The log squares were cut from *real wood* and the sets were complete with roofing timbers packed in metal canisters. It is most interesting to note that the real wood was an added attraction.

In 1960 there were many building toys and one kit supplied separate miniature bricks and window-frames and mortar that dissolved in hot water so that the materials could be used again and again.

Other kits were for making aeroplanes, one a scale model of the Scandinavian Air Lines Douglas D.C.-8 which was expected to make its first flight from Britain to Los Angeles in April 1960. There was also a moonship of a type which the firm said will eventually reach the moon; all of which goes to show that sometimes toys precede the actual event and are not necessarily mementoes which come afterwards.

In 1960 the hospital craze was here, this time with an 'invisible man' set, which enabled a child to assemble a man from his skeleton to his skin, inserting the various organs as he went along. This could be quite instructive, but some people remarked that it was just morbid.

Gamage's had a doll's house construction set in 1961 made of wood with windows of acetate.

The Seventh International Toy Exhibition was held in February 1968 in Paris. Amongst the thousands of toys on display was one consisting of a cardboard patient on which operations could be performed, and an electric circuit which lit up if the 'surgeon' was clumsy.

Nowadays, many toys are linked up with films and television programmes. To coincide with the launching of the Dr Dolittle film in December 1967, Happitoys brought out modelling sets for casting the clay animals. The kits included non-toxic modelling clay, modelling tools and moulds.

Some of the best construction sets of today are those put out by Lego, the Danish firm in Copenhagen. All kinds of houses can be built and extra parts can be bought separately and a whole village gradually assembled complete with station and other amenities. 'Legoland' itself is a paradise for children with toys and dolls, including the collection of Estrid Faurholt.

Another firm for building models is that of Fischertechnik, where the kits have many of the parts built of nylon.

385 Apple tree by Britains Ltd. England

145

11 Picture cards, puzzles, jigsaws

The origin of cards seems to be lost in obscurity and it is certainly as old as the beginnings of paper-making.

In A.D. 1120 the Emperor Seun-ho had dotted cards made for the amusement of his wives, and the Chinese made cards of pasteboard which were two inches long and one inch broad, with black and red characters on the face side. Circular cards came from India, and gipsies were mentioned as having told fortunes by cards during the twelfth century in Arabia.

From here, cards were imported into Europe through Spain by the Moors, and they were much used at the European Courts. By 1275, good paper was made in Italy and many cards were beautifully painted, some being done on horn.

The 'court' cards may have taken their name from the royal figures and the court jester, or from the coats and tabards worn at the time when court cards were termed 'coat' cards. Later, the dresses were based on fifteenth-century costumes.

In southern Europe the suits were termed 'coins', 'cups', 'swords' and 'clubs', whereas in northern Germany they were called 'hearts', 'bells', 'leaves' and 'acorns'. During the middle of the fifteenth century the French called the signs 'hearts', 'diamonds', 'clubs' and 'spades', and these names have become more or less universal.

Ulm, a German town noted for printing, applied wood engraving to the production of playing-cards in 1454, and soon English manufacturers petitioned that cards should not be imported from abroad, as they wished to improve their own trade.

The game of Piquet was said to have been invented for the amusement of Charles VI of France, and James IV of Scotland met his future wife while playing cards. She was Margaret, the sister of Henry VIII.

At the beginning of the seventeenth century, Thomas Murner of Strasbourg made cards to improve learning, and from these stem all those others concerned with history, geography and nature.

A set published in 1644 was for the purpose of instructing the young King of France and consisted of fables, famous women, geography and a history of France, all arranged by Desmarests and finely engraved by Della Bella.

The first English geographical playing-cards were issued in 1675, the king of each suit was a portrait of Charles II and the queen was his wife Catherine. The four suits were the countries divided into north, south, east and west. During the latter part of his reign more pictorial cards appeared, including illustrations of the Spanish Armada, and Dr Parry's plot against Queen Elizabeth. Later historical packs were of Guy Fawkes, Titus Oates, the Meal-tub plot and the murder of Sir Edmondbury Godfrey.

More peaceful scenes were pictured during the reign of Queen Anne, such as those featuring fables and heraldry, though it was during her reign in 1710 that cards were taxed in England.

The *Complet Gamemaster or full and easy instructions for playing above twenty several games upon cards* was printed in 1725. This was a little book for J. Wilfred at the Three Golden Flower-de-Luces, in Little Britain, London.

Historical cards picturing the history of England were published by Wallis sometime after 1760, beginning with William the Conqueror and ending with the death of George II.

Until now, the backs of cards had been left plain, but in 1769 John Berkenhout took out an English patent whereby the playing-cards were coloured on the backs in order to make the packs different, and by 1799 playing-cards were designed so that whichever way they lay the 'pips' looked much the same either way round.

At the time of the French Revolution, the kings and queens on the playing-cards were replaced by others, often labourers, the Dauphin being replaced by the figure of a gardener. People using cards with the royal figures and emblems were regarded as 'suspect', and certainly a thing to be avoided. Here the 'queen' has been replaced by 'Dame de Pique', in a pack by Lefer, of Paris, 1792, a stalwart maiden holding a club with which she has slain a dragon, possibly 'tyranny'.

One of the animals illustrated in the 'Cabinet of Beasts' was the 'kanguroo'. Each card was 2 × 3 inches and in the little booklet it says, 'This curious animal may be seen to great advantage in the King's garden at Richmond in Surrey. It is a native of a new discovered island in the Indian Ocean, called New Holland.' The booklet was $1\frac{1}{2} \times 1\frac{3}{4}$ inches and was published by John Marshall in 1800.

'The Mansion of Happiness' was published in the same year, and there were question-and-answer games with forfeits. One published by Darton about 1810 was 'Instructive Conversation', and had 32 biographical sketches of eminent British characters.

'Creswick' was a nineteenth-century game which, among others, was played with ordinary cards, and was popular among soldiers. I have noticed that often in a town where there is a barracks, in the museums there will be packs of cards preserved, especially from the years 1820–30. Dorchester, Salisbury and Winchester were such towns. This was the reign of George IV, a king who was fond of playing cards, and at this time a heavy tax was levied, the duty being 2s. 6d. a pack.

Hunt and Son made packs on which the pips were pricked in such a way that they could be used by blind persons. Henry Fawcett, the blind Postmaster-General, played with such a pack.

In 1823, indoor games were advertised in New York, including dissected maps and many games with pictorial cards having such subjects as botany, geography, astronomy and scripture.

386 Playing-card used during the French Revolution. France

387 'Changeable
Gentlemen'. England

The 'Panoramacopia' was invented in 1824 by an artist named T. T. Dales. This consisted of several upright aquatints cut up, which could then be grouped together in different ways to form beautiful landscapes. These were mounted on thin layers of wood so the pieces were quite strong, and as they were in colour, it was indeed 'a pretty toy'.

An early example of the 'Happy Families' kind of card game was 'Quartettes'. This was instructive, each set having some educational value, such as a picture of the author, his birthplace, and his works making up a set of four.

'Grandmamma's New Game of English History' was published in 1837, beginning with William the Conqueror and ending with Victoria. 'Dr. Busby' came in the U.S.A. in 1838, issued by W. and S. B. Ives.

Pretty cards were made in France; 'Flora', the game of flowers, came in 1820 and beautiful pictures of the Champs-Elysées in 1860. Lithographed plates were used for scenes such as the Palace of Industry, and the Bois de Boulogne, avenue de l'Impératrice, etc. One of the prettiest sets to be published in England was that of 'Botanical Lotto', about 1850.

Heads printed with an aquatint effect were on thick card and divided into threes – forehead, nose, mouth and shoulders. These could be so arranged that each feature fitted each face, with a comical result. Other unusual cards were those produced by R. Ackermann and others, in 1849. In these 'Diagrams illustrating the Sciences of Astronomy and Geography', the cards were pierced with holes and backed with coloured tissue paper. When the light shone through, it gave the illusion of the sky at night.

'Nap', after Napoleon, was played in 1850, and 'Blanchard' in 1860. Dickens mentions the game of 'Beggar my Neighbour' in *Great Expectations*. 'Old Maid' was played in Victorian days, it being almost an insult to be termed 'old maid' when there were so many spinsters about.

'Garden Flowers' was published in 1860, a matching game where the correct names had to be fitted to the picture cards.

Another well-known game was Happy Families. Those designed by Sir John Tenniel, the illustrator of *Alice in Wonderland*, were made about 1860, and depicted a father, mother, son and daughter. They were rather ugly families and each had a distinct family likeness, the son usually turning after the father. Each family had some trade or profession; there was Dr Dose the Doctor, Mr Bun the Baker, Mr Chip the Carpenter, Mr Soot the Sweep and so on. The cards were published by Jaques of London and were line engravings coloured by hand.

Queen Mary, in 1877 when she was ten years of age, wrote a letter to her mother saying that she had been playing a game called 'Happy Families'. Since then other 'happy families' have been printed including those of animals.

388 'Building Cards and Pretty Pictures'. England

A well-printed pictorial set was 'Capitals of the World', in fact a great deal of the child's enjoyment was in looking at the pictures; the same with 'Floral Lotto' which came about 1872. There is a set of these in the Cope Collection in the Old School at Evenlode.

Early in the twentieth century came more card games, Noah's Ark, Donkey, Snap, Brer Rabbit, and other packs known as 'Misfits'. These were cards in which three made a complete figure, the head on one, then the body, and lastly the legs. They were not interchangeable, the complete figure only emerged when the cards were arranged correctly. Many of the characters have now disappeared, such as the Tweeny-maid and the Butcher-boy. 'Maud' with her tiny waist and long dress showed a typical simpering female of the period.

Brer Rabbit and Brer Fox were two characters who appeared on playing-cards. They came from *Uncle Remus: His Songs and Stories* written in America by Joel Chandler Harris.

Zoo animals have always been favourites, and travel games show the vehicles of the period. 'Flight' was a popular game after the Second World War.

389 'Proverbs'. England

390 'Panko' or 'Votes for Women'. England

GOLLY MISFITZ.

HOUSEMAID

GOLLIWOG

MAUD

A LA PARIS

SOCIETY MISFITZ.

391 PICTURE CARDS
From two games of Misfits, 'full of Hilarious Amusement'

Mention must also be made of the fun in building houses with cards and of the special cards designed for this purpose. This is not a new pastime. Chardin has painted a boy playing at card houses, and in an eighteenth-century French engraving, a girl is building houses with cards which have been bent longways on. The actual cards are the ordinary ones with hearts and spades, but in Victoria's time special pictorial cards were printed with parts of houses for building card houses and these must have been tremendous fun to play with.

392   Card houses 'upon a novel plan'. Bavaria

PUZZLES, JIGSAWS

On the island of Crete a subterranean maze, known as a 'labyrinth', was said to have been constructed by Daedalus to hold the Minotaur. These large mazes are a form of puzzle, and there is an early maze cut out in the chalk on St Catherine's Hill at Winchester.

A maze at Hampton Court and another at Hatfield House are made of paths surrounded by privet or yew bushes. The idea was to follow the paths until one reached the goal, perhaps a seat, a grotto, or some sweet-smelling bushes, and then to return, possibly by some other devious route.

These large puzzles led to smaller ones which were constructed to hold in the hand, usually in the form of a circular tray. In these a marble was contained which had to be manipulated to roll into a depression in the centre. 'Pigs in Clover' was a noted maze made by Charles M. Crandall in 1889, and which became one of the best-selling puzzles of the nineteenth century. It was six inches in diameter.

Other kinds were the plain or decorated shapes cut so that they could fit together to form other shapes. For a long time these had been known in China under the name of 'Tangram'. There were usually seven pieces, which by careful arranging would form a square. Such

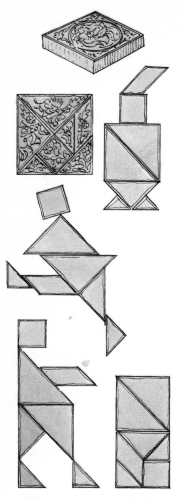

393 Tangram. England,
derived from China

puzzles may have led to the idea of sticking a picture to a piece of wood and then dividing it up by cutting in two directions.

The first cut pictures came in the eighteenth century, and were known as 'dissected maps'. In the *Universal Director*, published in London in 1763, appeared the name of 'John Spilsbury, Engraver and Map Dissector in wood, in order to facilitate the Teaching of Geography. Russel Court, Drury Lane'. This seems to be the earliest authentic date.

Dissected maps were produced by Wallis, the well-known London cartographers, about 1770–1880, and for several years they were published exclusively by them. Early examples had irregular edges, later maps had square corners, each map being mounted on wood before being cut.

The counties of England were cut into separate pieces surrounded by the sea, which was also cut into shapes, but the counties could be purchased without the sea and then the puzzle cost a little less.

One published by Wallis in 1788 with irregular edges was 'Wallis's Royal Chronological Tables of English History' on a plan similar to that of the dissected maps. Another cut with straight edges was a sheet map of the world showing new discoveries, and this could be approximately dated by the death of Captain James Cook in 1779.

Again education is linked with play, at first mostly historical or geographical. Natural History was also learnt from puzzles, one being a beautiful jigsaw of 1821 illustrating the 'Thirty-six Birds Commonly Seen in England'.

At the turn of the century the dissected maps became known as puzzles and later on as jigsaws, for the jig controlled the outline of the cut, which before had been done by hand.

The jig is the pattern, a form of template, which the saw follows. For example, when a dress is cut from a paper pattern with a pair of scissors, the pattern is the template, and the scissors the saw which follows the outline. After mounting the picture on wood, it would be cut in irregular lines from one side to the other, then the picture was turned round and cut from top to bottom in the same way, following the jig.

A fret-saw machine is one used for cutting frets, i.e. ornamental holes in flat sheets. It can cut a hole in the centre of a piece of wood and is a machine more for hobbies than the more industrial jig. When a puzzle is cut by hand with a fret-saw machine, a jig has not been used.

Many jigsaws were hand-coloured engravings, one of 'The Lord Mayor presenting the Sword of State to Queen Victoria at Temple Bar, Nov. 9. 1837', was complete with its box, and another beautiful and complicated puzzle was 'The Game of the Star-Spangled Banner or Emigrants to the United States', which was published about 1835.

'The Aerial Transit Company's Station in the Plains of Hindostan' was the impressive title given to a jigsaw lithographed about 1843. It was said to be a publicity stunt of Henson's who, with Stringfellow, invented the 'aerostat'. Henson also published prints, silk handkerchiefs and broadsides showing the machine in full flight.

About 1850 there were double puzzles, that is pictures on both sides. Some had a picture on one side and a map on the reverse, again adding a little jam to learning.

Japanese jigsaws were known as 'Chie-no-ita'. Here apart from the flat puzzles there were those solid ones, which were more in the nature of a 3-D jigsaw, and were sometimes known as 'breakdown puzzles'. This reminds one of an early ring of medieval times. This ring could split up into two or three interlocking rings when handled in a certain way. It was decorated in an ornate manner and was the forerunner of the disentangling puzzles made of metal, which are sold in the streets and in the shops of today.

Other puzzles were built on the early maze principle, in small boxes, or in tin lids during the Second World War. In these is a small silver ball which is manipulated along the route until the 'home' is reached. There are endless varieties to this kind of puzzle, which are based, more or less, on the earlier 'Pigs in Clover' of the U.S.A.

'Buffet the Bullies into their Billets', a First World War game, consisted of four square wooden bricks printed with four faces sealed in a box with a glass lid. The aim was to shake the bricks about until they were in their correct positions. The heads of the 'Bullies' were the Kaiser, Little Willie, Hindenburg and von Tirpitz. Probably our counterparts were made in Germany.

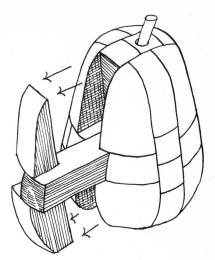

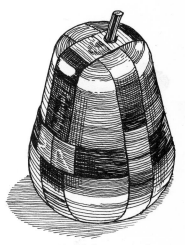

394   Breakdown puzzle.
Japan

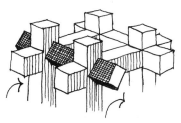

395   Breakdown puzzle.
Japan

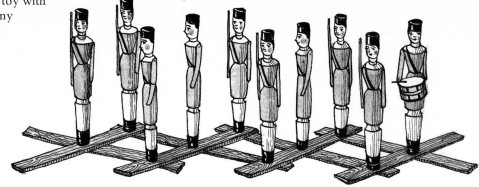

396　Scissors toy with soldiers. Saxony

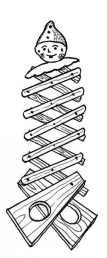

397　'Lazy Tongs'. Saxony

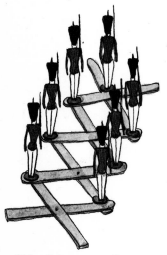

398　Scissors toy. Saxony

12　Novelties, lucky toys, teddy bears, golliwogs, characters, eggs and nests, banks

NOVELTIES

All toys when they are new are novelties, some come to stay and become traditional, others are here today and gone tomorrow. It is impossible to include every little novelty that one has seen, or perhaps has never seen, for who knows what little home-made toy lies away on the other side of the hill, or beyond the sea.

The scissors toys were mentioned in the sixteenth century by Silliman. They are sometimes known as 'lazy-tongs' after those used by confectioners and mentioned later by Mrs Molesworth. Some had merely a feather attached and cheaper variations are the hollow paper tubes which can be blown into. A spring enables them to roll up again and squeak on the return journey.

Jack-in-the-boxes were known in the sixteenth century and have been mentioned by Rousseau. Snake-toys are variations; when the box is opened a wooden reptile darts out and pricks the hand, a horrid toy, and even Jack-in-the-boxes are frightening especially those like Mr Punch, which reached the U.S.A. about 1825. Jack-in-the-box dolls were made by C. Bontempo in England, in 1898.

Other novelties are the figures of monks about six inches high which open to reveal an altar with candles, or a wooden doll whose skirts part and show a little kitchen complete with utensils. These were made in the eighteenth century, and the wooden stork who brought babies from Silesia came in the nineteenth century.

Pantins were first seen in children's hands in 1746, according to

154

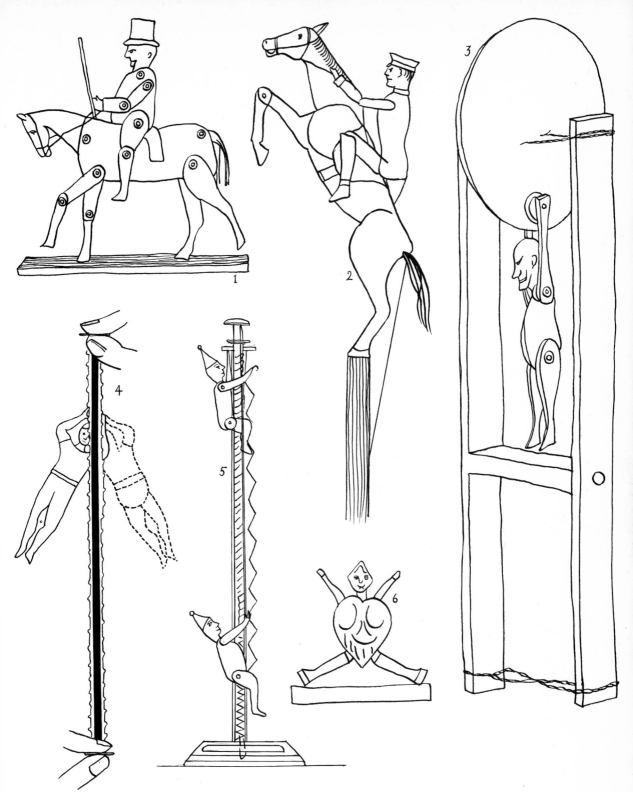

399 NOVELTIES
i Man on horse, registered by H. Jewitt. ii Mechanical rider, German patent
by W. Ziegler. iii Man balancing on a wheel. iv Acrobat, German patent by
E. P. Lehmann. v Clown, German patent by J. F. Wallmann. vi Clown,
registered by H. Jewitt

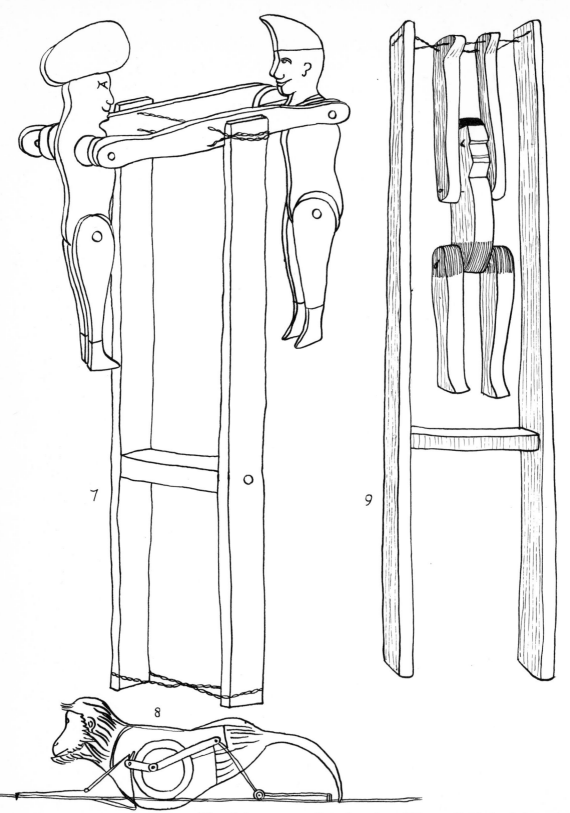

400   vii A more complicated version of No. 9. viii Mechanical monkey,
German patent by W. P. Shattuck, U.S.A. ix Traditional toy, called a
Jumping Jack in the U.S.A.

Max von Boehn and in 1747 they were played with by grown-ups. For the following ten years the craze persisted, until at last the police intervened stating 'the women were in danger of bringing children into the world with twisted limbs like pantins'.

The French aristocrats were enthusiastic players, and many of the sheets depicted the fashions of the day or theatrical personages. Others might caricature people. In the Collection of M. Roger Castaing is a 'pantin ayant le visage de Requetti, Vicomte de Mirabeau, tenant à la main un verre de vin' and called 'Mirabeau-Tonneau'. Mention of this is in *Jeux et Jouets d'autrefois*. Others might represent harlequins, colombines, shepherds or shepherdesses similar to those in the paintings by Boucher.

This idea of moving a cut-out figure by means of strings was the same as that used by the Egyptians for their toy dolls in ancient times.

About 1750 the pantins were made in five parts, the body and head, the two arms and the two legs. They were engraved on sheets of paper or card and could be cut out at home or bought ready cut and coloured. Later on they were printed by lithography. Cordier of France was well known for his pantins in 1889.

In Germany, a pantin was called a *Hampelmann*, and in Thuringia it was known as a *Zapplemann*. To act like a *Hampelmann* was 'to pull strings'.

Another name was jumping jack, and these were made in the Erz Mountains during the eighteenth and nineteenth centuries, small ones ten inches high and large ones $27\frac{5}{8}$ inches high. Usually made of wood, some depicted soldiers with uniforms and high hats.

The U.S.A. made jumping jacks in 1880, and in England an old sailor at Broadstairs made them on the sands to sell to children. There were also political jumping jacks which showed one person up when the other person was down, that is one in power when the other was on the decline.

By 1872 the importing of jumping jacks almost ceased in the U.S.A. as their own were so well made. Reuben A. Smith, who started the Toy Manufacturing Company in New Hampshire, made them his

401, 402   Merry Jacks. Erz Mountains

403   Merry Jack. Erz Mountains

404   Street vendor. China

405   Blow toy. Oriental

406   Street Pennyworths.
Germany

407   Jack-in-the-box.
German

own speciality. At first the figures were wooden, then printed paper on wood, then printed paper on cardboard. The early ones were held by nails, the later ones with wire staples.

Merry jacks, carved wooden animals or figures with the legs or limbs attached to two sticks were made at Oberammergau in the eighteenth and nineteenth centuries, and gave an appearance of movement.

Other novelties might appear when some historical event takes place, such as the models of the guillotine, and the little Sputnik of the Russians, the wobbly heads, including Mr Churchill of all people, and many of the penny toys of Victorian times to the more expensive playthings sold in the streets and markets at the present day.

LUCKY TOYS

Mascots, amulets and talismen are all objects which may be considered as lucky charms, and their history goes far back into the jungles of yesterday. Some were made to ward off illness, some for fertility, others to help in a confinement, or in teeth-cutting, some to help one in the world beyond, and all supposing to possess magic powers which would achieve that which the owner desired.

Many of these fetishes and objects of superstition are things which have ended in becoming children's playthings.

Dolls of straw such as the 'corn dollies' were to promote good harvests, dolls with a tooth attached were to help with teething. A little blue bead put in a child's hair, or a rattle made with coral were all to do with luck.

Knights of old would wear their lady's favourite colour, airmen in bombers of the Second World War might take a Teddy bear with them, there is no end to what could be considered as a mascot.

Acorns protected one from lightning and many of the cords on the blinds of Victorian houses ended in a knot enclosed in a carved wooden acorn. A belt with acorns attached would help one's tummyache, and a necklace of oak-galls would cure a sore throat.

A toy broom with the 'bristles' made from pins would be hung on a wall for good luck in parts of south London, and pretty little decorated hearts were sold in Whitechapel in 1910 at one penny each and were worn for love or good health. Other charms would be silver horseshoes, bent sixpences, coral brooches and four-leaf clovers made of enamel.

Different countries have their own superstitions, and today's mascots vary in other parts of the world, some being caricatures of humans such as goblins and trogs, others being real or imaginary animals.

409   Lucky broom.
England

A crude-looking doll from Afghanistan was called a 'Nawakee'. This was made of dried apricots strung together with eyes made of coloured cloth and was about ten inches high. Sylvia Matheson describes such a one in her book *Time off to Dig*. It was really meant to be hung up in the kitchen for luck.

Amongst the lucky toys mention should be made of those dangling objects hung inside the closed cars. All number of things could be seen, pixies, goblins, dolls, nodding tigers and even a skeleton. This object peering from the back would have a notice 'Ride on big boy, 'ell ain't 'alf full yet', which was rather clever as the occupants in the following car had to be fairly close in order to read the small print. The craze began about 1938 and has persisted with a certain type of driver ever since.

In June 1966, a leprechaun doll was found in a Dublin shop window, after much searching for a truly Irish present. It was resplendent in shamrock-green coat and hat and it had a curling white beard. When the doll was examined later it was found that neatly sewn to the sleeve of the little coat was a small label 'Made in Hongkong'.

However in October 1967, Sheila Scott, an air pilot, took off from Shannon Airport clutching a green leprechaun doll 'for luck'.

Today's television performers often seem to go in for mascots. In June 1968 Dusty Springfield admitted to going nowhere without 'Einstein' a battered Teddy bear.

> *See a pin and pick it up,*
> *It will sure to bring you luck.*

TEDDY BEARS

Much has been written about Teddy bears, but most people agree now that the first Teddy bears came from the U.S.A.

The story goes that when President Theodore Roosevelt was on a hunting trip in 1902, he had refused to shoot a little bear cub. A cartoonist, Clifford Berryman, made a drawing of this incident which was seen by Morris Michtom, the proprietor of a toy store.

Michtom made some toy bears of brown plush, with movable arms and legs and with button eyes. They sold well and he obtained permission from the President to call them Teddy bears, though at first they were known as Teddy's bear. One of these original bears is on display at Sagamore Hill, which is now a memorial to the President.

Margarete Steiff, in Germany, also made bears, but the word 'Teddy' seems to have come definitely from President Roosevelt. It was used in American advertisements in 1906, and by 1907 the Teddy-bear craze was in full swing.

Many firms incorporated a bear in their trademarks. There was Deuerlan in 1908, Harmus in 1909, also Fleischmann & Bloedel, followed by Winterbauer in 1910 and Otto Wohlmann in 1913, all these marks being registered in Germany. Margarete Steiff registered

410   Teddy bear. England

1, 2, 3, 4 Money-boxes. English. 5 Bird whistles. English

her mark of a stuffed animal with a bell in its ear, in 1907, but her animal was a cat.

The toy bears ranged in price from 98 cents to 12 dollars, and factories supplied them with sweaters, jackets and overalls. Little girls loved them as much as their dolls, and at last there was something for the boys apart from the old golliwog.

Early bears were made of the clip of angora goats, that is plush, the four paws were backed with felt and the nose was of black leather or worked in wool. The arms and legs moved as in a doll, for a true Teddy bear never crawls on four legs like an animal. Their noses were longer than nowadays, the expression more fierce, and they were always brown in colour, with a hump at the back between the shoulders.

Some bears were fitted with growlers and as the bear was turned over on its stomach it let out a growl. Later on, cheaper bears merely squeaked when pressed in the tummy.

During the 1950s it was suggested that the Teddy bear was on the decline, the poor Teddy who had comforted infant hearts beating in terror or in loneliness. It was said that modern houses with thin partitioned walls and laminated plastics allowed the sounds of TV music to lull the children to sleep.

But a writer in 1960 said that Teddy bears were more popular than ever, from a 2s. 11d. one with a squeaker, to a plush £9 one with a growl, and that they sold all the year round. This statement was backed up by several children.

In London, Caroline Collins wrote: 'I do not agree with you that teddy bears are dying out. My brother, my sister and I have about six teddy bears between us, including some old ones. As well I think all my friends and their brothers have teddy bears. Also I do not agree that teddy bears do not go with modern houses. My friend has rather a modern house, and her teddy leads a very pleasant life.'

Of all the toys to take to bed, the Teddy bear is the most popular. For 21 of them which are taken upstairs, there are four stuffed dogs, three golliwogs, two rabbits, and a panda, not to mention those disguised as hot-water bottles.

The bear has very gradually changed its appearance since 1911. Instead of a rather pointed nose coming forward like a pyramid, it now looks more like a ball stuck on the face. Some large ones still have shaped movable limbs and felt paws, others merely end in stumps like any old Jumbo. In 1960 at the British Toy Fair, there was even a Teddy bear with a tail.

The craze for pale blue, bright blue or pink furry material for bears' bodies seems to be over, but the brown fur of today is usually a man-made fabric such as imitation nylon fur. Handmade bears dressed in striped clothes are nearly £4 each, and a huge one for a Christmas display cost £65 in 1966.

In 1967 at the Victorian display in the Victoria and Albert Museum at Christmas there was an early Teddy bear, very small and really

411   Teddy bear, a Chad Valley toy. England

looking more like a rat or a mouse. It was claimed to be one of the first Teddy bears, but however that may be, until one is found previous to the year 1903 one must assume that they are all descendants from those first bears named after the President of the U.S.A.

Today some are called Rupert after 'Rupert the Bear' of the *Daily Express*, others may be called Winnie or Pooh after 'Winnie the Pooh' from the beautiful drawings made by Ernest Shepard illustrating the story by A. A. Milne, but most bears go under the simple name of Teddy.

GOLLIWOGS

Among the toys which are neither dolls nor yet animals, next to the Teddy bear in popularity would come the golliwog whose history goes back into the late nineteenth century.

In a letter to *The Times* in 1945, P. A. Lanyon-Orgill writes:

the word 'wogs' was derived from the letters 'working on government service' and the letters W.O.G.S. were worn on the armbands of the native workmen in Alexandria and Port Said. These armbands were worn as early as 1883 in Alexandria just after the city was occupied by the British. As these half-starved wretches were so thin, the wealthier Egyptians referred to them as *ghul*, an Arabic word for a desert ghost, and the British troops turned this word into 'golly'.

This account sounds authentic, especially the wog part, but others have said that the word was invented by an artist called Florence Upton who published *The Adventures of Two Dutch Dolls and a Golliwogg* in 1895. It remains for someone to find a golly before this year.

However, Florence Upton, an English artist living in Hampstead, also made toys, so there is just a chance that she actually made the first toy golliwog to use as a model for her drawings. In 1902 she published *The Golliwoggs' Airship*, for these black-faced figures had become popular.

Black all over, they had large white linen buttons for eyes with the pupil made of a black shoe-button. With the eyes placed fairly far apart and with a wide grinning red mouth, they presented a cheerful appearance. The black cloth bodies were stuffed, and were sometimes made of stockinet, or old stockings, for everyone wore black ones in those days, and their hair was either of black fur or black wool.

There is said to be a carved golliwog on Miss Upton's gravestone in a churchyard somewhere in Hampstead.

Gollies were usually dressed in butcher-blue open coats, red trousers, white collars and a black bow, presenting a smart appearance, and later on they wore striped trousers. Edwardian nurseries usually contained a golliwog, and often he was put in a pram along with the dolls.

In the 1920s, the golly was used as a trademark for Robertson's Marmalade, and a little cut-out paper figure was popped into the stone jars between a circle of greaseproof paper and the lid. During the late thirties these golliwogs could be collected, and when a certain number had been obtained they could be exchanged for a gilt enamel brooch. In their arms was a musical instrument or an implement of play such as a golf-club, so that there was quite a variety and this custom of collecting continues into the sixties. In 1960, a toy golliwog about ten inches high and stuffed and dressed was included in a set of Robertson's products.

Toyshops again display gollies as they did in Edwardian times, and they are much the same except that they cost more. Jolly Golly appeared at the end of 1960, and was a talking golly with a South American drawl. Girliwogs came in 1962, stuffed and dressed in black and white striped frocks, trimmed with red braid, matching pants and red shoes.

By 1963 a talking golly dressed in tartan trousers and with a corduroy jacket cost over £6, and in 1966 there were gollies with winking eyes. Much of the popularity of a golly is that he can be made at home, is soft all over, and has a cheerful grin.

412   Robertson's trade mark. England

CHARACTERS

London's policemen are often in the news, and about 1910 a stuffed toy was made in Paris to represent one of these. About 12 inches high with long legs and thin body, he had a flesh-coloured face and hands. There was a label attached saying

My name is Dicky Doo,
And my number's twenty-two.

In the U.S.A. about 1910, Rose O'Neill had been drawing áppealing babies with a little topknot. These were made into toys which were rather like cupids, and were called 'kewpies'. Genuine ones were made of celluloid, and little bisque dolls made in Germany were similar. Small gnomes with green glass eyes were also in favour, but the craze for kewpies lasted well into 1914 with their shiny tummies and two little blue wings behind their shoulders.

Sunny Jim, a character who appeared on packets of Force in 1909, was also made into a stuffed toy, with the word Force on him. He heralded a new kind of advertising soon to be followed by many others, such as the 'Campbell Kids' advertising soup in the U.S.A. in 1911.

The characters Pip and Squeak first appeared in the *Daily Mirror* in May 1919, and Wilfred shortly afterwards. They were drawn by A. B. Payne, Pip was a dog, Squeak a penguin and Wilfred a rabbit. Later these characters were copied as stuffed toys and were popular with both children and adults.

Teddy Tail of the *Daily Mail* appeared about 1920 as a cartoon strip, and Felix the Cat, who kept on walking, was a film character

413   'Wembley Willie', a 'Dean's British Rag Doll'. England

414 'Cheerful
Desmond'. English

invented by Pat O'Sullivan, an Australian, in about 1922. Both these characters appeared as toys, and there was also a dog called 'Bonzo', who was originated by Studdy, an artist.

About 1926 came another dog. Called 'Dismal Desmond', this was a stuffed toy in the shape of a Dalmatian puppy with a very mournful expression. Later he was followed by Cheerful Desmond, also a Dalmatian.

A nursery-rhyme character which has been made into a stuffed toy is Humpty Dumpty. In the latter part of the nineteenth century he appeared rather like a character from the drawings by Tenniel in *Alice Through the Looking Glass*, but he achieved a much more modern appearance when he staged a comeback during the Second World War. This was because he was easy to make, and all kinds of bits and pieces could go towards his make-up.

However, he could be purchased and became a Chiltern Toy in 1966. In this stuffed Humpty Dumpty was concealed a chiming mechanism made of wire. Unfortunately, when the toy was washed, the wires poked through, and he was banned, a far greater disaster than simply falling off a wall.

Rupert the dachshund, Dobbin the cart-horse, and all the animals which were created by Walt Disney were turned into toys. First and foremost was Mickey Mouse, then Minnie, Donald Duck, Pluto and a host of others, and followed by the seven dwarfs with their different expressions, until we come to the TV programmes with Muffin the Mule, etc., and Noddy of Enid Blyton fame, though the name of the artist who created him has been forgotten.

Snoopy Sniffer arrived in 1963. This was a jointed wooden dog who could growl and be pulled along on red wheels, and originated in the U.S.A.

Animals at the zoo have also become stars in their own right and have been massproduced in Toyland. There were the chimpanzees in 1936, Jubilee and Booboo, then a bear cub named Barbara, followed by Brumas the little white polar bear. The giant panda became a great favourite about 1939, and is still around in 1967 made in various sizes but remaining white and black like the original animal.

Other favourites have been the little tree bears from Australia who liven up the tourist shops as much as the toyshops, and look decidedly real.

Pipaluk, in 1968, was the first polar bear cub to be successfully reared at the zoo since Brumas in 1949. The name *pipaluk* is Eskimo for 'little one', and so commercial has this kind of toy become that a £1,000,000 sales campaign was launched in March 1968. He was to feature as a soft doll, badges for schoolboys, jigsaw puzzles, strip cartoons, books, and even Pipaluk mints and bubble-gum were to be on sale and also a possible design on nursery wallpaper.

415 'Funnybun'.
English

A 2,000-year-old custom in China was the presenting of eggs in spring, and Christianity has adopted the pagan practice and made it the symbol of the Resurrection.

From prehistoric times the egg has had numerous symbolic meanings, and often egg-shells have been found in ancient tombs and medieval graves. In some eastern European countries it is the symbol of the reviving powers of nature and its presence wards off evil spirits.

Many legends stem from the Crucifixion. In one from Rumania, the Virgin Mary brought a basket of eggs for the guards by the Cross hoping to move them to pity for her son, but the soldiers refused to touch it. Mary placed the basket at the foot of the Cross, and the blood dropped down on to the eggs.

Because of this, in many Christian communities the eggs are coloured red on Easter Day, by using dyes and wax, and some are decorated. In Yugoslavia, eggs may have the initials K.V. for *Kristos Vaskrese*, meaning 'Christ is Risen'.

Patterns on the Easter eggs include Christian symbols such as a cross or a fish mixed in abstract or geometric designs. In the Ukraine in 1963 there were specialists who made 60 or more designs, of which the majority were red against a white background. The Horniman Museum at Dulwich has a collection of these eggs.

In Hungary, flower motifs are used in the decoration, in Poland the goose and fish are included, the patterns often being repeated on other objects besides the eggs.

Various ceremonies take place. In Serbia the peasants put the red Easter eggs in their vineyards on Good Friday to ensure a good harvest. In Macedonia the men bury them in each corner of the vineyards believing that Christ will keep the crops safe from hail and thunder. They carefully mark the place and the next year when they dig the vineyards they even eat the eggs.

On Easter morning, in Yugoslavia, small children are told that a hare has made its nest in the stable and left some beautiful eggs as a present.

In the latter part of the eighteenth century in Maryland, eggs were boiled in logwood which dyed the shells crimson, and the patterns would be scratched away with a pin.

In Russia, little eggs of coloured porcelain were hung upon the arms of the crosses in the cemeteries in 1903 so that the dead would not be excluded from Christian rejoicing.

On Easter Sunday in Ireland, the children play a game in which they roll hard-boiled eggs down a hill.

In England most children have some kind of chocolate egg at Easter, and so nearly all over the world eggs have some significance whether they are mere hen's eggs, coloured eggs, chocolate eggs or containers in the shape of an egg, some of which can reach vast proportions.

These cases in the shape of eggs were made of papiermâché or wood.

416 Easter eggs. Yugoslavia

In 1874, Henry Cremer, the Regent Street toyman, advertised eggs which contained a 'Dolly and a Dolly's Trousseau', others might have minute glasses or tea-sets carefully packed inside.

The most valuable eggs were made for the Tsar of Russia, as presents for the Tsarina. These surprise eggs were made by Carl Fabergé. In 1892 he made an egg of gold, enamelled white, inside was a golden yolk and inside that again was a gold and white hen with ruby eyes. Little gems of fantasy reached the palace year after year, and a few may still be seen in the Kremlin armoury.

One egg contained a coronation coach, perfectly sprung, another had a clockwork train and on the 'shell' was a map of the Siberian Railway where each station was marked with a jewel. Yet another had a model of a cruiser from the Baltic fleet. However, the last surprise egg for the Tsarina was of plain steel with her initials, for Russia was at war.

In 1961 an egg which Prince Vassili had given to the Dowager Empress of Russia was sold for £11,000.

Nest toys originated in Russia, carved in wood by peasants, each toy fitting inside the next. Usually they are in the form of old women with handkerchiefs on their heads and arms folded across their fat bodies. The big one, perhaps ten inches high, opens to show another old woman in different colours, and in turn she opens until the last one is about a $\frac{1}{4}$ inch high.

Some open to disclose a set of babies, tumbling dolls with weights, or old men might open so that they could be used as money-boxes. Today the old women are very brightly coloured and perhaps have only four sizes, but Mr Khrushchev brought a large one over as a present when he visited England which contained many, many dolls. They are still pretty but not quite as pretty as the old ones, some of which carried a goose under their arm.

A beautiful paper toy made in Germany in 1860 was a nest of cardboard houses to fit one into the other and finally into a church. When each one was taken out and placed on a table, they formed a little village.

Jesse Crandall of Brooklyn and New York made nested blocks about 1870. These had five sides, each block was slightly larger than the other, being from about 12 inches square, down to a tiny one of $1\frac{1}{2}$ inches square.

They fitted into one another and were known as 'nesting blocks'. Nest boxes were also made in England of thin coarse wood and coated with a varnished paper picture, the five-sided blocks sometimes bore a relation to one another and sometimes had the alphabet down one side.

Toy nest eggs from Russia might contain as many as 12 different-size eggs. I had a beauty in 1928, but when toys were scarce in the Second World War, I gave it to my baby son to play with, which, after all is what toys are for.

Hilary Page founded a toy company which made toys to 'help a

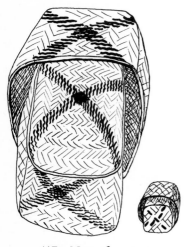

417   Nest of woven baskets. Madagascar

166

child grow up'. These were screws and things which fitted into one another when he found that his own children were interested in such things as cotton-reels and nesting saucepans. He was once a timber merchant, and he died in 1957.

In the Science Museum in 1968 the real trams and underground trains, instead of the usual seats, contained models of trams and models of underground trains, and are in fact, life-size nest toys.

BANKS

Pottery vases with slit holes were found in the catacombs, and these were said to be money-boxes. Similar ones are made in Peru today.

Cottage money-boxes, also of pottery, were made in the early eighteenth century at Staffordshire, England, pretty little decorated houses with a slot at the back of the roof to take the coins. They continued to be made in the early nineteenth century and may be said to be typically English, whereas those iron banks in the U.S.A. may be said to be typically American.

Penny banks were established in England in 1850, and from then on toy banks were numerous and of various shapes. They could be of historic or political significance, but the most popular toy banks were those of tin and shaped like a pillar-box.

These were painted red and black with a little white notice below the slit in imitation of the real ones. They were sometimes oval and sometimes round, the slit to take the letters being about the size of a penny, and there was no other opening. On the front the initials of the reigning monarch appear entwined, such as V.R. for Victoria Regina, G.R. for George Rex, and E.R. for Elizabeth Regina.

Other little coin-boxes could be of a diameter just large enough to take sixpenny pieces, and there were others made to take golden sovereigns.

A well-known manufacturer in the U.S.A. was J. and E. Stevens of Connecticut, a firm which specialised in iron and tin toys. One of the earliest mechanical banks made in the 1870s was known as the 'Cashier bank'. This was a model of a square building made to look like a bank, and when a knob was pulled, a cashier popped up through a door in the roof, received the coin and then popped back again.

Other U.S.A. models were the Magic bank, Lilliput bank, a Goat-butting bank, a Fat Man bank and so on, each one having some clever device which enabled the coin to drop into the receptacle.

The Frog bank of 1870 was a nice one. This was a large frog sitting on the bank roof, under one foot was a button, and if this was pressed the frog would open his mouth to receive the coin. Theodore Roosevelt's encounter with a bear also inspired a Bear bank as well as a Teddy bear. Here, concealed in a tree-trunk, was a bear which popped up when shot at by a man with a gun.

In 1909, the North Pole bank commemorated Robert Peary's

418   Money-box, earthenware. From the Catacombs

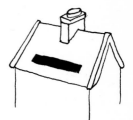

419   Back views of banks on colour plate, facing page 160

167

420 Model of the first Post Office letter-box. English

SHOWING MONEY-BOX

421 Iron bank. Probably American

discovery of the Pole. There are many other U.S.A. banks which are mentioned in the McClintock's book and with illustrations.

The craze for collecting banks is fairly recent. Walter Chrysler in the U.S.A. owned one of the finest private collections. There was a 'wanted' in *The Times* in 1968, for antique mechanical banks in good working order, and now and again they may be seen in museums.

At a recent sale the cast-iron bank called the 'Creedmoor Bank, 1877' was sold for 28 guineas. It was nine inches high, painted in colours and depicted a soldier firing coins at a tree-trunk. Another, the 'Tammany Bank Halls patent', showed William 'Boss' Tweed seated in a chair. He slips the coin into his pocket. This bank, six inches high, sold for 22 guineas. The story goes that when William Marcy Tweed was chief of a political party in New York, he gained control of the financial affairs and robbed it of millions of dollars. Later he was arrested in 1871, and since then the little banks must have given pleasure to many.

Other kinds of money-boxes are displayed on English counters in order for the customers to give their change to charity. Small children especially delight in placing a coin on a wooden tray held by a wooden dog who tosses the money into his kennel.

In the 1930s piggy banks became popular, pretty things of all sizes and made in white-glazed china with decorations in colour of clover leaves and flowers. In Peru, piggy banks were sold on stalls in the market-places, also birds, and some not so very different from the piggy rattles of ancient Greece.

A child, in 1967, was heard to remark 'quite apart from the effect on the children, money-boxes make parents into bank robbers'.

Talking of pigs, perhaps I could mention here the earthenware pigs which had grooves in both directions on their backs. We had one in our nursery at home and every year we watched the seeds sprinkled on its back, turn into mustard and cress. He began to look like a hedgehog, especially when the green tips were cut and put into sandwiches.

422 Money-boxes of pottery. Peru

13 Balancing, musical, automata, scopes

BALANCING

Tumblers, tilters and kellys are those toys which have a circular base with a weighted end. They sway to and fro and are not knocked completely over. They derive from the East and have various names, but most represent stability in some form or other.

In China a tumbling doll has a name meaning 'Stand up, little Priest', for Buddha cannot fall. The toy is usually painted red, and represents an old man holding a fan. In Japan there are the Ot-tok-I, that is the 'Erect-Standing-Ones'.

An old man named Daruma, now almost an idol, was said to have spent nine years in meditation wrapped up from head to foot against the cold, an ideal shape for a figure to be turned into a tilting toy. This toy is usually pear-shaped with the face painted on the 'stem' end. In Tokyo, the face may be indicated without eyes and he is said to be 'sold blind'. If one's wish comes true, one is permitted to paint an eye on his face, then if a second wish also comes true, the other eye may be painted in, and his value increases.

In France tumblers are known as *poupée boule* and one made in the eighteenth century represents a man wearing a cocked hat with his coat shaped down over a weighted ball. There is also 'La Poussah', made like a Chinese mandarin.

The tilter in Germany is known as a *Putzelmann*, and in England some tumblers have been made in the form of political figures. Kelly is the American name for this kind of toy with a curved base. Sometimes a Russian nest doll when opened discloses six tumbling babies all the same size, three wearing little red-painted scarves and three wearing yellow ones.

423   Tilting toy. China

424   Tilting toy. Japan

427   Tilting toy. Sweden

429   Tilting toy. France

426   Tilting toy. Spain

428   Tilting toy. U.S.A.

425   Tilting toy. China

169

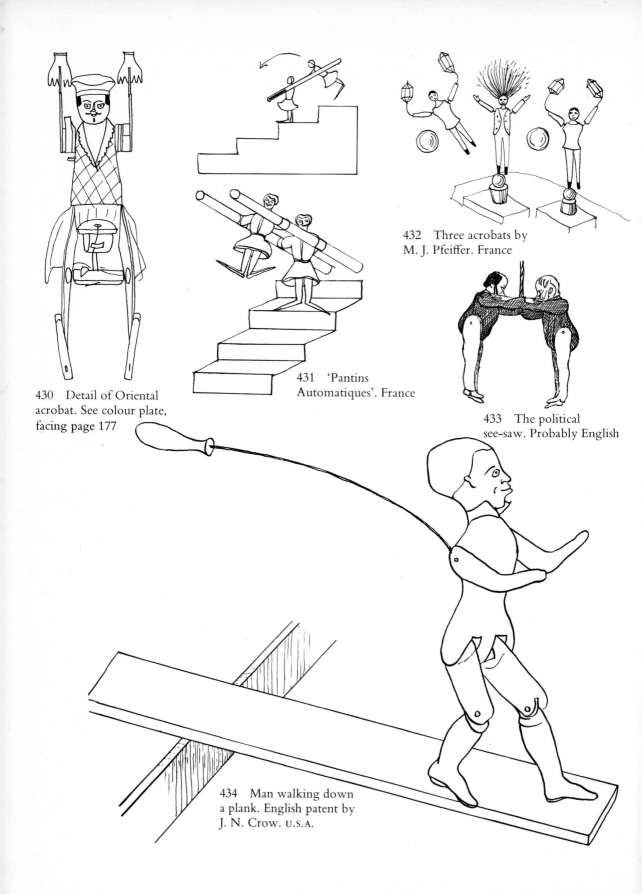

430   Detail of Oriental
acrobat. See colour plate,
facing page 177

431   'Pantins
Automatiques'. France

432   Three acrobats by
M. J. Pfeiffer. France

433   The political
see-saw. Probably English

434   Man walking down
a plank. English patent by
J. N. Crow. U.S.A.

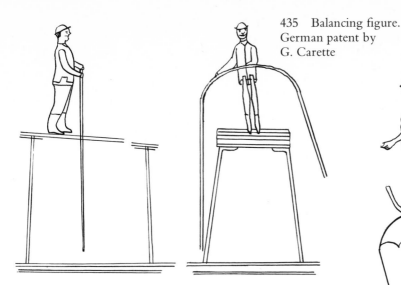

435 Balancing figure.
German patent by
G. Carette

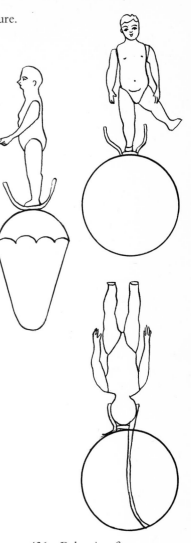

Other balancing toys were made in France during the reign of
Louis XVI in 1778, and many of these depended on mercury for the
balancing movement.

Little tumbling dolls made in Germany about 1850 were connected
by hollow rods containing mercury, the gravitational movement of
which pulled the dolls down a ramp as if somersaulting over one
another.

Some English toys earned much-needed dollars and among these
were the Hilly Billy drinking ducks. These Magnatex products
proved good exports. To make them work, their heads and beaks were
dipped in water and then stood beside a tumbler of water. They began
to sway and gradually they swayed backwards and forwards between
'sips'. The bodies of the ducks contained a volatile liquid which
normally rested in the lower portion. This liquid evaporated under
room temperature, and the ducks swung by gravity, pressure and
evaporation. They can still be seen sipping in the window of the
Magic Shop opposite the British Museum, and more modern
examples are made of brightly coloured plastic.

436 Balancing figure.
German patent by
K. Standfuss

437 'The Hilly Billy
drinking ducks'. A
Magnetex toy. England

171

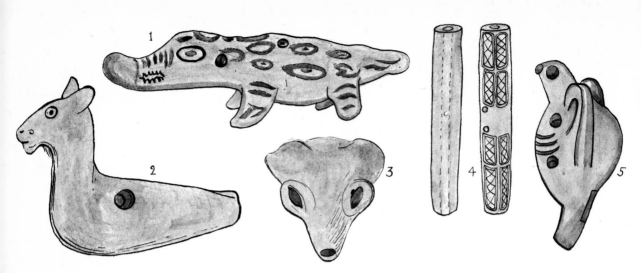

438   PRIMITIVE WHISTLES
i Pottery alligator. Chiriqui. ii, iii Pottery sheep. San Salvador. iv Decorated
bone. Chiriquano. v Pottery bird. Costa Rica

MUSICAL

Rattles with bells, whistles, trumpets, humming-tops and bull-
roarers could all come under the heading of musical toys, together
with all the small mouth-organs, little pianos and drums. Also all the
musical-boxes and polyphons of Victorian days which were especially
made for children.

Whistles have been unearthed from graves dating from 1100 B.C.
made in the shape of birds, which have already been mentioned.
Recent excavations in Jerusalem have brought to light many belonging to the years around 44 B.C. In addition there are different kinds of
native whistles found in various parts of the world.

The *Wasserpfeife* or water-whistle from Moravia was a bird whistle
made during the seventeenth and eighteenth centuries. The Mora-
vians who founded Bethlehem in Pennsylvania in 1741 made such
whistles and there is one in the Philadelphia Museum of Art. The bird
is of a grey and brown mottled glaze with sgraffito markings and
touches of green slip.

439   Bird whistles.
Chanhudaro

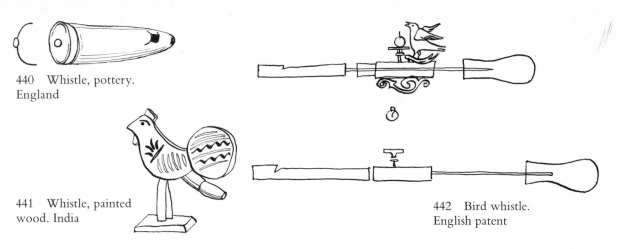

440   Whistle, pottery.
England

441   Whistle, painted
wood. India

442   Bird whistle.
English patent

In 1810 bird whistles in the form of cocks were made in Staffordshire, and in the Schreiber Collection at the Victoria and Albert Museum there is a woman's head on a dog's body which was possibly made by Ralph Wood.

Twittering bird whistles to be filled with water came from Japan and China, and many of these are much the same shape today except that they are now made of plastic.

In Korea also, there are toy birds which produce the note of a dove by blowing into the tail of the bird, which has a hole in its back for the noise to come through.

443   Water whistle.
England

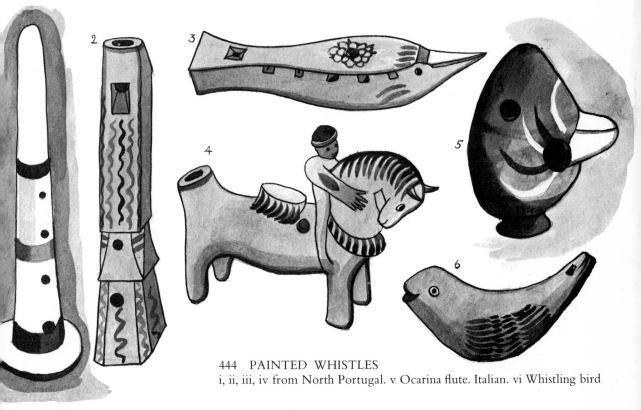

444   PAINTED WHISTLES
i, ii, iii, iv from North Portugal. v Ocarina flute. Italian. vi Whistling bird

445 Cuckoo whistle.
Switzerland

446 Drum with lizard
skin membrane.
Trobriand Islands

447 A Penny toy
whistle. Germany

Switzerland is the home of many musical toys and here were carved whistles in the shapes of birds. These cuckooed realistically when blown into, with the beak opening and shutting, and the tail moving up and down to produce the 'cuck' and the 'oooh'. These birds also had a little hole on the back and belong to the latter part of the nineteenth century.

The U.S.A. imported toy pianos from Germany, but when Albert Schoenhut arrived there just after the Civil War, he made toy pianos with sounding pieces of steel plates, and these miniature pianos were beautifully finished. His business grew and included glockenspiels, xylophones and metallophones, according to the McClintocks.

In England in Edwardian days every little girl or boy wearing a sailor suit, had a 'silver' whistle on the end of a twisted white cord tucked into the pocket.

On the night of 14 April 1912, the liner *Titanic* was sunk, and as the liner was going down 'gradually the passengers made themselves ready . . . some of the things they took with them were curious. Miss Edith Russell carried a musical toy pig'. This is mentioned in *A Night to Remember* by Walter Lord.

Primitive people make many kinds of musical instruments, from the beating of drums, the blowing of hollow reeds, to the various kinds of toys which make a whizzing noise; the last being found among ancient civilisations in the Old and the New Worlds.

Schoolboys in the 1940s bored holes in their wooden rulers with a compass point, threaded a cord through and twirling them around their heads produced a whirling buzz. These toys were known as 'bull-roarers'.

A mou mou used in the Grand Chaco is similar to that used by the Eskimos, but here it is known as a 'buzz'. Both a mou mou and a buzz are discs with two holes in the centre through which a string is threaded and twisted. Pulling in and out on the looped ends causes the disc to rotate and make a spinning or a buzzing sound. They are usually known as 'bull-roarers', but can also be called 'buzz saws'. When the edges are marked with teeth and bent alternately the buzzing noise is increased.

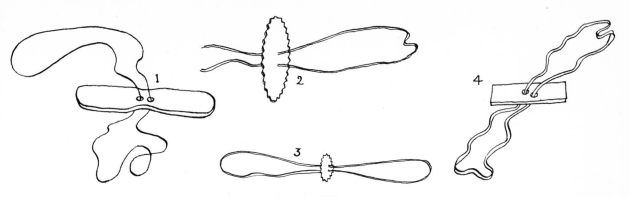

448   BULL ROARERS
i, ii Eskimo buzz toys. iii Mou mou from Rio Parapite. iv Japanese bun bun

In 1781, one made from a William III coin was discovered in the
U.S.A. at a former British camp and is now in the Museum of the City
of New York. At the end of the nineteenth century these toys
returned, made of metal discs, and later in the mid twentieth century
they were made of plastic.

Hollowed reeds for flutes were common in Japan and are favourites
because they are easy to make. With a hole for the mouth and holes for
the notes, they can be made by children.

In 1566, 30,000 trumpets were turned out yearly from the Nuremberg workshops and exported.

Musical-boxes were said to be invented by Louis Favre at the
beginning of the eighteenth century. The place of origin was the Val
de Jouz in Switzerland near the French border, the first toy musical-
boxes being made about 1835.

Nearly all the best musical-boxes come from Switzerland, and in a
recent sale prices ranged between 32 and 520 guineas. These prices
alone indicate that they were hardly toys for children.

Some would have a cylinder inside for playing a variety of tunes,
and others more properly known as 'polyphons' or 'symphonions'
had discs, the box itself often being made of inlaid walnut or rosewood.
In addition to the cylinder there could be bells, butterfly strikers or
drums. One Swiss musical-box with a seven-inch cylinder, had three
bells with bird strikers and two ballerinas pirouetting beside the bells,
and it could play eight different tunes. Twenty-one inches wide, this
sold for 55 guineas in 1967.

Nicole Frères, Geneva, and D. Boer et fils, The Hague, were
well-known makers and it is their musical-boxes which fetch the high
prices.

In the London Museum is a toy musical-box which belonged to
Queen Victoria and on the top, three tiny dolls dance.

Switzerland made cheaper musical-boxes in 1835, though many
others came from Germany. There is a pretty one in the London
Museum which was made in Leipzig about 1890. This one is rather

449   Bull roarer. Pueblo
Indian. U.S.A.

175

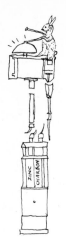

450   Musical toy. France

451   Under view of
bristle figure showing
legs. See colour plate,
facing page 177

like a doll's house but with a handle at the side. When the handle is turned, hidden bellows fill with air, and downstairs the doors open to show dancers pirouetting in the parlour, while whistles provide the music.

Early in the twentieth century many little polyphons came from Germany with the changeable metal discs, and were ideal nursery toys for a wet afternoon. My elder sister had one of these, but she never allowed us to touch it.

Other musical toys had large dolls standing on top of them often made by the firm of Jumeau.

Musical-boxes are now made in Sorrento as souvenirs for tourists.

The following advertisement appeared in March 1855, in the *Illustrated London News*:

Musical Box Repository, 32 Ludgate St. London.
Wales and M'Culloch are direct importers of Nicole Frères' celebrated *musical boxes*, playing with unrivalled brilliancy of tone the best Popular, Operatic and Sacred Music.

Large sizes,   four airs £4
six airs £6-6-0
eight airs £8
twelve airs £12-12-0
Snuff boxes, two tunes . . . . 14/6 and 18/–
three tunes 30/–
four tunes 40/–

There were other musical toys apart from musical-boxes, where animated figures or birds arranged in groups could move and make songs, and there were the poupards, already mentioned.

In the mid nineteenth century, troubadours sang and guitarists moved their fingers, little birds in gilded cages could turn their heads and sing, and monkeys performed conjuring tricks. Various mechanisms were used, and in some a musical-box was hidden in the base.

Many were in the form of a picture in a frame, others were in bower-like structures and placed under glass domes. The result was pretty, for the moving objects were surrounded by artificial flowers and grasses and perhaps ornate pillars, or there could be performing musicians in the entrance to a grotto. Another favourite subject was a sailing-ship tossing on a rough sea, perhaps with a lighthouse near by or a tower containing a clock.

A hundred years later the picture has somewhat changed, although these old things are now greatly appreciated.

A glance at a Fisher Price catalogue gives an idea of the toys in 1959. A sweeper which actually picks up dust can play 'Whistle while you work' as it is pushed along, the turning wheels providing the mechanism for the music. 'Merry Mutt' can play the xylophone, and Donald Duck, the drum, and although the characters from Walt Disney are not exactly things of beauty, they have brought a great deal of happiness to a great many children.

1 Oriental acrobat. 2 Balancing clowns. Probably German. 3, 4 Dancing bristle figures. English. 5, 6 Paper toys from China. 7 Man on a bicycle. East Brazil.

452 A musical sewing
party. European

AUTOMATA

Something which could move on its own, and appear to be alive
seemed to be the aim of inventors and many ways were devised to
achieve this effect.

Water, sand and quicksilver were used to alter the position of an
object's centre of gravity, and these were employed by the ancients to
produce the movement of figures and animals. The Chinese and the
Greeks used quicksilver for this purpose, although water was the chief
controlling force, and there were many complicated systems using
wheels and weights.

Daedalus made self-moving statues which were small figures of the
gods. Plato remarked that they were so realistic that unless they were
securely fastened they would of themselves run away. This led
Socrates to say that one should hold fast to scientific truth in order
that it may not fly away from us.

Hero, in the third century B.C., described syphons, clackvalves,
steam-engines, and even a kind of penny-in-the-slot automatic
machine from which one could obtain a drink or maybe a change of
scent. He had moving toy ships with which to amuse his guests, and in

453 Nursery clock.
Probably Switzerland

27 B.C. the rich Romans also had automata when men were entertained at banquets.

Before A.D. 1000 the Byzantines and the Arabs mentioned automatic birds which could sing and flap their wings.

Between these times and medieval days, hardly a thing is known. Partly because the makers of moving things were in danger of being punished as magicians, and even if the maker came to no harm, the thing itself was in danger of being destroyed.

There were monsters in many of the medieval plays and in the civic processions of which the populace was fond. The huge figures could move and the jaws could snap and the eyes roll, but at the time of Cromwell many of these objects were destroyed.

Real performing bears and jugglers abounded, travelling about the country, but in the cities children could see automatic figures moving on the clock towers.

There are several famous ones, the one in Berne having many figures and animals moving round when the clock strikes. There is a jester who rings his bells while bears march in procession, the cock opens his beak to crow, the lion moves his head, and Father Time opens and shuts his mouth as he counts the strokes.

My sisters, brother and I used to be taken to St Mary's Steps in Exeter to watch the moving figures high up in the tower as the clock struck, and I have taken my children to St Albans City Museum to see a pretty toy clock strike the hour and the little figures move round. The museum shut prompt at 4 p.m., but the curator, Mr Poulton, would also wait and watch, before shutting the heavy door behind us.

In London today, there is the clock on Liberty's where the dragon is stabbed by St George, and the recent clock on the façade of the famous Fortnum and Mason shop where the figures move as the hour strikes, and a pretty carillon sounds when one is near Old Bond Street.

Italy, Germany and Sweden also have their clocks. Lund Cathedral has such a one reconstructed in 1923 where, once a day, a procession files past a statue of the Holy Virgin and Child, each figure bowing as it passes.

In the sixteenth century, automata worked on hydraulic systems were perfected by Bernardino Baldi. The Spanish king, Charles, had little figures of armed men and mechanical horses which played upon his table to amuse him.

Automata, driven by water-power, were still being made during the seventeenth century to decorate the elaborate gardens of nobles. Fountains of water cascaded down over rocks and grottoes, the sculptured figures moved and birds warbled and sang.

Sand toys were made in the reign of Louis XIII of France, where figures moved by means of shifting sands instead of by water.

At the time of Louis XIV, 1643, the King was amused by clockwork toys, which is no wonder considering the poor mite was only four when he came to the throne.

178

François Camus, born at the end of the seventeenth century, made mechanical toys in which horses and figures were said to move naturally. Many of the early automata found their way to the East, some being made especially for the rich and royal personages which would account for the rather Eastern appearance in some examples seen today.

Jaques de Vaucanson, born in 1709 at Grenoble, spent his life making mechanical toys, which moving by clockwork were elaborate toys more for grown-ups than for children. Three of these brought him fame about 1738, the flute-player, the drummer, and the duck who could perform all kinds of natural things including drinking, quacking and digesting its food.

Pierre Jaquet-Droz travelled to Spain in 1758 with six extra-ordinary clocks which he showed to the King. Ferdinand VI was so delighted with them that he bought them all. The Droz brothers also made sand toys.

In 1774 Jaquet-Droz, his son Henri, and Leschot made automatic figures with very complicated machinery. The 'Draughtsman' could do drawings, the 'Writer' could write with a pen, and the 'Musician' could play the piano.

Apart from the cleverly made toys, there were others which were nothing but frauds. Small persons were hidden within to work the mechanism at performances when crowds were watching.

James Cox made complicated clocks with intricate mechanisms for wealthy people and some were for the Imperial Palace at Peking and others went elsewhere in the East.

The majority of automata was made in Switzerland and many of these beautiful toy-like objects had animated scenes with musical mechanisms. There were snuff-boxes, scent-bottles, brooches and so on, all made to delight the eye with their beauty and animation. Pistols could spray scent from a flower-head and caterpillars could crawl in a realistic manner, but these animated toys were more in the manner of the Chelsea trifles and were expensive.

In the museum at Neuchâtel is a watch with a dog which can bark, and birds which could come out of their cages and sing.

A Frenchman, Jean Maelzel, made a trumpeter in 1809. He is the same man who made the first talking doll, and in the early part of the nineteenth century there were toys worked by magnetised needles.

At the Paris Exhibition of 1844, M. Guillard of Paris was mentioned for his well-made mechanical toys, and M. Sawrey, also of Paris, devised a mechanical method whereby theatrical scenes could be changed in a simple way.

In the mid nineteenth century curious groups were made in France, in a most elaborate manner. Clowns on stages with curtains and pillars performed tricks, and monkeys dressed in silks and satins did conjuring under bowers of flowers surrounded by artificial flowers and leaves. These mechanical toys were finished with much detail and were kept under glass domes of about 18 inches high. They were more

454 Figures at a forge. France

179

for ornamenting a gentleman's study than for amusement in the nursery. The mechanism was in the carved base, and also a musical-box, the whole affair being wound up with a key. Today's prices are about 500 guineas.

Scenes made in the Late Victorian era were also kept under domes or glass cases, some with a musical-box base. The groups often included a clock built into a tower or château, and perhaps a windmill. There were seascapes with moving boats, lighthouses, Gothic churches, sentries marching round castles, soldiers marching over bridges, all kinds of things against a painted background of mountains and rivers. Artificial flowers, stuffed birds, leaves and dried grasses added to the crowded scenes, and many had shells which the Victorians were so fond of collecting, and using.

A toy worked by sand was brought out in England by Brown, Blondin and Company. This represented Leotard, a French trapeze artist, 1830–70. It was exhibited in the Victoria and Albert Museum in 1967.

The first cheap mechanical toys for children were made by Cruchet, about 1862, who made little carts where the limbs of the drivers were set in motion when the wheels turned. France became famous for this kind of thing, many of the toys having a musical accompaniment. Nuremberg also became famous for automatic toys about this time.

Walking figures pushing toy Bath chairs and worked by clockwork came in 1868. Newton patented such a figure in England and another well-known name was that of William Goodwin. Dolls would push small go-carts and doll-carriages which were usually of the three-wheeler type.

There was a toy lion in 1871. When a crank was turned, the lion swallowed a figure, either a Russian soldier or an Indian sepoy.

In 1875, a pretty toy was a box on which little figures danced and moved about by means of clockwork. By 1878, rubber was used as a motive power, and toy figures moved by magnets were patented by H. Kamprath in England in 1879.

455 Squirrel in a cage. German patent by W. J. Wilcox

In 1896 cut-out figures on metal stands danced about by means of a magnetic needle.

Another method of movement was by string and of course elastic, and when these methods are used, a broken toy is far easier to mend. Today many toys are operated by electric batteries.

456 Preacher, clockwork. U.S.A.

During the seventeenth century in England, Holland and Sweden, sets of mica transparencies were made for use as a fashionable amusement. Each picture was laid over the first one, showing changes in the costume or a sequence of history, and consequently were quite instructive.

An original portrait, about $3\frac{1}{2} \times 2\frac{1}{2}$ inches and usually oval, would be painted in oils on copper, and transparencies to fit over the top were of the same size and shape. Sometimes there were as many as 18, but by the eighteenth century, glass was being used in place of the mica.

One of the mica sets depicting the various stages in the life of Charles I is in the Jacobite House at Chastleton, Gloucestershire, and others with portraits of women are in the Victoria and Albert Museum, the Cluny Museum, Burgundy, and the Rijksmuseum at Amsterdam.

Beautiful peepshows with hand-coloured engravings by Martin Englebrecht, 1684–1756, were produced in Augsburg about 1740. The box, about six inches cube, contained slots to take four cut-out scenes, the front of the box had another cut-out, and the back was painted with a landscape, making six 'curtains' in all. There are some in Bethnal Green Museum, with views of gardens with intricate cut-outs, and there is also a complicated battle scene.

457   Peepshow. England

Panoramas made of stout paper could be landscapes where one was placed alongside another, or they could be those which when looked through and along, as in a peepshow, gave one an idea of perspective. The perspective views were cardboard toys which opened out and were viewed through a peephole. Sometimes these were called 'areaoramas' or 'regiaoramas' and included views of the London parks or theatre scenes. The most popular were those of the Thames Tunnel, which were actually on sale before Brunel's tunnel was finished.

Other popular ones were views of the Great Exhibition of 1851 and are some of the prettiest toys imaginable.

These coloured paper pull-out panoramas with concertina action could be quite a length, beautifully drawn and worked out so that the perspective appeared correct. A peepshow of 1830 was of St Mark's Place in Venice. It was engraved and carefully coloured by hand, and was probably Austrian or German.

Harvey and Darton in 1822 published such things, a well-known one being the Geographical Panorama which showed 'characteristic representations of the Scenery and Inhabitants of various Regions'. It consisted of 20 coloured cut-out figures and the backgrounds, which were all in a cedar box with a grooved lid, together with two uprights to fit the corners. On the lid was a floral border surrounding the title.

The one of the Thames Tunnel, 'a Picturesque View taken from nature', commemorated the opening in 1828, and one of the Industrial Exhibition Palace of 1851, 'showing a soirée in the Crystal Palace', by G.W., in a cloth board box, were both sold for 36 guineas in 1967.

There were many panoramas to do with this exhibition, and

another simple cardboard one showing the interior of the Crystal Palace in a box with a print on the lid, sold for 14 guineas in the same year.

The motion picture began its life in the form of an optical toy. About 1660 Christian Huygens, a Dutch physicist, made what was probably the first magic lantern. When it was introduced into England, Pepys described a demonstration in 1665. About 1800 a strip of glass with coloured pictures on it was moved across in front of a light, and projected on to a screen, and things such as these amused children well into the twentieth century.

Kaleidoscopes came about 1814, and were perfected in 1817. The Thaumatrope was based on the persistence of vision. The disc of card was rotated so rapidly by means of threads attached to it that the eye saw both sides of the card simultaneously. If say a bird is drawn on one side of the disc and a cage on the other, when the card is revolved the two pictures are seen together and the bird appears to be inside the cage.

These little cards fitted inside a circular box on which were the words 'Seeing an Object which is out of Sight'. There was a jockey on one with a horse on the reverse side, a cat on one watching a bird on the other, a man signalling with flags and so on. The Thaumatrope was invented in 1826, some say by Dr J. A. Paris, others say by Sir John Herschel. This toy was a fundamental fact which formed the basis of every mechanical apparatus that has been contrived for producing an appearance of motion.

The Stroboscope or Phenakistascope was invented by two people in 1832 independently of one another, the first by Stampfer, the second by Plateau. The device consisted of a cardboard disc with a series of slightly varying diagrams on its face.

These are observed in a mirror through slots in the periphery of the disc. When the latter is rotated rapidly, an impression of continuous movement is observed. The number of slots was equal to the number of diagrams. Pretty coloured discs were printed by Ackermann and Company in 1833; another name for this device was the Fantascope.

The Zoetrope, sometimes called the 'wheel of life' had slightly varying diagrams on a strip of paper which was placed inside a hollow cylinder. When the cylinder was revolved, by peeping through a slot, the slots revolve quickly and seem to be as one. The little pictures then appear to be moving on the inside of the cylinder opposite the viewing slot.

It was first described by Horner in 1834, but did not become

458   Thaumatrope by Dr J. A. Paris

459   Zoetrope strip. Milton Bradley, U.S.A.

460 Zoetrope. Described by Horner, introduced by Desvignes

461 Magic lantern, lit by candle

462 Magic lantern, lit by oil wick

popular until 1860 when introduced by Desvignes. There are several in museums today, the Science Museum, the Folk Museum at Cambridge, Pollock's Toy Museum, etc. and the Zoetrope belonging to the Princess Victoria is now in Kensington Palace. Milton Bradley patented one in the U.S.A. in 1867, and one of these is at Bethnal Green Museum.

The Praxinoscope patented by Reynaud in 1877 had the pictures inside a more shallow tin than the Zoetrope and in the centre was a series of mirrors, the number of mirrors being equal to the number of pictures. By rotating the cylinder and looking in the mirror facing you, a series of moving pictures was provided.

Animated lantern slides came between 1850 and 1890. The Choreutoscope was a lantern slide with six images which were shown in such rapid succession that they appeared to move. A shutter interrupted the light while the slide was in motion.

A less expensive method of achieving movement was by those books which had a series of little pictures printed singly up in the top corner. By flipping over the pages very quickly, the little figure or animal appeared to move.

Victorian Stereoscopes amused both children and grown-ups from 1867 onwards. Many of these optical toys are arranged in the Science Museum and can be worked by pressing a button. The Viviscope of 1890 showed a youth eating a slice of lemon.

A Panorama Panoptique which consisted of six translucent pictures viewed through a bellows, and day-and-night effects obtained by opening the back or top, was sold in 1967 for 38 guineas. It was $14\frac{1}{4}$ inches wide, and the original green box was marked with the vendor's label of Spurin's Toy Warehouse, New Bond Street.

A Zoetrope in the same sale fetched 26 guineas. The revolving drum, 12 inches in diameter, was black japanned, on a turned wooden base, and there were many coloured strips. Another with a cardboard drum, $10\frac{1}{2}$ inches in diameter, had a central candle and a patterned floor, on a turned wooden base, also with a quantity of coloured wooden strips.

A collection of 21 wood-framed double lantern slides, painted in colours with humorous subjects, where the different images were obtained by sliding one glass over another, and made in England in the mid nineteenth century, was sold for five guineas in 1967.

14　Outfits

463　Boy with bow and
arrow

464　Figure disguised as
a stag. England

465　The Hobnob.
Salisbury, England

The game of pretence is enhanced by dressing-up, and it is natural for a child to copy some grown-up hero. The game was also played by all those people who have attended masques and fancy-dress parties and by Marie-Antoinette when she played at being a milkmaid, it is only the fashion which had altered.

Miniature suits of armour preserved in armouries indicate how small boys emulated their elders although they did not participate in the actual battle. Five-year-old soldiers complete in every detail, may not necessarily join the army when they grow up, though young princes will probably follow in the footsteps of their fathers. Minute drummer-boys, policemen, and little boys dressed as members of the Salvation Army will most likely change their minds before they have outgrown their suits.

There must have been hundreds of children since the days of Robin Hood, about 1190, who have played in imaginary forests dressed in leaf-green and carrying bow and arrows. Others with feathers in their hair have been fearsome Red Indians, or desperate cowboys with pistols in their belts.

At weddings small boys may be dressed in uniforms, and girls as little 'Kate Greenaways', a fashion which has persisted for many years in England. Bishoff, a firm noted for their tin toys, had two toy swords for their mark in Nuremberg, which was registered in 1899.

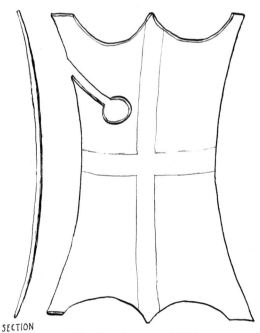

SECTION

466　Toy jousting shield.
English

184

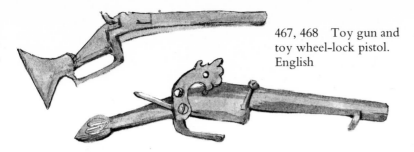

467, 468   Toy gun and toy wheel-lock pistol. English

469   Boys playing soldiers. England

Until the turn of the nineteenth century children's clothes were much the same as those of their elders. In the 1960s and 70s, it is the parents' clothes which have become childish. Mothers and children alike pull on nylon-stretch trousers, little anoraks and pixie hoods, the silhouette of both being almost identical except for the size.

Children themselves are supposed to be bigger nowadays. Patrick Murray of the Museum of Childhood, Edinburgh, remarked that only a child of seven could get into a Victorian suit made for a boy of 14 years old.

The Quartier Saint-Martin, Paris, specialised in 'outfits' where the individual items were displayed on cards.

Schoenhuts of Philadelphia marketed a set for playing at soldiers in 1904. This consisted of a breastplate, helmet and sword, and also a hobby-horse on which to ride, complete with two wheels.

470   Bean- or pea-shooter. Choroti

471   Outfit for a boy by Schoenhut. U.S.A.

Nowadays children seem to copy one another and the various crazes come and go. In recent years there was a craze for being Davy Crockett, an American pioneer who wore a kind of fur cap. In 1956 a film was shown, and children rushed around wearing weird fur hats with a furry tail hanging down behind. Enterprising mothers used up odd pieces of fur, and caps were also displayed in the toyshops, and a shortage of cheap fur was rumoured.

Domestic cats were said to have been rounded up, people feared for their pets, especially those with fine tails, and cats were kept indoors for fear they should be snatched.

Lord Scarsdale, President of the Derby branch of the R.S.P.C.A. suggested that the makers of Davy Crockett hats should go to the R.S.P.C.A. inspectors for cat-skins because for reasons of kindness, 1,338 cats had had to be destroyed during 1955, 'I think this would put an end to any suggestion of back street cat snatching.'

But the Davy Crocketts soon disappeared, and the fur hats gave way to space suits and equipment. Boys wore over their heads transparent beehive contraptions and carried weird implements. This time they were not imitating the past, they were looking into the future for as yet no real man had ventured into space.

'Every lad can be an astronaut' declared the spacemen sets with tunic helmet, trousers in a silver material, complete with spaceman guns to fire 100 caps.

However, a spaceman was rather a lonely occupation, and soon cowboys and Red Indians returned and many small girls pictured themselves as nurses. They dressed in either home-made uniforms or ones from the toyshop costing about £2. These included minute cases containing queer instruments, and not many believed that babies were found under gooseberry bushes. In 1960, the little 'doctor' outfits actually included hypodermic needles.

There were archery sets and suits of armour for lucky boys, but a feather would still be enough for a child with imagination and with plenty of chairs for a deep forest.

Many a craze started from television programmes. In 1966 the 'famous emergency ward set' was supplied with the nurse's uniform, white apron, regulation red cape, and head-band with Red Cross emblem.

472 Boy dressed as 'Batman'. English

But the big craze from this source in 1966 was for a Batman outfit. This consisted of a large black cape, shaped cowl and pants with belt, with 'shimmering P.V.C. contrasting bat decorations'. So for 29s. 6d. a child was disguised and pictured himself flying over the tree-tops and in fact, with slit eyes and a nose-piece, a child did not look himself at all, and knew that his appearance was frightening.

Many of the new man-made materials are not fireproof. A toy military jacket worn by a Welshpool girl burst into flames when her brother fired a cap-pistol at her back. In 1967 the Fire Service was instructed to look into this kind of thing, and parents were warned against buying inflammable toys.

The best 'let's-pretend' outfits were designed by Robert Heller, a fastidious man, who made everything authentic, at first for his grand-sons and their friends, but now making 30 different kinds of suits. B.O.A.C. asked that their uniforms be included in his range, and all his outfits are tailored copies of the originals.

15   Soldiers, space toys

473   Warrior with club.
Italy

SOLDIERS

Of all the ancient examples of miniature soldiers it is difficult to decide which may be a child's plaything. Some may be votive offerings, some part of a lost chess piece, or even a collector's sample, pilgrim's badge or token. However, it is certain that Roman children had model soldiers in 27 B.C.

In the legend of Troy, the Trojans conveyed the hollow wooden horse into Troy and in the night the Greeks stole out, opened the gates to their friends and Troy was captured. This happened in 1190 B.C., and six centuries later, model Trojan horses made of wood and hollow were sold at the gates of the city of Troy.

Perhaps Roman children kept their own toy soldiers within these horses, in much the same way as animals are kept in a Noah's ark. They had flat soldiers of tin and lead, about one to three inches in height.

474   Soldier, tin. Roman

Naturally there were toy knights in the twelfth century, and elaborate clocks in Germany showed knights in armour striking the hours. European children played with knights, some of which were on horseback and possibly there were small guns, for the Chinese had invented gunpowder in A.D. 1160.

The toys show contemporary costume; skull-caps and vizors were used in 1216, and the horses were covered with a coat of mail. The Battle of Crécy was fought with bows and arrows, and in England Edward III had 100 men armed with lances, each man wearing a tunic and mantle.

475   The Quintain.
England

In 1383, Charles VI of France was given a little cannon made of wood, and in England about 1388 Queen Isabella, wife of Richard II, introduced side-saddles for ladies when riding horses. In 1400 men used spurs for the first time, they were made of gilt for a knight and silver for an esquire. Such things as these give a clue for a date and are a help in reconstructing a toy.

The Battle of Agincourt was fought with archers, and black armour was worn on the field as well as for mourning. On the bridges over the

187

476 Knight. Wood.
England

Seine in Paris were built booths and stalls containing articles for sale. Many people passed over, and under one of the booths a little tin knight in armour was found in 1466, the forerunner of all tin soldiers, and mentioned by Karl Gröber in his *Children's Toys of Bygone Days*.

Tournament toys of bronze with the horses hollow were made about 1400.

By the year 1500, it was becoming clear that the old stone castles were insufficient protection against cannon, and a new type of un-protected castle began as residences for kings and nobility. Gradually with the use of guns, the moat-surrounded castle was useless and this form of fortification fell out of use.

Martin Beheim gave his little son a pea-shooter together with 300 shot, and years later Sir Hiram Maxim, the inventor of the Maxim gun, amused himself with a toy pea-shooter, shooting actual peas across the street at his neighbour's house.

In 1512, Henry VIII's soldiers wore a shirt of mail, over this a shirt of red cloth laced up the front, and on their legs they wore tight hose. He gave each soldier a badge, and some were armed with halberds. Toy knights were made of bronze and some were painted.

In 1544 soldiers wore 'blew clothe, like fotemans cotes, and garded with redde clothe'. No silk was worn except upon the left sleeve and 'everyman had the right hose red and the left blew, with one stripe of three fingers broad, redde, upon the outside of his leg'.

Soldiers wore a 'sad green' colour or russet uniform in 1584 and over their armour they wore shirts.

Gunpowder had done away with bows and arrows, spears and javelins, castles and walled towns, and in 1594 the Privy Council decreed that bows should never again be used as weapons of war.

In 1606, the future King of France was given amongst other things a toy soldier riding on a black horse; this, and others with it, was made of lead. About 1650 Louis XIV played with a toy fort and soldiers in the garden of the Palais-Royal, some modelled in silver.

Later his son, the Dauphin, inherited from his father an army made of silver. The toys he played with came from Augsburg and Nurem-berg, the home of little horses with riders and infantry soldiers. These were the movable soldiers on which the War Minister, Sebastian de Vauban, had given his advice, actually travelling to Nuremberg for the purpose. They were modelled by Hans Hautsch and his son Gottfried about 1672 (Gottfried died in 1703).

James I, in 1618, said that 'armour not only saved the life of the wearer, but prevented his hurting anyone else', and by the end of his reign armour terminated at the knees. The pikemen, musketeers and infantry wore helmets on their heads, and backplates and breastplates on their bodies.

During the Civil War, the troops of Charles I wore helmets and scarves to distinguish one side from the other. Horsemen were of four classes by 1635 – the lancier, cuirassier, harquebusier, and carabinier – these were the Dragoons who all wore a cuirass, their coats were of a uniform colour, but their breeches could be of any hue.

Red coats were worn by the King's Life Guards and Queen's Life Guards in 1645, while other regiments wore white, blue or grey. Prince Rupert's Footguards wore scarlet, and in Cromwell's army some wore scarlet coats with different facings.

Actually the Guards officers mostly wore what they fancied, there being more silk coats and plumed hats among the Cavaliers than among the Puritans. By the time of Charles II, the officers wore no other armour than a large gorget, which was later commemorated as a diminutive ornament.

Tight breeches, fanciful boots and fur caps were worn by soldiers in 1666, which was known as 'Hungarian costume'. This included horizontal barring on the breast and fur-trimmed jackets slung over their left shoulders. At this time English toy soldiers were made of wood.

The use of armour almost disappeared in 1689, when the Royal Horse Guards were ordered to march from Winchester to Salisbury to oppose the Prince of Orange. They were instructed to leave their breastplates behind, for a long march was before them.

Furthermore, by 1689 the steel helmets were replaced by large hats with, of all things, feathers! These gradually turned into tricornes which were later worn atop the periwig. When the soldiers charged, the evitable happened, both hat and periwig were likely to be lost in the fray, and yet this curious headgear lasted more or less during four reigns, and many went for one another bald-headed.

The Battle of Blenheim in 1704 resulted in Blenheim Palace being built for the victorious Duke of Marlborough, and here in one of the 'stately homes of England' can be seen a case containing toy soldiers arranged as on the battlefield of Bavaria.

During the Napoleonic Wars, the English troops wore their hair well larded and sprinkled with white powder. The Ramillies tie developed into a long pigtail, and many soldiers turned up the thick plait with a leather strap, leaving a knot of hair below.

By 1759 square-cut coats were worn, turned-back cuffs, lace ruffles and long waistcoats with pockets. They wore stockings over their knees but with the garter below. Square-toed shoes had buckles, coats and breeches were grey, soldiers' coats were red, and they all wore their three-cornered hats.

Later it was found impossible to sling a rifle over one's shoulder while wearing a hat like this, so Grenadier caps were substituted. These were soft and mitre shape, later they turned into stiff high structures and were worn by the horse regiments as well as the infantry.

Andreas Hilpert, a tin-founder and pewterer at Coburg, cast flat figures of toy soldiers in 1760, sometimes signing them with his full name, and often with his initials A.H. The flat figures were then placed on little stands, but they were still known as 'flats'. Single pieces such as generals were made separately. Later on, during the nineteenth century, these were copied and sold as genuine. That is what happens when the signature is on the actual article, as in so many of Rembrandt's etchings. Now it is the custom to sign the print below in pencil, and to give the number of the proof and the edition number. The same thing has happened with dolls' heads, when the original cast has been found.

In 1768, a Light Dragoon wore a helmet with horsehair crest, a scarlet cloak with a white lining and blue half-lapels, and the sleeves turned up with blue. The breeches and waistcoat were white, there was a blue cape, and long white boots were worn to the knee. In England in 1784 a short jacket was worn in place of a coat.

477 Frederick the·Great, by J. Hilpert. German

Max von Boehn says that all authors are agreed that the tin soldier owed its being as an 'echo of the victories of Frederick the Great'.

Johann Gottfried Hilpert made models of tin about 1775, two to three inches high, and he is best known for his models of the soldiers of Frederick the Great. Other makers were Ammon, Besold, Haffner, Stahl and Gottschalk.

Russian soldiers were much like those of the English. The officers wore three-cornered hats on their thickly powdered heads, the false pigtails worn by the men were kept in place by iron grips and they plastered down their hair with a mixture of glue and cornflour.

At the end of the eighteenth century toy soldiers were made at Aarau in Switzerland. The tin-founders William Gottschalk and Johann Rudolf Wehrli made soldiers rather like those of the Hilperts. There were soldiers marching, drumming, holding flags, rifles, swords and pennons.

One-sided figures of lead were replaced by those of tin, and later by an alloy of tin and antimony, the latter being even more poisonous to lick than lead. The silver plate used in the French churches was transferred to the mint and coined, and model armies of silver were melted down to pay for the real armies.

Among the treasures of the Royal Family is a bill for toys in 1797 and a receipt to the Princess Charlotte of Wales, daughter of George IV. This is from A. Loriot of New Bond Street, and amongst the items are a regiment of soldiers 2s. 6d., a dressed wax doll 8s., and a conjuring clown 5s. At this time the little princess was a year old.

By 1800, wigs had vanished from the British Army, though pig-tails treated with pompatum or candle-grease were worn until 1808, when the pigtails of the entire army were ordered to be cut off.

The three-cornered hat also disappeared. A cocked hat for officers took its place, with the brim folded into two instead of three. Napoleon wore his in square-rig style, but the Duke of Wellington placed his fore and aft. The infantry wore felt caps with a brass plate, similar to a brimless top hat, and between 1808 and 1814 the breeches were changed for trousers, long gaiters to short gaiters, the army following Beau Brummell's fashion for tight trousers.

In 1812 when Napoleon took Moscow, the fur caps worn by our soldiers were divided round the middle by a cord, the Hussars had more buttons than ever, and the Heavy Dragoons none at all.

A quantity of lead 'flats' painted in colours was sold recently for 14 guineas. They were in a box containing 27 infantry, three Hussars, and a gun-carriage, and consisted of Austrian, Russian and Turkish troops.

Small toy armies in 1816 read like a list from a game of spillikins, their arms consisted of the club, mace, battleaxe, pike, spear, javelin, dagger and even bows and arrows.

Lancers wore Dragoon jackets with embroidered cuffs and collars, enormous epaulettes and an aiguillette. They wore very high Polish caps with square crowns, with a brass plate in front and topped with a plume. The officers wore Cossack trousers.

In the early part of the nineteenth century, J. Hilpert was succeeded by Hilpert and Stahl. Most fine soldiers were of lead, but there were others made of papiermâché.

George IV revived the breastplates of the Household Brigade in 1820, which now wore steel helmets with bearskin crests. The bear-skins of the Footguards were so much 'improved' that taller sentry-boxes had to be put round the Palace to accommodate them.

William IV liked his army to be dressed in red. In 1837 the Lancers wore red uniforms, the Household Cavalry 'weeping plumes' and the Light Dragoons had blue coats. At the Kaffir War in 1844 the Highlanders wore long trousers, and low-peaked caps.

Firms making toy soldiers made them any size whether they were of papiermâché or the lead flats, even the Hilpert ones had not been made to any set scale. Those made by Gottschalk and Wehrli, in the

478 'Flat' soldier. Lead. Belgian

191

private collections in Zürich, could be $2\frac{1}{8}$, $3\frac{3}{4}$, $4\frac{5}{8}$ inches high and smaller soldiers on horseback were sometimes only $2\frac{3}{4}$ inches high during the middle of the century. They were difficult to play with by fastidious boys, unless placed in a kind of panorama with the larger ones in front.

However, soon a scale was agreed upon known as the 'Nuremberg Scale' in 1848, when it was decided that the infantry should be three centimetres high and the cavalry four centimetres high, that is roughly $1\frac{1}{3}$ inches. The two largest firms, Heinrichsens of Nuremberg and Allgeyer of Fürth decided this, and thus was added an extra inducement to the collecting of armies. Heinrichsen, who was a skilful designer and engraver, had started making 'flats' in 1839.

J. C. Haselbach of Berlin was another well-known maker. Others were Deuecke of Brunswick, Weygang of Göttingen, Haffner of Fürth, and Rieche. Allgeyer, Haffner and Söhlke of Berlin made semi-solids, and later on Söhlke made toy trains almost as soon as the real ones appeared.

During the Indian Mutiny in 1857 the soldiers were greatly hampered by the leather stock which they wore round their necks, the band being so stiff that they could hardly bend to look along the sights of their rifles.

About 1858, the son of Napoleon III had a small cannon given him which was made of wood and bronze. In 1859 the first patent for a toy gun was issued in the U.S.A. to J. Johnson of New York City.

The firm of Mignot made a large collection of lead soldiers for the son of Napoleon III. The Empress Eugénie kept these for some time after her son was killed in Zululand in 1879. Mignot are now the oldest toy soldier firm in the world, making knights, archers and bowmen.

Apart from soldiers in the flat and soldiers in the round, there were sets printed on card for cutting out in the same manner as dolls. They were instructive toys depicting the various uniforms. The sheets were engraved about 1744 in Strasbourg, but round about 1860 they were printed by lithography. Board games also taught boys the art of warfare, while their younger brothers rushed about with trumpets and drums.

A large collection of lead flats painted in colours, and comprising an Austrian army of 1866, with Uhlans, Hussars, musicians and sappers, together with a large proportion of infantry in various uniforms was sold in 1967 for 70 guineas. These were made by Ernst Heinrichsen of Nuremberg, labelled and catalogued and were in 39 cardboard boxes, the average height of the figures being $1\frac{1}{3}$ inches and thus conforming to the Nuremberg scale.

Another set in a fitted box, late nineteenth century, sold for 30 guineas. This contained French lead soldiers, painted in colours, and consisted of a troop of Horse Artillery, comprising three guns and carriages with horses, two field-carts with spare wheels, three ammunition units with horses, 12 mounted soldiers, two officers with swords, and also a carabinier and a bugler.

479 Tin soldier. German

480 Tin soldier. German

1, 2 Metal engines and trains. 3 Wooden engine and truck. 4 Tree, wood. 5 Tree, lead. 6 Seven festival figures, tin. 7 Boat on trolley, wood. 8 Fandango, wood. 9 Dog, wood. 10 Horse-drawn water-cart, wood

About 1870 Heyde of Dresden was famous for his solid figures which were in a variety of postures. He sold boxed sets of assorted figures, and about the same time, Haffner turned from making flats to semi-solids and made soldiers of lead.

By 1870 all British troops carried rifles, and German soldiers wore spiked helmets. The scarlet coats of the British Army, beloved by so many, facilitated its defeat by Kruger in South Africa in 1881–82.

Towards the end of the nineteenth century, boys who had pretended soldiers down through the centuries, now changed their pikes and swords for toy pistols. There were 'caps' made on strips of pink paper which went off with a bang and a smell of gunpowder. Guns could also fire small lengths of steel, and a gun called a 'Daisy Airgun' cost 3s. 6d. These were made in the u.s.a. at Plymouth, Michigan, and when they were first produced in 1888, the company made about two gross per day.

The early cap-pistols are now collected, and they vary somewhat in size and shape. The early Hubleys are smaller than the later models, and unusual pistols were made by Stevens in the u.s.a. towards the end of the nineteenth century.

Most boys played with toy soldiers. Winston Churchill and his brother Jack collected lead soldiers; they had about 1,500 which they arranged for battle on a long table in their playroom. De Gaulle also played with his three brothers. Even as a boy he was a great patriot, and always insisted that the French soldiers should be his when they played at armies.

The year 1893 was very important. Mr Britain invented hollow toy soldiers in place of the flat lead ones from Germany. The German ones, now commercial, were thin and soft, and the Britain soldiers took the trade away from there to here almost suddenly. These little models were correct in arms and uniform, hand-finished and coloured, in fact everything to appeal to a boy or to a grown-up, and were of standard size.

A box of eight infantrymen cost one shilling and a box of five cavalry men the same; there were Lifeguards, Horseguards, Bengal Lancers, and West Indian regiments with dark faces, white turbans and red Zouave jackets, and also colourful Highlanders correct in all their detail.

The horses were well made and in natural colours, some trotting, some prancing; some soldiers could move their arms to use their swords or point their pennoned lances. There were also mules and sentry-boxes. The smaller guns were muskets with hammer percussion, complete with miniature ramrod.

Later on, when khaki was worn for the first time in 1898 during the Egyptian campaign and the South African War, particular small boys were busy painting over the bright colours of their toy soldiers with khaki paint to bring them up to date.

Many patents for toy soldiers and toy pistols were registered in 1914, the year the 'Great War' broke out. New toy soldiers depicting the

481   Lead soldier. German

German Army wore field-grey with spiked helmets and later on steel helmets. There were all the things to go with an army, horses, Red Cross ambulances including some motor ones, and mechanised lorries carrying soldiers in khaki; white tents and later on khaki tents were also sold in boxes. Blaise Castle, near Bristol, has a fine collection which is well arranged.

The grandson of Heinrichsen made soldiers of the First World War, and this famous firm did not close down until about 1945.

In *A Choice of Ornaments*, Nicholas Bentley tells about his childhood toys: 'there was a whole regiment of cuirassiers complete with trumpet major which came from Le Nain Bleu in Paris. How I loved them.'

During the 1930s the best-selling toy was the Buck Rogers gun, made by the same firm as the Daisy.

An interesting economy was practised in the pre-war German flats. The figures were cast with three legs and with arms and weapons in two or three positions. Thus the purchaser could cut off the extra item and obtain more variety in the figures.

At the beginning of the Second World War, there were still lead soldiers, lead submarines and the like, but gradually lead toys disappeared and plastic took its place. Heyde's factory was eventually destroyed, and in 1946–47 there was an acute shortage of lead soldiers.

When the war ended, the toy soldiers for sale in Germany were those which were made in the U.S.A., and in 1948 even the bombers, aircraft-carriers and missiles were imported. German boys could buy South African soldiers and realistic tanks which came from Britain.

In 1957, at a trade fair, British toy soldiers were still reputed to be unbeatable, but ones which were attired as if for a Trojan war brought groans from enthusiasts who thought that this was going too far back into history.

By 1958 many toy soldiers were made to a new scale. This was in order to match up with the popular 'OO' gauge railway trains. An exhibition of model soldiers was also held this year in Park Lane, London.

Today's forts are much the same as those of the 1920s, with a platform, some walls, a drawbridge and a slope.

482   R.A. Gun, No. 1201.
by Britain's Ltd. England

Now, for a moment, we leave the toy soldiers, for there was 'rocket-fever' in New York in 1958.

A soldier was put on full-time military assignment, who was described as 'keeping rocket interest alive in boys and at the same time keeping the boys themselves alive'. He gave various facts and said that since last October 368 rockets had been launched within a 20-mile radius of Manhattan by young enthusiasts. One rocket had risen to a height of 1,500 feet, and another was as much as 14 feet long.

In the New England–New York area there had been at least 1,000 launchings, rockets had shot up from city rooftops, even from front-door steps on the streets and in one afternoon five rockets were sent up from a single vacant lot in Brooklyn.

But nasty accidents were numerous. One boy was pouring gunpowder into a three-foot aluminium pipe when it exploded and carried him to the ceiling, burning his left hand while he assembled a 'multi-stage' rocket. In the March *New Yorker* was a cartoon showing four children in a backyard, with a strange barrel-like contraption by the side of them, whilst the eldest is telling the others, 'By this time tomorrow, fellows – if our calculations are correct – Ralphie Sanford here will be in orbit.'

However, these space toys were looking into the future, for it was not until April 1961 that Gagarin, a Russian, was the first man to be sent in orbit.

In England in 1959 were cannon-trucks which were rocket-launching guns with caterpillar tracks and revolving gun-turrets. The missiles and caps could be fired separately or simultaneously and were controlled by an electrically operated panel.

The Ric-o-shay was a life-size six shooter, firing caps with a loud bang, followed by a most realistic whine. Another atomic cannon-truck was complete with rockets which could be fired with deadly accuracy and were stated to be painless.

However, all these toys, warlike and otherwise, came in for criticism. In September, under a heading in *The Times* 'Toy Re-armament at Nuremberg' there were apparently models of the Heinkel 111 for less than five shillings with all the appropriate markings. Stukas, v1s and v2s were also for sale, though the latter were advertised as pioneer rockets.

There were many guns and pistols about. In 1960 there was one which produced smoke from a muzzle, and small boys would jump from behind telephone-kiosks yelling 'Stick 'em up' and even babies in prams would wave heavy pistols of shining metal.

In 1961, a Bill was prepared to prohibit the use of air-guns by children under 15. Since 1958 2,712 children had been injured, compared with 388 injured children and one killed in the three years ending 1954. At the Harrogate Toy Fair, Mr Maudling recalled that when he was a small boy, he possessed a toy howitzer with shells, with which he shelled his nannie.

483 'Spacemen'.

Toy soldiers are collected by grown-ups, and in 1960 the first toy-soldier convention was held in Southampton by Donald Featherstone, who had 7,000 lead and plastic soldiers. Members enacted battles such as the Wars of the Roses, the Boer War and the Indian Mutiny.

A year to remember in the history of toy soldiers is 1966, for this was the year in which the last of the metal models were for sale. From then on, all toy soldiers were to be made of plastic.

Every sort of firing weapon was around in 1967, tanks, armoured cars, troops and aircraft, and children continued to get injured at play.

Mrs Anne Kerr, in the House of Commons, tried to get a ban on war toys, even on toy soldiers and imitation tommy-guns. She said that her mother had shopped for her and returned with bombs, flame-throwers and booby-traps. However she was treated with ridicule by Mr Cranley Onslow, who said one might as well outlaw golliwogs, cowboys and Indians, Grimm's *Fairy Tales*, and cops and robbers.

There were protests also in the U.S.A. in 1968 by parents known in the toy industry as 'bosom-beaters'. A British psychotherapist said there was no connection between the toy gun and the criminal, in fact 'one murderer told me that when he shot his victim he expected him to get up again, and was dismayed when he didn't', and a reprieved murderer had said the same on television. However, if they had never played the game of shooting, perhaps they would never have done it in real life.

Norman Newton Ltd were the people for miniature soldiers in 1968, with a shop in Paris, two in London and agents in Europe and the U.S.A. Their models were expensive, the little painted figures starting at four guineas each. The Napoleonic period was the most popular, but any figures could be made, from Roman soldiers to Indian dancing-girls, accurate in every detail. Collectors could buy figures which they could paint themselves, and also dioramas for the backgrounds.

A toy for grown-ups was sold for £6,950 in 1965. This was a figure of a Lancer, $5\frac{1}{4}$ inches high, dated 1914–15, with the mark of the workmaster Henrik Wigström, a Fabergé craftsman.

In July 1969, Hamley's window display included a lunar module, complete with scoop for picking up 'moon dust', which was working forwards and backwards. The model was built with Meccano, and there were more elderly gentlemen looking at it than boys, who had probably sat through the night of the 21st watching the actual moon landing taking place on television.

484 Lancer, by Fabergé. French influence

16 Doll's houses, rooms, furniture

The Greeks and Romans made models of rooms furnished with all manner of everyday articles. They were like a three-sided box and were made of reddish clay, each being about 18 inches long and one foot high.

Inside was placed furniture of baked clay, pinkish and yellow-ochre colour, with bowls of fruit on the tables and little dressing-sets in the bedrooms, the whole conveying a good idea of a room of about 300 B.C. These were the forerunners of many little shops and rooms which have appeared off and on continuing to the present day.

Other models show the kind of things in use at the different periods. A clay toy of a woman sitting in a bath was made by the Romans about A.D. 100 and at this time furniture of lead appeared; little chairs, tables and settees which convey a perfect idea of their contemporary fittings.

Although there is no record of rooms and furniture for many hundreds of years, children surely must have played with models or imitated the houses of the day. According to Stow in 1189 'all men in this city of London should build their houses of stone up to a certain height, and to cover them with slate or baked tile, in order to prevent fires'. How easy to play in a garden with toy houses such as these real ones.

The Munich doll's house, built in 1558, is an early example, but only the inventory of its contents has survived. In 1625 there were a few in the Netherlands complete with miniature furniture. Separate rooms were made in 1630 also, and Cardinal Richelieu gave one of these to the Princess d'Englieu.

Dolls' houses at first were not intended to be exact models of a large house. The rooms were placed where they would be most convenient and where they could display their miniature objects. Practically, they were mere cupboards divided up, later with the front modelled as the façade of a house, though usually each division was provided with one or more windows.

It is said that the Dutch originated the doll's house, and the Cabinets, or *Puppenhuizen* as they were called in Holland, are some of the most costly ever produced. Again they are made on the cupboard principle and date from the seventeenth century.

In 1631, an elderly spinster of Nuremberg, Anna Koferlin, put together a doll's house so that children would see what an interior should look like, and she also produced a pamphlet on how the household should be managed. In fact, the doll's house was of educational value to the small girl, and was intended to teach her house management until she became a bride.

So as early as the seventeenth century, spinsters spoke out on the bringing up of children. However that may be, these early dolls'

485   Chair. Made of lead. Roman

486   Woman with rolling-pin. Greek

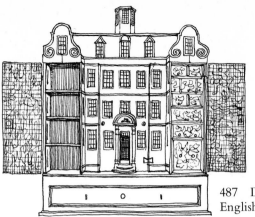

487 Doll's house. English

488 Doll's house. U.S.A.

489 Dumb-waiter with set of pewter. English

houses do give an idea of the interiors of the period and many depict with great accuracy the everyday objects then in use.

English dolls' houses conform to the German and Dutch pattern, but an Italian one at the end of the seventeenth century has a square ground-plan and can be viewed from all sides through large windows. The Christmas cribs of Italy are meant to be seen from the front and front sides only as on a stage.

In 1716 it was fashionable in England to own a doll's house, or baby house, as dolls were known as babies at that time. In 1754, the Prince of Wales mentioned building baby houses at Kew, and many wealthy parents followed the royal example.

In 1772 Horace Walpole sent some verses to the Lady Anne Fitzpatrick when she was about five years old, together with a present of some shells: 'May these gay shells find grace and room, both in your baby house and sight.'

In the first place, much of the beautiful miniature furniture was made as a model for a client from which to choose, though eventually some royal child might become the possessor of such a piece.

Albert Bentley was an upholsterer at Buckingham Palace about 1754 and he also made miniature furniture. Chippendale and other well-known makers made such pieces which could be used as trade samples, though pieces were known to have been made especially for dolls' rooms or dolls' houses. There are some wonderful examples in the Bethnal Green Museum, together with pieces known as 'exercises by industrious apprentices'. These were sent to clients much in the same way as fashion dolls had been sent to display dresses.

Miniature Nuremberg kitchens complete with all the utensils were said to teach children the elements of housewifery. Historically they are of tremendous value as are all the other contemporary rooms of different periods, for they represent faithfully the households of their time, and in some instances include little objects which cannot be found today even among their full-size prototypes.

Some rooms are literally architectural models with wonderful panelling, textiles, etc., others might be simply a box stood on one side. Booths and shops were favourite toys, a butcher's shop being popular with boys, and a haberdashery with the girls. In 1842 such a shop could have painted wooden joints of meat and large chopping-block with a fat, red butcher in a striped apron, whereas the haberdashery might have a minute chest of drawers behind with displays of ribbons and laces and stands to show intricate bonnets.

In 1844, the year of the Paris Exhibition, M. Kopp of Paris, in the rue du Temple, was mentioned in the 'citations favorables'. This was for 'a collection of playthings, and above all for his gay model of a dining-room with sideboard and furnished table'. An honourable mention was awarded to M. Colin – 'he makes playthings and households with care, which he exhibits as models. A furnished kitchen and a dressing-table which showed the perfection of the products of his factory.'

There were posting-inns of solid wood, and stables for horses. Market-stalls which copied those in the market-place, and sold fish and cakes. A little model toyshop, in the Folk Museum at Cambridge, was saved from Sharman's toyshop in the Market Hill fire of 1849. It is similar to a market-stall with toys hanging up, including a banjo and some wooden sheep.

The models built like shops sometimes had an upstairs also, and were more like a doll's house with a cupboard front.

Beautiful fittings could be seen inside the dolls' houses, and drawing-rooms full of knick-knacks which needed dusting with minute feather-mops. Small china or bisque dolls performed various duties, nurses with tin baths, maids with master's shaving water in copper or tin cans, and the cook would be in the kitchen with the tweeny-maids. When looking at dolls' houses, I always look for a staircase and doors which can open and shut. Why is it that so few of them have a back door?

A doll's house in the museum at Peterborough is named Jubilee House, 1887. By putting a penny in a slot, the interior lights up to show all the contemporary furnishings and occupants within.

Although all these early things are very interesting, they are not always beautiful, some being in fact quite hideous. Such a set, made in 1880, was furniture for dolls' houses, made of wood and covered with printed and varnished paper.

In France, household toys and models were made by Merlin et Cie, in 1887. Other toy-makers were Bane and Rossignol. Rossignol in 1890, followed by his widow in 1905.

While the mothers dressed dolls for their children, some fathers would make furniture and models for a doll's house, or get the local carpenter to make some pieces. Lewis Carroll made a little tool-chest with tools for one of his sisters. About 1900, reproduction furniture was made by a boy who later on became Lieutenant-Commander Style R.N., his little 'antique' pieces were carved and somewhere on them was the signature s.

Mr Walter Lines remembers making a doll's house for Mr Hamley

DETAIL

490 Doll-house furniture made from horse chestnuts. England

491 Doll's house by Jouet Belge. Flanders

and charging him £30 for it, 'a lot of money in those days'. A Rothschild bought it furnished for £120, and it was a gift for the Queen of Spain.

At the coronation of Edward VII, wooden copies were made of Edward the Confessor's chair as souvenirs of his coronation. In the small drawer under the seat were chocolates. This was remembered by Rachel Ferguson in her book *We Were Amused*.

And now just as the Victorians collected the minute objects with which to fill these houses, so today grown-ups are paying large sums for these bygones, while the children are given more modern houses to play with.

It is interesting to note in 1956 some of the prices paid for these things of the past. About half a dozen were sold at Sotheby's, and one from the eighteenth century went for £580. This was an elaborate affair, fully furnished and with everything to scale. The floors were carpeted with Persian needlework, and the walls hung with miniature pictures. There were eighteenth-century Chinese glass portraits, Wedgwood medallions, and about 400 miniature objects in malachite, ivory, lacquer and ormolu.

A second doll's house went for £165. This one had Georgian chimney-pieces, green panelled walls, and the rooms contained some very beautiful furniture.

For £130 there was a house with fine panelling of pinewood and furnished with everything of the best, there was even an ivory piano and a miniature ivory chess table set out with chessmen.

A fourth doll's house was £155, and this one had an eighteenth-century needlework carpet, a pinewood chimney-piece and furniture of walnut.

In contrast to these early dolls' houses, one was given to Princess

Anne in 1956 which was equipped with electric light, radio and running water. This was three feet high, three feet wide and six feet long, and was offered to the Duke of Edinburgh by Sir Herman Lebus.

In 1959, for a girl there were toy cookers in clinical white stove enamel, with a time clock set in the splash-back, and with two hot plates which really worked by using special fuel tablets which burnt from ten to 15 minutes. These complete with a kettle and saucepan cost 48 shillings.

One of the nicest toys for a small girl in 1960 was a kitchen utensil set made entirely of wood. There was one in the Norwegian Exhibition of 1967, slightly different from the English version with the rolling-pin along the top of the rack. The wooden rack fitted to a wall and contained a meat-pounder, whisk, pestle, patterned roller for marking butter or little biscuits, and a wooden spoon, and of course a rolling-pin.

In 1961 came a toy hospital complete with operating-theatre and carved-up patients, surely a most weird kind of toy, especially when added to this, spectators could watch real operations nearly every week on their television sets, and by the way there were refrigerators with ice-cube trays, and miniature television sets for dolls' houses. In addition, there were model washing-machines containing a large tank with a realistic pulsator, and a wringer with independently sprung rubber rollers, in fact everything for a small girl who happened to be that way inclined.

A magnetic-action doll's house sold for $10 in the 1963 shops, in which a whole family of dolls came to life. Mother got food from the refrigerator, father worked outside, and the dog and the cat played, all done by magnets, but surely not half such fun as doing it by hand.

In 1966 there was a washing-machine which really worked and dolly's washing could come out cleaner than clean. There were also electric stoves with saucepan and frying-pan complete.

The most fabulous doll's house of all was sold for 30,000 guineas in 1967. This was Titania's Palace, designed by Sir Neville Wilkinson, begun in 1907 and in the beginning intended for his own daughter, but she was grown up before it was finished. Sometime in the future it will be seen near Wookey Hole Cave, in Somersetshire.

17   Tableware, silver toys

TABLEWARE

Of all the things in miniature, the little objects made for tableware are among the most beautiful, and although they may not all be playthings their history goes back a long way.

The figurines and toy pots made at Jarno in Kurdistan in 4750 B.C. were made from clay pressed out or rolled in the hand. A flat round

492   Two vessels. Britain

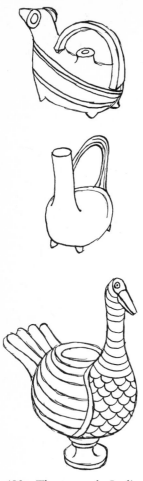

493 Three vessels. Lydia

blob of clay would be the base of a pot and a long flat rectangular piece rolled out like pastry would make the sides.

Between 3000 and 2000 B.C. the potter's wheel was discovered. Craftsmen found that by putting a lump of clay in the centre of a horizontal disc, and rotating the disc, they could press and pull the clay into a shape more beautifully symmetrical than before, and by pressing the thumb well down into the exact centre of the clay lump, hollow pots with thinner sides could be made.

The houses in Mohenjodaro and Harappa about 2500 B.C. had pipes made from pottery, and a number of pottery models have been found in the drains. Wood also would have been used but naturally clay objects and sculptured marble lasts much longer.

The Egyptians made many little objects in clay, both figures and buildings, and little bowls of fruit which may have been childish playthings or may have been to put in a grave so that they could be used in a life beyond.

During the Shang dynasty in China about 1400 B.C., the potter's wheel was also used, but by 700 B.C. everywhere there were so many potters and carpenters that the industries were crowded and thus began competition, 'Potter competing with potter, and carpenter with carpenter.'

Some of the little dishes, plates and jugs were made in miniature to place before the gods of the Romans, and may later be mistaken for playthings.

From the child's tumulus at Gordium, 500 B.C., were found Phrygian vessels, these were painted and were in the shape of birds and animals. Miniature Greek vases containing pebbles or brass balls were found along with other toys near the skeletons of children dating from 364 B.C.

Excavations at Jerusalem have brought to light whistles, rattles, miniature cooking utensils, and pottery models of furniture and animals, dating from about 44 B.C.

Two toy pails belonging to the T'ang dynasty, A.D. 618–906, show that these little miniature playthings were also made in China, just at a period when there is such a lack of toys in the West.

In 1664 some kitchenware was sent across the Atlantic and in a detailed inventory there was no mention of a fork. Actually three-pronged forks came into use in 1667 and forks with four prongs came in 1726.

It must be remembered that some of the most beautiful miniature dinner- and tea-sets were not intended for children's hands. In 1709 the porcelain factory at Dresden made samples to show their wares, and as in the case of 'silver toys' some pieces marked as toys would be fabulous trifles for the wealthy.

In 1740, Thomas Whieldon of Little Fenton made 'toys' in either the clay or biscuit state. They were coloured with zaffre, copper, manganese, etc. and glazed with black, red or white lead. Zaffre is a blue pigment made from cobalt ore and silica.

202

Many Staffordshire tea-sets were of salt-glazed stoneware and were made about 1745 to 1750. They were beautiful little things in a cream colour with a raised pattern, exquisite miniatures with intricate designs, and with no handles on the tea-cups. The Joicey Bequest in the Victoria and Albert Museum has a wonderful set, and also a toy coffee-cup with a handle.

At the Minerva Works in Park St, Fenton, children's toy sets were made and also toy mugs in the mid eighteenth century.

John Sadler of Liverpool was said to have had the idea of decorating pottery with printed pictures in 1756, because he had given broken pots to children from which they built dolls' houses.

'Chelsea toys', which were derived from Meissen novelties, won a European reputation in 1754. An advertisement for their sale stated: 'Porcelain toys consisting of snuff-boxes, smelling bottles, etwees and trinkets for watches.' 'Etwee' was an anglicisation of the French *étui*.

About 1752–53 Whieldon and Wedgwood had orders for 'Blue-flowered cups and saucers, plates and image toys.'

By 1760 beautiful miniature dinner-services and tea-sets were made which are now collectors' pieces. In the British Museum is a wonderful dinner-service in white with a raised pattern, and another where the pattern is of raised leaves.

'Glass Toys for Young Ladies' were advertised by John Peploe of Birmingham in 1764 as gradually the demand for silver toys diminished. Glass toys, though breakable, were possibly more permanent for the young ladies as the silver toys were sometimes melted down to pay off a family's debts.

In the *Boston News Letter* of 1771, in America, there are among other things mentioned 'several compleat tea table sets . . . children's cream-coloured Toys'.

During this century there were many wonderful dolls' sets belonging to royal children and others who became well known later on. A son of George III had a doll's tea-service made of silver, and the son of Marie-Antoinette, the Dauphin, had a doll's dinner-service and a doll's coffee-set of Sèvres china.

Elizabeth Cure, about 1750, had a Georgian tea-set and Elizabeth Fry, born in 1780, had a toy dinner-set and a tea-service of blue and white pottery. When the mother of Charlotte M. Yonge was a child she had a toy tea-set made at Worcester, with the initials 'M.C.' entwined in gilt flowers and sprigs, and when Byron was a boy he also played with a doll's tea-set.

In 1795 many of these miniature sets were made at Worcester and at Caughley. Thomas Frye was another who made sets for dolls. In 1800 toy tea-sets were made by Spode and by G. F. Bowers of Tunstall, and Thomas Whieldon also made perfect sets. Other places were Lowestoft, Rockingham, Leeds, Bow and Swansea, and in France at Saint-Cloud and Chantilly. More tea-sets were made than dinner-services.

The Princess Charlotte of Wales in the spring of 1800 caught the

494 Toy tea-service. Staffordshire

STOOL
ONE INCH SQUARE

OIL
CONTAINER

INCH

495 and 496   Kitchen set.
India

measles. During her illness she was visited by the Queen, who presented the little girl with a superb service of china, manufactured on purpose from drawings selected by Lady de Clifford, the governess of the Princess. This was mentioned by John Watkins in 1819.

In 1828, Queen Charlotte who was very fond of children ordered, in the King's name, two miniature tea-sets for dolls. She also sent dolls to greet little friends on their way home from a visit to the dentist. The little Princess Victoria's tea-set was of Lowestoft china.

There were now 12 makers of glass toys in Birmingham as these tiny fragile things were popular, some were child-size for a child to play with, some were doll-size to put in a doll's house, and the same applied to the china toys also.

Many beautiful toy dinner-services belong to the 1850s, complete sets are mostly in museums. There are some in the Victoria and Albert Museum and a particularly fine one in Staffordshire ware is in the British Museum. The Minerva Works at Park St, Fenton made toy sets in 1830, and these are among some of their earliest productions. They continued making them until 1876, saying that 'the toy sets are still popular'. Since 1859 their trade went under the name of M. Green and Company.

In 1852, according to *Hogg's Instructor*, many toys at this time were made of copper. One toy-maker who specialised in these things could make 5,000 a year, little toy kettles, toy coffee-pots and suchlike.

Later on in 1878, pewter was the favourite metal and in England at this time, 2,500,000 articles were made yearly. A girl worker could turn out 2,500 small tea-cups in a day, but factory hours were very long, and many of the 'girls' were but children. Little tea-sets of pewter were made in 1888 by Bull of Newington Causeway, Surrey.

Queen Mary, when she was a child and staying at the White Lodge, played with a toy set of table-glass and a doll's tea-set of 17 pieces. One can imagine the delight when the little things were brought out.

In India, the kitchen is of great importance and the children play with little utensils in the same way as those who delighted in the kitchens of Nuremberg. Each article shows the contemporary in miniature and whereas those in Germany were made of pewter, these in the East are made of brass.

The popularity of dinner-services and tea-services has continued and many sets well worth keeping belong to the end of the nineteenth century and the beginning of the twentieth and show household things in miniature. Breakfast dishes with little rivers down which the fat runs, gravy-boats almost like boats, vegetable dishes with two handles and ornate lids, finger bowls and special salad containers, even cucumber dishes and junket saucers, all beautiful to look at, even if not in their entirety.

The little tables and the large dining-room table in Titania's Palace were laid with magnificent sets of china and wine-glasses, thin and transparent, with some of Bristol glass amongst them.

204

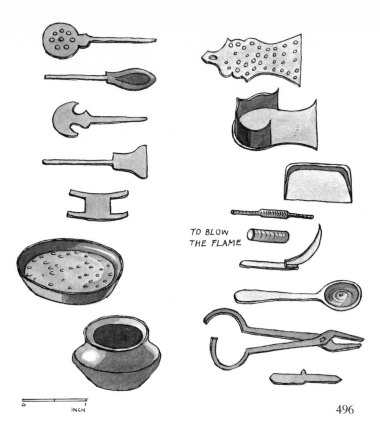

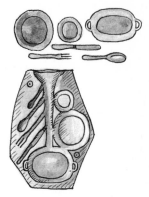

TO BLOW
THE FLAME

INCH

496

497   Doll's dinner-
service, by G. F. Rhead.
England

498   Decanter with
glasses. English

Many sets were also provided with trays of china on which to place the things, and which were decorated to match.

About 1910 there is a picture by Renoir at Cagnes in which the child is playing with a porcelain dinner-set belonging to her doll. Most children about this time would have possessed or have seen the sets of plates on which tempting dishes were laid out, so tempting was the ham that the two bad mice of Beatrix Potter fame, smashed it to pieces when they found it unfit to eat. I had a turkey on a dish when I was small which certainly did not improve with carving.

In the 1950s there were sets for children made of thin aluminium, and some of china, soon to be replaced by plastic. A rather pretty toy was a picnic-basket for two, with napkins, cloth and crockery and a 'vacuum' flask for cold drinks, and in 1966 there were 'Kiddies' China tea-sets 'prettily decorated, just like mummy's, containing four each Cups and Saucers, Tea pot, milk jug and Sugar basin, all in a pretty gift box'.

205

Here the word 'toy' means an extravagance, a trinket or a trifle, and at first the little silver toys of the prosperous seventeenth century were exact replicas of the everyday articles in use. The later examples of the nineteenth century did not always reproduce contemporary types.

At La Paz in 1660 a silver-mine was discovered, so rich that often the silver was cut out with a chisel. Maybe this had something to do with the spate of silver toys which became so popular about this time.

Holland excelled in these toys, and minute silver coaches were made in Amsterdam, complete with horses. There were many Lilliputian pieces, acrobats being a favourite subject, but the pieces were rarely marked with the maker's name. The toys were one of the minor extravagances between 1649 and 1660, when Charles II entered London, a period known as the Restoration.

499 Silver with black handle. English

Makers of silver toys in England were R.G. in 1672, George Middleton about 1685–1726, and George Garthorne about 1697. David Clayton entered his mark in London in 1697, though his toys were mostly made during the reign of George I. In 1700, the notable makers were the gold- and silversmiths. There was Isaac Malyn in Gutter Lane, John Clifton in Foster Lane, and Augustin Courtauld in St Martin's Lane about 1708–20.

In Germany, Peter Winter made 'toys' about 1702 and all these minute articles show those in use at the time. A toy chocolate-pot with a molinet is in the Victoria and Albert Museum, and most full-size examples gave up these stirring-rods when coffee was used. Silver plate-stands were for warming plates in front of the fire, but full-size ones were commonly made of iron.

There were small toys made for furnishing dolls' houses, and larger examples for use when playing with dolls. Some of these are actually engraved with the doll's initials arranged as monograms or even in the manner customary for husband and wife.

500 Chocolate-pot with molinet. English

Both in Holland and England there were many little figure subjects, soldiers, servants and travellers with luggage. These 'toys' were sometimes kept in the parlour arranged on velvet in glass cabinets. A special privilege of small girls was to be allowed to clean these treasures when visiting elderly relations, with rouge, whitening and water mixed together in a saucer.

The tiny sugar-tongs in the shape of a stork, the minute ink-stand with the sand-sprinkler, the jar with the silver quill, the tea-urn with tiny tap, all these things accurate in every detail would be cleaned with loving care.

In 1750 John Sotro, goldsmith, jeweller and toyman, made toys for children, and John Medleycott made gold and silver toys, but unless the word 'children' appeared, these toy-makers were the makers of trinkets and trifles for grown-ups and which were often of considerable value.

Two notable collections are in the Victoria and Albert Museum. These are those of Miss Mabel M. Bloore, and Miss Phoebe Marks.

501 Teapot. English

502 Pikeman. Dutch

503 Dog and kennel. Dutch

504 Chestnut-roaster. Dutch

505 Gridiron with fish. Dutch

Any children helping Miss Mabel or Miss Phoebe would see the doll's monogram on the doll's silver toys.

In 1818 there were six silver dolls' spoons engraved with the initial 'L', and a wonderful silver doll's service was given by the Earl of Oxford, in 1741, to his granddaughter Lady Henrietta Cavendish Bentinck. This consisted of one cruet, lantern, one coffee-pot, six cups and saucers, one kettle, one stand for silver plates, one candlestick and snuffers, two candlesticks and one fire-grate and three fire-irons. Everything for a midnight feast except for the food.

506 Mousetrap and cat. Dutch

507 Pan with brown wooden handle. English

508 Gold table with utensils

18 Dolls, ovens, sewing-machines, cradles

DOLLS, OVENS, SEWING-MACHINES

Much has been written about dolls, and yet there is still plenty to discover, and as recently as 1960 dolls have been unearthed from the Biblical city of Gibeon.

Little figures from Kurdistan were usually females and were often just the upper part, for a cloth skirt could be added. The details were indicated with clay pellets and both pots and figures were left unbaked.

By 2900 B.C. gods of Indian mythology were made in miniature, the god Brahma rode on a goose, Shiva on a bull and Durga his wife on a tiger. Figures which went up and down sticks came about 2400 B.C. Earthenware scale-pans which looked like toys were made by children, and if any textile was used it was sure to be cotton.

509 Shabti box.
Egyptian

509a Detail of
decoration

It is nice to be able to show an Egyptian Shabti box to contain the Answerers or Ushabti dolls made to serve the dead person in another world. The earliest examples were during the Eleventh dynasty, about 2100 B.C. This one belongs to the New Kingdom, about 1250 B.C. The Shabtis were made of wood, clay or wax, and were about ten inches long, that is about the height of the compartment in which they were placed. Later they were made of blue glaze faience.

An Egyptian doll made of string and with a head-dress of bright blue beads was found at Beni-Hasan of the year 1900 B.C.

In Africa, dolls have been made in the shape of jars, within which was some special medicine used for warding off snake bites. Others had hair fixed to their heads so that coconut oil could be placed on them.

Sealing-wax was used in England as early as 1556, and in Victorian times little dolls have been made as pen-wipers. Using a wishing bone from a fowl or a turkey as a body, a blob of sealing-wax made the head and by dressing the 'body' in a kind of Red Riding Hood effect, the two ends of the wishing bone stuck out below the skirt like a pair of feet. The petticoats of flannel were used for the wiping part. There is a collection of these sealing-wax dolls in the museum at King's Lynn.

Mr Swinford, who owns the museum in the tiny stone house at Filkins, told me that jointed wooden dolls were made near by about 1810, and were fixed to a small stool with their legs dangling.

In *Jane Eyre* by Charlotte Brontë, the best wax doll was laid between silver paper in a drawer.

208

1 Pails. 1¼ ins. and 1½ ins. diameter. 2 Jug. 1½ ins. high. Cup. 1 in. high. Plate. 1¼ ins. diameter. 3 Cup. 1 in. high. 4 Dishes. 2¾ ins. long. 5 Teacup and saucer. 3 ins. diameter. Milk-jug. *c.* 2¼ ins. high. 6 Hot-water can. 2 ins. high. Foot-bath. 2½ ins. long. 8 Saucer. 3½ ins. diameter. 7, 9 Tray. 9½ ins. long. Cups. 1⅛ ins. diameter. Saucers. 2 ins. diameter

At the Great Exhibition of 1851, dressed dolls were eightpence a dozen, and undressed dolls of composition were 2½d. the dozen. Although a penny was worth more in those days, these dolls must have been the results of slave labour. A cheap doll in Scotland was known as a 'laaly'.

Cremer, in 1875, wrote that 'in the matter of toy cooking stoves, we have proof that at a remarkably early date, the coppersmiths of the Old city of Abydos were quite as handy as those of London, Berlin or Paris at the present day. Look at that toy stove covered with kitchen utensils of divers shapes, all in bronze, once the property of an Egyptian named Atai, and of the family of little Atais.'

Iron stoves were manufactured in the U.S.A. in the 1890s. Some were models, others were toys with every necessity, kettles, pans and hot-water containers. The Hubley Manufacturing Company in Pennsylvania made cooking-stoves with every detail correct. The firm started making steel and iron toys in 1894.

In *The Longest Journey* by E. M. Forster, published in 1907, he mentions the Roman Catholic church near the station in Cambridge. He says that the legend is that it was built by a Papist who made a fortune out of movable eyes for dolls.

Florence Upton, when a child, opened up some of the bodies of rag dolls, sewed red hearts inside them, and then stitched the body up again. These were probably cut in the shape of the hearts on playing-cards, and possibly of red flannel left over from petticoats of this material, for those of red flannel were *de rigueur*.

510 Old woman sewing, worked by string. Central Europe

511 Metal oven. U.S.A. or German

512 Singer sewing
machine. U.S.A.

A large Victorian doll made to open like the monks of earlier days,
contained a kitchen complete with brass articles, and later novelties
have been dolls made as tea-cosies or in the late 1920s as covers over the
'Daffodil' type of telephone.

All the well-known bisque dolls with marks, resided in the Late
Victorian and Edwardian nurseries, and during the reign of George V
and Queen Mary. There were paper patterns and knitting instructions
for dressing dolls of various sizes, and most English children had at
least one doll, and perhaps a cooking-stove.

Other toys beloved by small girls are the various kinds of sewing-
machines, which usually do a kind of chainstitch as they do not have a
shuttle. As they are light in weight, they work better when clamped
to a table.

With the coming of plastic, the doll scene changed, and their little
faces became less natural. Long thick eyelashes, far too thick, flapped
up and down on the eyelids as the dolls were pushed along in prams,
gradually looking more like film stars than babies. In fact, the dolls
grew up, busts arrived, and long stiff legs, but not one could compete
with those beautiful slightly busted dolls of the Queen Anne or
Georgian types of the eighteenth century.

By 1957 the shapely dolls seemed as if they had come to stay. Based
on film stars such as Marilyn Monroe, they were unbreakable with
nylon-clad legs, lacy negligées and diamond engagement rings.

Dolls with the proportions of Brigitte Bardot were dressed in the
latest fashions in 1960, and their wedding-dresses could cost anything

between half a guinea and eight guineas. Some dolls made in Italy had eyes which could follow one about, others made of felt had their hair dressed and dyed in grey, silver or blonde, and wore velvet drainpipe trousers and lace brassières over their slightly busted fronts. A new doll more likely to appeal to a younger child was a hush-a-bye crying doll with a battery-operated cry, which stopped when she was lifted from her cot.

Twenty-five pounds was the price asked in the U.S.A. for dolls' nylon fur coats, but of course this was a headline hit for 1961. Many dolls were made to look like Mrs Jacqueline Kennedy, and other dolls could screw up their faces and offer a kiss. From Italy came a sophisticated doll called a Sweetnik.

By 1962 dolls could have a complete wardrobe of wigs, blonde, brunette and platinum, or a queer pink known as 'strawberry blonde'. Modern dolls from Japan could play roulette, French dolls could dance the twist, but nearly all the little dolls dressed in national costumes came from Hong Kong.

A paper doll in 1963 was called Liza. She was 18 inches tall, made of jointed pasteboard, and had six different paper outfits. Made by a firm called Goods & Chattels, the price was 55s. 6d., a high price indeed for a paper doll.

The Tressy doll came in 1964, with waist-length hair which could be made shorter or longer by inserting a key in the doll's back, and there was great competition among firms selling dolls' clothes, which could be purchased for every possible occasion.

A 'Dolly's Beauty Set' was for sale in 1966, in a 'make-up' case 8 × 5 inches. This contained 19 beauty aids comprising hair-drier, brush, comb, mirror, lipstick, eye-pencil, and hair-slides, etc. Most dolls by now had rooted hair which could be washed and set, and special doll shampoos were sold for this purpose. Modern mothers seem not to have time to make dollies' wardrobes from scraps of this and that. As most of their own clothes are bought off the peg, not many scraps are available, and indeed many of them cannot sew. Glamorous dolls can have 28 swinging outfits in 1966 from the 'leather look' to 'soda pop cutie' and 'wild enchantment'. Ridiculous words for small children, but dolls such as these may be heading for the same fate as those green-faced Teddy bears.

In Tudor times, it was said at Court that Mary was given a wax doll and a silver pin with which to prick it. This was in order to harm her half-sister Elizabeth, but that she was too kindhearted to use it. This piece of sixteenth-century history, if true, is enlightening, for at school we always knew her as 'Bloody Mary'.

Tucked away on a shelf in the museum at Bury St Edmunds is a witch doll. Dressed entirely in black, her skirt is made up of leaves of paper containing spells – evil spells, perhaps.

Jane Carlyle, who died in 1766, played with dolls. When she was ten years old she burned her doll on a funeral pyre, having learned about the fate of Dido from her early study of Latin.

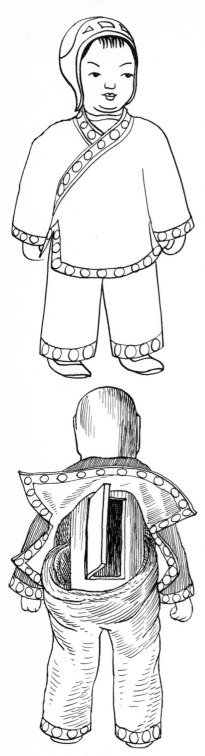

513 Doll used for smuggling. China

Apart from witch dolls, dolls have not played many sinister parts, though some were used in code language to impart information to the enemy during the Second World War.

However, in 1960, the picture changed and heroin was put inside the hollowed-out backs of the local Chinese dolls. Large numbers of children were seen clutching these as their parents carried them past the customs. This drug traffic is mentioned by Donald Fish in his book *Air Line Detective*.

More sinister dolls appeared in 1965. These were from Vietnam, and were fitted with explosives by members of the Vietcong. These were sophisticated dolls, *à la* Bardot, wearing evening coats over long dresses, and with straw hats, they were likely to appeal to soldiers looking for a souvenir.

From Ottawa in 1966 came a warning about explosive dolls from Poland. These dolls had hair of vegetable fibres and their faces were alleged to be made of highly inflammable material. Their bodies were covered with cotton clothing and filled with straw and sawdust. So dangerous were these dolls that the fire chief of Winnipeg issued a warning about them on a TV programme, and consequently these dolls were banned by New York City and Newark fire departments. These dolls had not been intended as harmful; it was merely the fact that the new man-made materials had not been sufficiently tested. However, the worst dolls were in the nature of a horror comic.

These were ghost dolls which could talk, or remote-controlled robot dolls which could walk about. When a command was spoken into a microphone, they either hurled grenades with their swinging arms or they shot out rockets from the top of their helmets.

Dressed dolls representing different countries became more and more popular, especially among schoolgirls. Five hundred dolls were produced at the invitation of the Inner Wheel Club of Ryde, New South Wales, from the neighbouring town of Wollongong, Australia, and these travelled 50,000 miles raising more than £3,500 for charity. Among them was a doll representing Granny Smith, famous for her green apples.

In 1959 a present to our Queen Elizabeth was a contemporary fashion doll dressed by students from Leicester College of Art, and a felt doll representing Robin Hood came from a junior school in Nottinghamshire and was a present for Princess Anne. Princess Margaret also received gifts of dolls dressed in local costumes when on holiday near Lisbon.

Princess Beatrix of Holland was presented with a doll in 1967 which was dressed in the costume of Urk, a former island of the Zuider Zee, in fact dolls today are presented as gifts almost as much as bouquets.

It is pleasant to know that the early dolls are much appreciated and the one burnt by Jane Carlyle may have been one of those wooden Georgian dolls dressed in cotton. Such a one was bought by Spinks in 1967 for £60, and dolls need have no fear, for their value is increasing.

A fine eighteenth century doll of carved and painted wood with brown glass eyes, carved wooden hands with the usual stuffed upper arms had legs jointed at the knees and hips. She was 24 inches high, and made about 1740. She wore a white chemise, satin boned corset, an open robe and a petticoat of deep red with white stripes. She also possessed a dress of green silk. These beautiful dolls are rare, and in 1969 this one fetched the fantastic sum of 420 guineas, in a London sale.

514   Doll lying on a bed or cradle. Pottery. Tel el-Amarna

CRADLES

When the gods were young, they were cared for in cradles. It is said that the baby Zeus had his cradle suspended from a tree so that it could rock to and fro in the wind, and he had a many-coloured ball to play with. The baby Hermes had a portable cradle, and Dionysus was cooled by a winnowing fan when lying back in his. The father of Heracles let his baby lie in a shield as befitted the child of a warrior, and many of the new-born Greek infants were bathed in cold water, preferably in a river.

In Peru, babies were kept in four-legged cradles until they were old enough to walk. The cradles could rest on the ground or be carried on the mother's back with two sticks to protect the baby's head and prevent suffocation when wrapped round in a blanket. Native dolls are made with the same contraption on their doll cradles.

It must be remembered with things such as toy cradles, rocking-chairs, utensils and so on, that there are always two kinds. There are those which are made for a large doll to sleep or sit in as the case may be, and there are those smaller ones possibly to go in a doll's house. There are various sizes in each category but most show the everyday articles in use at the time.

Many cradles have been made of wickerwork from the time of Moses until the present day when a kind of plastic seems to be taking its place. Others were of wood, which could be carved, but they nearly always had rockers.

Blue ribbons for a boy and pink ones for a girl have been the custom for a long while, and these were threaded through the wicker cradles and baskets accompanying them. The baskets contained miniature hair-brushes, powder-boxes, etc. and a baby doll with all these accessories is the well-known Princess Daisy at Bethnal Green Museum.

The little Moses baskets of the 1930s made of plaited straw were beautifully copied in miniature for dolls, embroidered with raffia and lined with muslin. Today in the 1960s they may be of coloured waterproof material and lift in and out of prams like the real ones. The dolls are pushed into the village by day or put on the seats of a car, and rest in the nursery bedroom at night.

Wooden beds were made as replicas of large ones, some carved in walnut, others in mahogany and with elaborate head-pieces. There were four-posters draped with curtains to pull and bedspreads to match, much beautiful hand-sewing and embroidery going towards their manufacture.

There were also wooden cots with sides to let down and today some of the nicer plastic toys are small cots from Hong Kong complete with figured mattresses.

I would like to end this chapter with a quote from *Treetops, Window on the Jungle* by Katherine Drake:

> The junior baboons are bewitching. Like children the world over, they romp and show off, while mothers sit indulgently by, cuddling new babies, gossiping, retrieving mites from near-by mud-holes. The toys of these jungle fry are simple; a tug-of-war vine rope that breaks, sending half a dozen sprawling; a branch left over from an elephant's dinner that serves as a 'kite'. One infant, so raw-looking it resembles an embryo, is hugging a 'doll' – a piece of dried elephant dropping – to its scrawny bosom, scolding it tenderly.

Not exactly the thing for doll-collectors, but the mention of mud-holes takes me back to where I began and the fun of making primitive mud-pies. However, there is no space here for the early wooden pails, the later galvanised iron buckets, and the gaily painted tin buckets of yesterday. Already rubber and plastic have arrived and those of today are made from the mould of a square castle with four square turrets at the corners.

515   Sand Toy

19 A note on printing

A study of playthings shows that many are closely connected with printing, and a short summary of the methods of reproducing illustrations will be useful. This applies not only to toy books but also to building-bricks, board games, jigsaws, paper dolls and many construction sets.

There are three main kinds: *relief*, where the printing surface is raised, such as in woodcuts; *intaglio*, where the printing surface is incised, such as in etching; and *surface* printing, such as in lithography.

516   Woodcut section
Metal plate section

I. RELIEF, SUCH AS ENGRAVINGS AND WOODCUTS

Omitting marks on pottery or linen, woodcuts were first used for figures on playing-cards, and for cutting type. The first printer to use actual illustrations with type was Albert Pfister of Bamberg in 1461. The printing was done by rubbing the back of the paper on the inked block, so it was printed on one side only. When a book was made, the single sheets were stuck back to back, and thus the book was known as a 'block-book'.

Many woodcuts showing children holding dolls and toys are those of Lucas Cranach, born in 1472, and a painter to the Saxon Court. Later, woodcuts were coloured by hand or made from a number of wood blocks, one for each colour, its invention being ascribed to an Italian, Ugo da Carpi, born about 1486.

Japanese woodcuts are all done on the plank-way of the wood with a gouge, and not on the end grain with a graver as in later wood engravings. Each black portion is pure black, each colour a pure colour though a wash manner may be used for Japanese colour prints.

In the sixteenth century, books began to be illustrated by copper-plate engravings. In 1744 John Newbery published his 'Pretty Little Pocket Book for 6d., or with a ball or a pincushion for 8d.' He had new woodcuts made for his alphabets and he also used copper-plate engravings, and covered his books in flowery Dutch papers tinged with gilt.

The discovery of end *wood engraving* as opposed to plank-cutting was attributed variously to Papillon, a Frenchman, and to Thomas Bewick, born in England in 1753. They used the white line on black for the effect and the cross-hatching thus appeared as little squares rather than as black lines.

517   Portion of Litho stone

518   A Wagon, woodcut. French

519   Cradle, woodcut. German

520   Marble, wood engraving. English

521   Straw horse, scraper-board. Mexico

215

Toy-theatre sheets influenced the early nineteenth-century books with cut-out figures to put into slots in the pictures.

Artists such as Caldicott and Kate Greenaway had their work reproduced by wood blocks cut by professional engravers, and the prints were either coloured by hand or by the use of separate blocks for each colour. Edmund Evans produced children's books and excelled in this process of reproduction.

2. INTAGLIO, SUCH AS STEEL ENGRAVINGS, ETCHINGS, ETC.

The second method of reproduction is a process where the printing surface is incised, known as 'intaglio', and the presence of the plate line surrounding the illustration distinguishes an *engraving* from a woodcut or a lithograph.

The word 'plate' refers to the metal on which the engraving is done, such as iron, copper, zinc, etc.

'The Master of the Playing Cards' lived near Cologne about 1446. His manner of shading was parallel lines in a vertical direction with no cross-hatching. In books of the fifteenth century, the engravings were printed on separate pieces of paper and then pasted in. Acid is not used in an engraving, for the lines are incised into the metal with a tool known as a 'graver'.

A set of instructive cards was made in north Italy depicting 'The Sorts and Conditions of Men', and Spain also produced playing-cards. 1479 is the earliest date found on Dürer's engravings, and in the early sixteenth century he was the pioneer of *etching*, which he did on iron.

In an etching a ground is laid on the plate, the lines drawn through with a needle exposing the metal, which is then bitten away with acid. Ink is pressed into the grooves, paper laid on the plate and a print taken under heavy pressure. The process of etching was practised by the armourer, the gunmaker, and the goldsmith long before it was used for the production of prints.

Etched plates of children with dolls and toys are those of Zost Amman, who lived in the second half of the sixteenth century. Lucas van Leyden used copper, and Dirick Vellert produced a pure etching in 1523 called the *Drummer and Boy with Hoop*.

When passing one's hand over an etching with the eyes closed, it is possible to feel the lines under one's hand. The same with an aquatint, where the tones are bitten away with acid through a porous ground, thus giving a kind of dotted effect seen better through a magnifying glass.

Aquatint plates date from about 1768, and early in the nineteenth century various aquatint views were published. *Colour prints* are those where separate plates are used for the various colours, whereas *Coloured Prints* are those which are coloured by hand, including etchings and engravings. The colour aquatints of Ackermann are well known for their beauty of tones and also the pictorial playing-cards which were printed by this method.

In a *mezzotint* the engraver works from dark to light on a grained plate thus obtaining a deeper dotted effect with lines and with much contrast between dark and light. The decay of mezzotint was due to the perfection of photogravure.

William Blake had his own means of reproduction, that is the etching of text in relief, leaving the lines raised and the background bitten away. The plates were printed in one colour and then tinted by himself and his wife, his *Songs of Innocence* coming in 1789.

During the latter part of the eighteenth century, rather dull line engravings were the universal medium, though woodcuts were still used for ballad sheets, chap-books, and many ABCs.

Daniel Chodowiecki, an eighteenth-century German illustrator, sometimes strengthened his etchings with *drypoint*, that is drawing on the plate itself with the graver and not relying on the acid. Many of his subjects were of children at play, as also were those of Tomkins in England who used much stipple in his engravings.

Steel plates, at first used for bank-notes, were brought into use about 1810 and machine ruling was commonly used. Between 1815 and 1860 steel facing protected the copper-plates, but the ruled lines tended to give a very monotonous effect.

In 1835 George Baxter patented a method of printing in oil-colours which was a combination of a copper-plate with wood blocks for the various tints, using between ten and 20 blocks. He worked from 1834 to 1860, but some of his prints were unpleasant and glossy.

In the third quarter of the nineteenth century wash drawings by artists were rendered into line by engravers of astonishing achievement, and by the 1880s the camera was used in order to reproduce the drawing on the block or plate, which was a great advantage. Apart from being more accurate, the original drawing would still be to hand from which to copy.

Soon the camera was used for reducing large drawings on to small blocks and the background was eaten away by acid. These *line blocks*, as they were known, revolutionised reproduction methods, and by 1886 drawings were first used in a book by this method. 'Commercial' wood engravings disappeared soon after the 1890s, and at this time William Morris began printing at the Kelmscott Press.

The first book illustrated by photographs came in 1844. In 1852 Fox Talbot patented photo-engraving on steel, his second patent on copper came the following year. In 1864 Swan patented his autotypes. The most practical and successful method of photo-engraving was known as *photogravure*.

The three-colour process where the blocks are broken up all over into dots of various density is a method of using three halftone blocks in order to produce a coloured illustration. The dots on the picture can easily be seen through a magnifying glass – the three colours being red, blue, and yellow, each colour needing a separate block.

The screen of ruled lines to break up the masses into dots was patented by Miesenbach in 1882, and was finally perfected by an American, Max Levy.

522   Copperplate engraving

523   Engraved initial

524   Jack-in-the-box, three-colour process

Illustrations by the three-colour process were printed on what is termed 'art paper', and were usually tipped into a book, or the whole book printed on this paper as in the case of the little Beatrix Potter books. Note, in these reproductions, that there is no solid black.

3. SURFACE PRINTING

This includes all the various methods of *lithography*; the principle being that ink, greasy ink, is repelled by water and vice versa. Briefly the drawing was done in ink on a smooth stone, the stone was wetted, and when printing ink was rolled over the stone it adhered only to those parts where the drawing had been done in greasy chalk or greasy ink. Paper was laid on the stone and a print taken under pressure.

The process was invented by Aloys Senefelder in Germany in 1798. In 1818 he began to write the history of his invention, and his claims were proved by Ackermann in England, Engelmann and Lasterie in Paris, and by Schlichtegroll in Munich, the word 'lithography' being first used in this year.

At first the prints were pale colourless drawings, the later ones had sharp outlines and many were reproductions of chalk drawings, while other effects were obtained by scraping.

Englemann experimented with washes at Mulhouse and invented the name *chromo-lithography*. By 1860 it was being used less for illustrations, and hardly at all in France.

Polyautography was the name sometimes used in England. The first lithograph used as a book-illustration here was in J. T. Smith's *Antiquities of Westminster* in 1807. The drawing was ruined after 300 impressions.

The first successful lithos came in 1826, and Edward Lear's *Book of Nonsense* was printed by this method in 1846. The years 1846 to 1865 were the great period for lithography in England, though artists thought it a vulgar way of reproducing drawings and a high price was put on them to secure a sale. Professional lithographers trained others to do their work for them, and thus the litho artist became a copyist and was consequently looked down upon. Gradually, the unwieldy stones gave way to zinc plates which could be put on rollers and by the use of rubber blankets the offset process began.

Photo-lithography is now used extensively for book-illustrations, maps and board games. Art paper is not necessary and no dots show through a magnifying glass though, various mechanical tints may sometimes be observed where a paler colour is needed.

In general, the early illustrations were woodcuts, hand-coloured engravings were used between 1767 and 1860, hand-coloured woodcuts between 1790 and 1835, children being employed to do the colouring. Lithographs were hand-coloured between 1835 and 1843, and coloured lithos used between 1840 and 1870. Chromo-lithos were the accepted method between 1870 and 1905, and from 1910 onwards the coloured print took their place.

Stamped metal sheets for toys came in 1877 and 1886. In 1887, the firm of J. Schön in Germany registered a mark for their sheet-metal toys which were coated with enamel. Péan Frères of France also made metal toys in 1887, and another well-known maker, Lehmann of Brandenburg, made sheet-metal toys in 1909. Gebruder Sauer of Nuremberg had a metal-toy factory in 1908, and early in the twentieth century the German tin toys flooded the market. Many of the metal sheets were printed in colours direct on the tin, whereas the earlier tin toys had been sparsely decorated with hand-painting.

A FEW GAMES WITH THEIR METHOD OF REPRODUCTION

The Game of Besieging. German. Early 19th century. Hand-coloured etching.

Cut-outs. La poupée-modèle. English (pretty). 1830. Hand-coloured etching.

Peep-show. St Mark's Square in Venice. Probably Austrian or German. About 1830. Hand-coloured engraving.

Reynard the Fox, in three languages. German. 1840. Hand-coloured litho.

Toby Toft and Christmas-pudding, with a cardboard spinner. English. About 1845. Hand-coloured etchings.

Tom Thumb, a merry game. English. About 1845. Hand-coloured litho.

The Cottage of Content. English. Spooner, 1848. Hand-coloured lithographs.

Cut-outs. Ranks of the Female Sex. German. Mid 19th century. Hand-coloured etching.

Grandma's New Game of Natural History. English. Mid 19th century. Coloured by hand.

The Adventures of Don Quixote. English. Mid 19th century. Hand-coloured litho.

Alphabetic dominoes or Child's Play. English. Mid 19th century. Hand-coloured litho.

Happy Families, designs by Sir John Tenniel. About 1860. Line engravings coloured by hand.

Outward Bound. English. About 1865. Hand-coloured litho.

Alphabet picture-making blocks. American. Second half of 19th century. Chromo-litho.

The Counties of England. English. About 1870. Coloured wood engravings.

Floral Loto, a new round game. English. About 1872. Coloured woodcuts.

Game of Members of Parliament or Government and Opposition. English. About 1875. Process engraving.

525 Jack-on-strings

20 Marks

The country of a manufactured toy will be marked on the toy itself, after 1898. Most other information will be printed on the box containing it, and in some cases the box itself will be part of the toy.

The first registered name in Britain seems to be that of Jaques, an English firm who apart from card games made table-tennis sets, croquet sets, etc. Ayres is another name connected with card games and outdoor activities.

It is curious to note some of the occupations of the persons registering, such as a naval lieutenant and the many Clerks in Holy Orders. Firms such as Pears, Bovril and Birds appear, and marks vary slightly in different countries. Sunny Jim appears here under the German marks in 1922, whereas he had been registered in England in 1904 (*see European and American Dolls*) and the little Rose O'Neill doll is here registered in Germany in 1913 under the name of a Kewpie.

The firm of F. Ad. Richter of Rudolstadt which had made the stone bricks between 1886 and 1914, appeared again with the addition of '& Cie' in the years 1917 and 1918, and again using their trademark of an anchor. By 1922 they were making dolls, stuffed dolls, leather dolls and ones of porcelain, and the firm of Bing also made dolls at this time. Richter's devised various new games and for each of these they used their anchor sign, sometimes more than one anchor and often with the initial 'R' entwined.

SOME MARKS REGISTERED IN ENGLAND BETWEEN 1849 AND 1910

JAQUES

1. Jaques
Games and chessmen
1849

BROUAYE

2. Pascal Tasso
16 rue Lefort, Paris
Rackets
1850

JEFFERIES

3. Jefferies
Wood Street, Woolwich, Kent
Racket balls
1855

4. T. & C. Clark & Co.
Shakespeare Foundry,
Wolverhampton
Toy cannons, balls, etc.
1861

F. H. AYRES

5. F. H. Ayres
Balls
1864

SNAP

6. Jaques
102 Hatton Garden, London
The game of snap
1866

7. Henry Jewitt
Toys and games
1870

THE ROYAL CABINET OF GAMES

8. Chapman, Son & Co.
2 Charterhouse Buildings,
Aldersgate, London
Games
1872

9. Richard James Secundus Joyce
18 Aldermanbury, London
Toys
1873

10. Salford & Irwell Rubber Co.
Fenchurch Street, London
Games
1876

11. De la Rue
Games of all kinds
1876

12. William McBurney
Toys and games
1776

13. Robert Whyte
Games
1876

14. Weintraud, Joyce & Co.
Uses the word Protector,
also Semper Adastra
1873

15. William Meyerstein
Toys
1876

16. James Asser
Manufacturer of games
1876

PEARS

17. Pears
Games of all kinds
1876

BOVRIL

18. Bovril
Games of all kinds
1876

19. Reason, Mann Co. Ltd
Brighton
Toys and games
1876

20. Berthold Eck
Germany
Toys
1877

21. William Farini
74 St James Street,
Westminster, Middlesex
Games
1878

22. Ferdinand Rosing
Billiter Square, London
Toys
1878

23. Edward Henry Vero
Westgate, Dewsbury, Yorkshire
Toys
1878

24. George Gibson Bussey
Museum Works, Rye Lane,
Peckham
Roller-skates
1878

25. Shoolbred & Co.
Tottenham House, London
Toys
1878

26. John Lilly
Manchester
Games
1878

UNIVERSAL PROVIDER

27. William Whiteley
Toys
1878

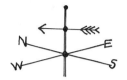

28. Alfred Bird & Sons
69 Worcester Street, Birmingham
Games
1878

29. John Shaw & Sons
Wolverhampton, Staffordshire
Toys
1878

30. William Beale
Ravenstone House, Farquhar Road,
Upper Norwood, Surrey
Games
1879

MERZBACH, LANG, & FELLHEIMER

31. Merzbach, Lang & Fellheimer
1 and 2 Snow Hill
and 57 St Mary Axe, London
Games and toys
1879
Sign, a coat of arms with watches
coming out of a cornucopia

32. Ihlee & Horne
31 Aldermanbury, London
Toys
1879

33. Carl August von der Meden
4 Jeffreys Square, London
Toys and paper kites
1879

34. Robert Smith Bartlett
Abbey Mills, Redditch
Toys
1879

35. John S. Elmore & Co.
77 Coleman Street, London
Games
1879

36. Frederick Henry Ayres
111 Aldersgate Street, London
Rackets
1879
'Fellkoropalon' (the bat is lop-sided)

37. Koeber & Co.
28 Great St Helen's, London
Toys
1880

38. Leon Hernandez
2 Talbot Court,
Gracechurch Street, London
Toys
1880
Sign, two elephants running
round a tree

ANTI-CORRODO
TR & G I
Co
W B

39. The Rustless & General Iron Co.
97 Cannon Street, London
Toys
1880

40. A. & F. Pears
Great Russell Street, London
Toys
1881
Sign, a boy being scrubbed
by an old woman

41. Humphreys & Co.
High Holborn, London
Toys
1881

C. LILLYWHITE & CO.

42. C. Lillywhite & Co.
Cricket-bats, etc.
Frederick Ough
1881

43. Koeber & Co.
Great St Helen's, London
Toys
1882

44. William Warne & Co.
29 Gresham Street, London
India rubber goods. Games
1882

45. John Turner
Albert Villa, Tiverton-on-Avon,
Somersetshire
An outdoor game
1882

46. William Meyerstein
6 Love Lane, Aldermanbury,
London
Games and toys of all kinds.
Paper Chinese lanterns
1882

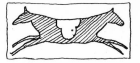

47. Oscar Moenich & Co.
Coleman Street, London
Toys
1882

48. Duplex Electric Light Power
& Storage Co.
Toys
1882

H. B. MUIR & Co.

49. H. B. Muir & Co.
26 Old Bread Street, London
Toys
1882

50. Ihlee & Horne
31 Aldermanbury, London
Toys
1882

WANKENPHAST & Co.

51. Wankenphast & Co.
60 Haymarket, London
Toys
1883

52. Thomas Murray Gardiner
Hoddesdon, Hertfordshire
Games
1883

53. Frank Bryan
38 Charterhouse Square,
Aldersgate Street, London
A game
1883

54. Edward Falkener
Carmarthenshire
Game of the Bowl, Senat and Tau
1883

COUNTY

55. Frank Bryan
38 Charterhouse Square, London
Games
1884

56. Cole & Co.
6 Falcon Square, London
Toys made of tin, brass, iron, steel
or lead, being children's playthings
1884

57. Caroline Manby
Oakhill, Bath, Somersetshire
A game
1884

58. Slazenger & Sons
56 Cannon Street, London
Games
1884

59. The Continental Caoutchouc
& Gutta Percha Compagnie
Hanover
Games and toys
1884

60. J. S. Elmore
79 Coleman Street, London
Balls of paper pulp,
substitutes for glass ball targets
1884

LA SOCIETE MEIFFRE, NEVEU ET CIE

61. La Société Meiffre, Neveu et Cie
82 rue d'Hauteville, Paris, France
Games and toys
1884

WILLIAM CURIE

62. William Curie
India rubber balls
1884

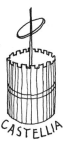

63. Caroline Manby
Oakhill, Bath, Somersetshire
A new game
1884

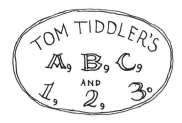

64. Louisa Hammon (spinster)
3 Sudeley Terrace, Kemptown,
Brighton
A toy
1884

THE NORTH POLE

65. Davidson & Co.
Games
1885

EUROPA

66. Deverell Bros.
73 Cheapside, London
Games
1885

THE GAME OF SANDRINGHAM

67. Slazengers
1885

68. Oscar Moenich
Games
1885

69. Harburg & Vienna
India Rubber Co.
Prussia, Germany
Balls
1885

70. The Hanover Caoutchouc,
Gutta Percha & Telegraph Works
Linden near Hanover
India rubber manufacturers
1885

CLIMAX
DRAGON   THAUMA

71. Felhausels
52 Little Britain, London
James Rice
Bats, balls, tennis, cricket
1885

THE RATTLUM SNAKORUM

72. The Economic Electric
Supply Co.
Wood Green, London
A toy warranted harmless
but hideous
1885

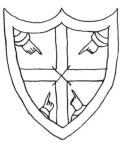

73. The London & Provincial
Novelty Co.
24 Great Crosshall Street, Liverpool
Serpents' eggs, imitation lightning, etc.
1885

74. James Rain (mathematician)
1 Napier Villas, Waldegrave Road,
Upper Norwood, Surrey
Games
1885

THE TOBOGGANING CO

75. The Tobogganing Co.
Palace Chambers, Bridge Street,
Westminster
A game with picture of toboggan
1885

76. Parkins & Golto
54 Oxford Street, London
Toys and games
1886

THE BIRMINGHAM TOY MANUFACTORY

77. The Birmingham Toy
Manufactory
George William Herbert
1886

PRESIDENT

78. Frank Bryan
38 Charterhouse Square, London
Games
1886

79. Richard Daft
1 Lister Gate, Nottingham
Football, etc.
1886

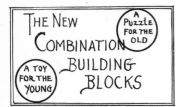

80. William Richardson
Poultry, London
1886

81. William Salmon
5 Clayton Street, London
Cricket
1886

82. Mowbray Fitzroy Bailey
Gracechurch Street, London
A parlour game
1886

OPTIMUS

83. Charles Fotherly Bagley
Barbican, London
Tennis, etc.
1886

THE WOOD STREET BALL

84. Charles Malings
18 Cockspur Street, London
1886

REX

85. David Moseley
Manchester
India rubber manufacturers
Tennis balls
1886

86. Hyman Abraham
Abraham's Tennis
1886
Sign, 'a spider on a web'

87. Chas. Macintosh
Rubber balls, billiard-balls
patented in 1886

JOHN BULL

88. William Howard
Footballs
1886

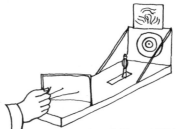

THE JUBILEE GAME OF SKILL

89. Richard Henry Douglas Hart
(gentleman)
Tokenhouse Yard, London
1886

90. Thomas Blenkarn
62 Fenwick Road, Peckham
Games and toys
1886

JUMBO

91. James Pascall
Blackfriars Road
Manufacturing confectioner. Toys
1886

92. Co-op Wholesale Co.
1 Balloon Street, Manchester
Games, but no dolls
1886

93. Chas. Macintosh
India rubber manufacturers
Games
1886

TIP

94. Hale Bros.
Sheffield
1886

95. Harry Woodham
109 London Road, Tunbridge Wells
Cricket-bats
1886

KANGAROO

96. Chas. Macintosh
Manchester and London
Games
1886

THE DURABLE

97. Deverell Bros.
73 Cheapside
Balls, toys, etc.
1886

RINK CROQUET

RINK CURLING

98. Hugh Dalziel
Games, toboggans
patented in 1886

99. F. Ad. Richter
Rudolstadt, Thuringia, Germany
Games and toys
1886

LA FUREUR
M. P.
TOUPIE DU NORD DEPOSÉE

100. Mordacq Plamont
Lille
1887
Sign, a spinning-top printed
in violet

101. Amorces-jouets
Au petit pioupiou qualité supᵣᵉ
(a foot-soldier)
1887

102. Robert Fuller (potter)
Lavender Hill
Toys
1887

CURLING STONES

103. Ayrshire
1887

PATCHESI

104. John Jaques
102 Hatton Garden, London
A game
1887

ROMETTE

105. Edwin Leworthy
(gentleman)
Bromley, Kent
A game for board and pieces
1887

QUILLETTE

106. John Thomas
Clerk in Holy Orders.
Manorbier, Pembrokeshire
An improved game of skill
analogous to croquet
1887

BILLIATELLE

107. 1887

108. Shin guards for protecting
ankles at football
1887

ENDLESS PUZZLE

109. Perry & Co.
Birmingham
1887

REVERSI

110. Lewis Waterman
Bristol
Boot and shoe manufacturer,
a game similar to draughts
1887

111. George Lutticke
Hove
Toys of all kinds
1887

KALMUTATOR

112. Alfred Spencer Jones
(model-maker)
Ipswich
Engine
1888

Anchor Box

113. Friedrich Adolf Richter
Rudolstadt, Thuringia, Germany
Games and toys
1888

114. Thomas Lidster
(patternmaker)
Hull, England
Games
1888

"REVERSI"

115. Lewis Waterman
Bristol
The original game of Reversi
for the chess board
1888

116. Bingley
Nottingham
Metal toy, 'The Grand National
Hurdle Race'
1888

HALMA

117. Ayres
1888

118. Eliza Jane Fairless (spinster)
Brixton Road, London
An outdoor game
1888

119. Hanks & Harley
Liverpool
Toys
1888

120. Thomas Hardman (artist)
Liverpool
1888

TESSELLA
ROYALE

121. R. G. Powell
Manchester
Toys
1888

228

SHUTTLE TENNIS

122. A game
1888

Britton's SETOW

123. Canonbury
(Professor of Music)
A game
1888

Anchor Box

124. F. Ad. Richter & Co.
Rudolstadt, Thuringia, Germany
Building stones in three colours
1888

BIG BEN BANK
E. A. Tice

125. Edward Albert Tice
Middlesex
Toys
1888

FICHE-MARBRE

126. Samuel Webb Thomas
(clergyman)
Southease Rectory, Lewis
A game
1888

OUR STILES

127. Frederick Reynolds
Birmingham
1888

MUSICAL PNEUMATIC
TOYS

128. William Henry Brown
1888

TIDDLEDY-WINKS

129. Joseph Assheton Fincher
(gentleman)
114 Oxford Street, London
1889

NAVAL BLOCKADE

130. Henry Chamberlain
(Lieutenant, Royal Navy)
Greenwich
Games
1888

FLITTERKINS

131. Jaques
A game
1889

132. Henry R. Hughes
Long Lane, London
Games
1889

MINIATELLE

133. The Toy Manufacturing Co.
5 Oxford Street, London
1889

SPINNAKER

134. Henry Glanville Barnacle
(clergyman)
The Vicarage, Holmes Chapel,
Cheshire
A game of skill
1889

LADY BLOWAWAY'S VISIT TO THE ZOO

135. Emma Susanna Windsor
(manufacturer and saleswoman)
150 Soho Bazaar, Soho Square,
London
A game
1889

THE EIFFEL TOWER ASCENT GAME

136. Ernest de Lima Bird
Peckham
1889

THE BROWNIE BLOCKS

137. Palmer Cox (artist)
Broadway, New York
1889

SPOOF

138. Ayres
The new game of spoof
1889

COZARI

139. James Morrell (engineer)
A game
1889

CROBILLE

140. Jaques
An outdoor game
1889

141. Wankenphast Ltd
Sign, a man striding along

FLICKEM

142. Hildesheimer & Faulkner
Games
1890

143. James George Ingram
Games
1890

QUOITAC & ALSO SLIDIT

144. Edward Mortimer
Ten table games
1890

LABYMAZE

145. Jules Pierre Cavallier
(accountant)
A game
1890

BASILINDA
BUFFALO JACK
COZZARE
DUC DAMÉ
JAQUITTA
KAN HOOPLAR

146. Games played in 1890

147. Ménard & Moss
Greenock
Péronnelle games
1890

BOOMERANG

148. Robert Owen Allsop (architect)
Strand, London
A game
1890

PALMERETTO

149. Emma Barker
Gwendur Road, Kensington
Games
1890

PLIFFKINS

150. Played in 1890

151. Ernst Paul Lehmann
Brandenburg on the Havel, Prussia
Toys
1890

152. Henry Thomas Jarrett
(model brick maker)
1890

FLIPPERTY FLOP

153. Oppenheimer & Sulzbacher
Nuremberg, Germany
A game
1891

154. Eugène Lavignac
Négociant à Bordeaux
1891
Sign, black on a white background

155. Dorothy Annie Garner
West Kensington, London
A cup and ball game
1891

156. Thomas Farrar
Manchester
Skipping-ropes
1891

157. Ephraim Samson (collector)
Houndsditch, London
Games
1892

PANOPE

158. Sir George Strong Nares
A kite
1892

159. Louis Gervais
Médecin à Rouen
1893
Sign, stamped on the playing-cards
for the use of blind people

SPIRAL NATIONAL

160. Georges-Paul Gérard
Désigneur des rouleaux de
papier pour fêtes
1893

161. The Laripino Game
1898

162. Schlesinger
The Toy House, London
1898

163. Max Dannhorn
Nuremberg, Germany
Metal toys
1899

Chemin roulant

164. Georges Dreyfus
Négociant à Paris
1900

165. Regnald-Stansell Williams
Paris
1902

SNAKES AND LADDERS
166. 1904

Geo M Kelsons

167. George Mortimer Kelson
Westminster
1904

Neige de Riz

168. Douglas Farquhar Glennie
Knightsbridge, London
Games
1907

MECCANO
169. 1908

BUMBLE PUPPY
170. 1909

BLÉRIOT

171. Gabriel de Lapeyrouse
Paris
Toys
1909

BOLO

172. John Green Hamley
(toy merchant)
86 High Holborn, London
A toy animal in the form of
a grotesque dog
1910

SOME MARKS REGISTERED IN GERMANY BETWEEN 1910
AND 1922

DAISY TEA SET

173. Sontag & Söhne
Bayern
Kinder-service aus Porzellan
1910

174. Bruns Ulbricht
Nuremberg
Puppenküchenart, Kel
1911

Campbell Kids

175. Jos. Süszkind
Hamburg
1911

CLAUSS

176. Robert Gaszler
Zittau-i.-Sa.
Unbreakable wooden figures
1912

Ludo

177. J. W. Spear & Söhne
Nuremberg
1912

MECCANO

178. Meccano Gesellschaft
Berlin
1912

179. Ernst Luckhaus
Drusberg
1913

Kewpie

180. Borgfeldt
Berlin
1913

SCHWARZER PETER

181. J. W. Spear & Son
Nuremberg
A card game
1913

HAPPY FAMILIES

182. also 1914

183. Arthur Galle
Dresden
1916

ROYAL LUDO

184. J. W. Spear & Son
Nuremberg
1916

DIABOLO

185. A. Zehnfenning
1917

MÄRKLIN

186. Göppingen
(No dolls)
1919

187. Hahn & Co.
Nuremberg
Stoff und Leder Spielwaren
Fabrikation, Stoff Tiere und
Werf-puppen
1920

188. Ernst Vanoli
Freiburg
1920

Lothar Meggendorfer.

189. Lothar Meggendorfer
Krottenmühl
Wooden toys
1920

ℱ S

190. Freiburger Spielwaren Fabrik
Freiburg
1920

191. Margarete Martin
Hanover
1920

KnallFritze

192. Edmund Mätzig
Spielwaren
1920

Pixat

193. W. Gustav Voigt
Zwickau
1920

194. S. Günthermann
Nuremberg
Mechanische Blechspielwarenfabrik
1921

195. Erste Schlesische
Puppenfabrik
Heinrich Schmuckler
Liegnitz
Puppenfabrik, Gekleidete Puppen
und Gestopfte Tiere
1921

POGO

196. The Game of Pogo
Hanover
1921

MUTT & JEFF

197. Borgfeldt
1922

„Sunny Jim"

198. M. Kohnstam & Co.
Fürth
1922

199. C. H. Müller, junior
Olbernhau
1922

Marks index

Notes on illustrations in colour

Facing title page

1   Poupard. Wood and cloth. The doll by Schönau and Hoffmeister, Porzellan-Burggrub, Bavaria. Height 14½ ins. *c.* 1889. *Lent by Mr David Blaylock*

2   Doll's house. Four wallpapered compartments, two up and two down, no staircase, no doors, movable fences and posts. 22 ins. to ridge line; 17 ins. wide. Victorian. Brought from Falmouth for the *Collection of Mrs Evelyn Harvey*

3   Snow-storm. A glass ball 2½ ins. diameter, on a stand decorated with three shells. The blue sky is painted on the back of the glass sphere. Total height 3½ ins. *Lent by Mr. J. D. Fordham*

4   Spinning-top. Metal, painted. 19th century. *Salisbury Museum*

5   Goose. Plastic. By pressing slightly down on the bird's back, the wings flap up, and from between its legs an egg drops out. Repeat again for second and third egg. 4 ins. high. *c.* 1946. *Belonging to A. Moreton Moore*

Facing page 14

1   Baby's rattle of coral, with gold filigree and enamel of blue and green. 3 ins. high. Italian. *c.* 1600. This baby's amulet is in the Jewel Gallery of the Victoria and Albert Museum. *Given by Dr W. L. Hildburgh*, F.S.A.

2   Tarocco counters, very thin and with various designs in original box, wooden with sliding lid and freely painted pattern on gold background. Box 4 × 2½ × 2½ ins. *St Albans City Museum*

3   Lead soldier. Total height 4½ cms.; stand 2½ cms. long. German. *St Albans City Museum*

4   Animated figures. Carved in bone and painted in colours, standing on a bone box with a brass handle. Box 5 ins. long. One figure bangs the anvil, one hammers in the bung, and the soldier beats the drum. Made for Captain Lincoln Barker, last Governor of Norman Cross Barracks, and now in *Peterborough Museum*. There are many intricate toys here, carved by French prisoners-of-war, between 1797 and 1815, including models of boats, many versions of the guillotine, some double, and beautiful little figures with bonnets and hats in thin bone showing the costumes at the time of the Napoleonic Wars.

5   Part of a Set of soldiers, comprising thin printed paper stuck to blocks of wood, 3¼ ins. long, 1½ ins. high, the officers being on separate blocks. This set was put together by Richard Cuming when Captain of the Newington Volunteers, 1798–1803, during the threatened invasion of England by Napoleon, and the toy was possibly used by him for recruiting purposes. *Cuming. Museum, Southwark, London*

6   One of 22 hand-painted 'Lotterie plates'. On wood. *c.* 9 ins. × 3 ins. To them belong little round wooden pieces with the same paintings behind glass, a game played in Denmark and elsewhere. Danish. *From the collection of Mrs Estrid Faurholt*

7   Peacock. Wooden. Carved and painted in the shape of a boat. 7 ins. long. Early 20th century. A folk toy from India, where it is known as 'mayurpankhi' or 'peacock boat'. *Given by H.M. Queen Mary to Bethnal Green Museum*

8   Toy soldiers. Made of terracotta and decorated by hand.

Facing page 49

1   Mouse. Glazed composition. 1½ ins. high. From Egypt. 2000 B.C. *British Museum*

2   Pig. Clay, pale ochre with brownish marks. *c.* 4 ins. long. North Syrian civilisation. 1780–1190 B.C. *British Museum*

3   Horseman. Clay, pinkish white. *c.* 4½ ins. high. Made in Athens about the 7th century B.C. *British Museum*

4   Dog. Clay, brownish stripy with ochre-coloured eyes, and with a hare in its mouth, ochre colour *c.* 3 ins. long. Found at Thebes. Boeotia. 580 B.C. *British Museum*

5   Monkey riding on a mule. Clay. 4½ ins. high. From Tanagra. Made in Corinth. 380 B.C. *British Museum*

6   Monkey. Clay. *c.* 4 ins. high. From Sar Dheri. 1st century B.C. *Given by Major-General H. A. L. Haughton. Victoria and Albert Museum in 1939*

7   Goat. Clay, painted. *c.* 5 ins. long. *British Museum*

8   Animal. Clay, with spots. *c.* 4 ins. long. *c.* 120 B.C. *Horniman Museum*

9   Camel. Painted terracotta. *c.* 5 ins. high. A.D. 100. *British Museum*

10, 11   Animals. Papiermâché, highly coloured and light to hold. *c.* 6 ins. long. Made in China. *Pitt Rivers Museum, Oxford*

Facing page 64

1   Noah's ark of painted wood, with dove on roof. The side slides open and inside are Noah, his wife, and four members of the family, about 120 animals, birds, insects, together with a piece of

green baize and three palm trees. Ark 23 ins. long. *From the Gilchrist Collection of Victoriana, sold at Sotheby's in December 1968. End view shown also*

2   Ark of carved and painted wood, together with animals and people. Ridge of roof 12 ins. long. Early 19th century. *Given by Oswold Dobell Esq. to the Bethnal Green Museum*

3   Set of ninepins. Consisting of papiermâché frogs. Height 6¼ ins.; captain 7 ins. Five are painted green, four are painted brown, the captain is the one with his 'hand' up. Each standing on a round wooden base with the detail of painting varying on each frog. Probably German. Late 19th or early 20th century. *Lent by Miss Ruth Wainwright*

Facing page 161

1   Money-box. Pottery. The 'Shakspere Saving Bank' (note spelling). 5½ ins. wide. English. *Cuming Museum, Southwark, London*

2   Money-box. Pottery. Made like a cottage trimmed with flowers and creepers. 5 ins. high. Staffordshire. English. Back view on page 167. Early 18th century. *Victoria and Albert Museum, London*

3   Money-box. Pottery. c. 7 ins. long; 7 ins. high. Money slot in roof at back. English. *Peterborough Museum*

4   Money-box. Pottery. c. 4 ins. high. Staffordshire. English. Early 18th century. The brush strokes on the ground and the tree up the side of the cottage indicate Pratt Ware. Back view on page 167. *Victoria and Albert Museum, London*

5   Two cock and hen bird whistles. The red amongst the flowers is the mouthpiece. c. 4 ins. high. English. 1810. *In the Schreiber Collection of the Victoria and Albert Museum. Near these two is another whistle*

made in the form of a dog with a woman's head, this may be by Ralph Wood.

Facing page 176

1   An Oriental acrobat. Figure c. 6 ins. high, very fragile and light. The figure somersaults backwards from the three levels as its centre of gravity is changed by a shifting weight. The little stand, figure and lower step shut up into the box containing them. c. 1790. *St Albans City Museum*

2   Two clowns balancing on a wire frame. 10 ins. high; clowns 3¼ ins. high. Probably German. c. 1900. *Lent by Miss Ruth Wainwright*

3   Bristle figure. The little figure appears to dance when placed on a vibrating surface such as a drum, harpsichord or piano. 1⅝ ins. high. 17th century. *St Albans City Museum*

4   Bristle figures. Yellow one 2 ins. high; green one 2½ ins. high. Of a later period than No. 3. *St Albans City Museum*

5   Fairground paper toy with whistle. 15 ins. long when blown out. Made in China and sold for 1s. in England in 1968

6   White rabbit. Made of folded paper with dab of red paint for eyes and nose, on a cardboard base, eating a paper carrot. 2½ ins. to tip of tail. Made in China and sold in England for 1s. in 1969

7   'Man on a bicycle'. c. 6½ ins. high. From Garanhuns, Pernambuco, East Brazil. *Pitt Rivers Museum, Oxford*

Facing page 193

1   Metal train. 18 ins. long. c. 1840. *Gunnersbury Museum, Middlesex*

2   Metal train. Thin tin, with wheels of 1½ ins. diameter, overall length of train 21 ins. The name

NERO appears on the engine. c. 1850. *Folk Museum, Cambridge*

3   Wooden train with cast-iron wheels. London, Brighton and South Coast Railway. Engine 19 ins. long from buffer to buffer; truck 13 ins. long. c. 1880. *Folk Museum, Cambridge*

4   Seiffen wooden tree. In various sizes. c. 1850

5   Tree. Cast lead, painted. 3 ins. high. German. c. 1860

6   Seven tin figures. All 3 cms. high, i.e. the Nuremberg scale. Second half of 19th century, possibly made for a festival held in 1848. Back views on page 62. *Lent by Miss Janet Dunbar*

7   Wooden boat on wheeled trolley. c. 4 ins. long. Bought at Bartholomew Fair, 1849. Part of the Cuming Bequest. *Cuming Museum, Southwark, London*

8   The Fandango. Wooden. Posts 3½ ins. high. Bought at Bartholomew Fair, 1849. *Cuming Museum, Southwark, London*

9   Little dog on a stand. Painted wood. Stand 1 in. × ½ in. Indian. Second half of 20th century

10   Horse-drawn water-cart. 21 ins. long. English. Late 19th century. One of many large toys popular at this time. *Bethnal Green Museum, London*

Facing page 208

1   Toy pails. 1¼ ins. and 1½ ins. diameter. T'ang dynasty, A.D. 618–906. *Victoria and Albert Museum, London*

2   Blue and white pieces from doll's dinner- and tea-services. Jug 1½ ins. high, cups 1 in. high, plate 1¼ ins. diameter. Also there are many larger cups and saucers, dishes, teapots and jugs, all very beautiful and some with s in underglaze blue marked on them. *Alfred Darby Gift. Victoria and Albert Museum, London*

3 Blue and white cup. 1 in. high, no saucer for this size. Larger cups have saucers, and there are also teapots, etc. The pieces are marked s in some cases and sometimes accompanied by a cross in underglaze blue. *Bequeathed by Mrs M. A. Wise. Victoria and Albert Museum, London*

4 Three toy dishes. Earthenware. One has two fishes, another has two cauliflowers with raised centres, the third is a sauce-boat. Coloured plates have raised edges. The dishes are about 2¾ ins. long. English, probably Leeds. Late 18th

century. *Bequeathed by Mr Legh Tolson. Victoria and Albert Museum, London*

5 Teacup and saucer. 3 ins. diameter saucer, cup has no handle, and toy milk-jug, *c.* 2¼ ins. high, of earthenware. Staffordshire. Early 19th century. *Given by Mrs Kate Bentley to the Victoria and Albert Museum, London*

6 Hot-water can and foot-bath in copper with enamel finish. Can 2 ins. high; foot-bath 2½ ins. long. *Peterborough Museum*

7 Detail of saucer from tea-set below

8 Cup and saucer. Palish cream colour with painted flowers. Saucer 3½ ins. across. Swansea. *c.* 1790. *From the Collection of Mrs J. C. Bishop*

9 Toy tea-service. Consisting of porcelain tray with large bowl, sugar-bowl with lid, teapot, milk-jug, two cups and saucers, decorated in shaded pinks and gold on white. Tray 9½ ins. long from handle tips; cups 1⅛ ins. diameter; saucers 2 ins. diameter. Swansea porcelain (could be Derby). First half of the 19th century. *Bethnal Green Museum, London*

Notes on the illustrations in black and white

1 Italian sweetnik. *c.* 10 ins. high. 1961

2 The Salisbury Giant. A figure of St Christopher used in pageants, first recorded in 1496. *c.* 7 ft. high. *Salisbury Museum*

3 Ball of stone. *c.* 3 ins. diameter. From Old Deer, Aberdeenshire, Scotland. *c.* 3000 B.C.

4 A bone needle. Made from the bone of a bird. 2 ins. long. Tel el-Amarna, Egypt. 1380–1360 B.C. *British Museum*

5 Mud gaming board with pieces. From a Pre-dynastic grave near Abydos, Upper Egypt

6 Bull. Fawn clay with red markings. *c.* 6 ins. long. From Kulli, India. 2900 B.C.

7 Boy with a toy cart. Greek

8 Toy doll made of bone. 4½ ins. high. Found at Wollaston field, Dorchester. Roman, A.D. 9. *Dorchester Museum, Dorset*

9 Chess piece of carved bone. *c.* 1½ ins. high. Probably of Late Roman or Dark Age date. *Cirencester Museum*

10 Draughtsman made from a horse's tooth. Found in the King's Field Cemetery, Faversham, Kent. *British Museum*

11 From a Chinese scroll painting 'The Hundred Children'. Ming dynasty, A.D. 1368–1644. *British Museum*

12 Juggler. MS. Cott. Claudius B. IV. 11th century. *British Museum*

13 Figure with animal. German. 14th century

14 Boys playing at water quintain. 14th century

15 Toy bean-shooter. 13½ ins. long. Choroti

16 Figure of carved boxwood. *c.* 4 ins. high. From Augsburg. A.D. 1516

17 Detail from Rubens painting of his children. *Galerie Royale, Dresden*

18 Rider. Made of Siegburg pipeclay with the help of moulds. Found at Cologne. 15th century. *Victoria and Albert Museum, London*

19 'Boyes-sports'. Woodcut from Charles Hoole's translation of Comenius's *Visible World*, 1659

20 Toy booth at Bartholomew Fair. 1728. The booth was known as 'Pickpockets' Harvest', and a small child is seen picking the pocket of the old gentleman

21 Guillotine of wood. French

Revolution. 1794. From Karl Gröber's *Toys of Other Days*

22 Child with a butterfly-net. 19th century

23 One of eight figures forming a German band. Made of plaster and coloured, natural flesh colour, black suit, striped trousers, wire musical instrument. 5½ ins. high. Said to have been a wedding present to Queen Victoria. *St Albans City Museum*. These German bandsmen of the early 19th century are similar to the little figures in a Biberach catalogue of 1836. Another set is in *Bethnal Green Museum, London*

24 Child with skipping-rope. 19th century

25 Tin lid. *c.* 3 ins. across. A toy of the First World War

26 Horse and man of plastic, with weight on end of string. The horse moves forward when weight is put over a table's edge. Blue all over. 1¾ ins. long, 2 ins. high. Legs marked LF, LB, RF, RB. Given away in Kellogg's Cornflakes packets

27 Stone ball. *c.* 2½ ins. diameter. From north-east Scotland. After 2000 B.C.

28 Ball of twisted rushes. 3¼ ins.

diameter. From Thebes, Egypt. 12th dynasty, 1786 B.C.

29   Leather ball. 4 ins. diameter. Six segments of red and white tawed leather sewn together. From ancient Egypt. *c.* 1500 B.C.

30   Putting the stone

31   Girls playing catch. Egyptian wall-painting. 1786 B.C.

32   Ball with 12 sides

33   Ball game, where a ball is rolled down a sloping board and falls into a depression a few feet away. Greek

34   Porcelain ball with deep blue and cerulean stripes alternately. 1400 B.C. *British Museum*

35   Ball of split cane. 8 ins. diameter. From the Malay Peninsula. *British Museum*

36   Ball. Romano-British period

37   Tossing the ball. From a 14th-century manuscript

38   A game of bowls near Smithfield, London

39   A game of ball using 'bats', near Smithfield, London

40   The game of bandy, also known as 'golf' or 'cambue'. 14th century

41   The game of trapball. 14th century

42   Piggy stick. A game still played in Yorkshire in 1910. The nose, eyes and ears were sometimes drawn on with ink. 10 ins. long

43   The game of trapball. From an engraving by F. Bartolozzi, R.A., after a picture by William Hamilton, R.A. 18th century

44   Bat, trap and ball in wooden box. Wooden bat 14 ins. long, wooden trap 9 ins. long, 2 ins. high. Ball of composition. Box about 17 ins. long. *Folk Museum, Cambridge*

45   Boys playing with ball and mallets. Note the notched post. 15th century

46   Bat and stick

47   The game of bowls. 16th century

48   Four carpet bowls or 'woods', played with in the 'long galleries' of country-houses. The ones shown are made of porcelain. 3 ins. diameter. *Gunnersbury Museum*

49   Curved mallets and ball for the game of paille maille

50   The game of paille maille, St James's Park, London

51   Cricket-ball of mangrove wood. The seams and stitches are imitated by carving. $2\frac{1}{2}$ ins. diameter. From the Trobriand Islands. *British Museum*

52   The 'locust ball' of Joseph Pracy. A football with 12 identical panels, sewn by hand and then turned inside out, so that no stitches show. 1903. *Leathercraft Museum, London*

53   Ball containing nuts, used in the game of tocoro, by the Chorotis. $1\frac{3}{4}$ ins. diameter. South America

54   Bouncing ball and Japanese girl. The kind of ball sold at fairs in England. From a print by Hokusai

55   Ball of plaited cane. Modern, in the traditional style and very light to hold. $2\frac{1}{4}$ ins. diameter. 1968

56   Marbles found in a child's grave. Made of stone, of a mottled colour. $\frac{9}{16}$ in. diameter. From Nagada, Egypt. Later 4th millennium B.C. *Ashmolean Museum, Oxford*

57   Three 'choice marbles or taws' made of glass, with white threaded centres, red and blue stripes, or red and green stripes. $1\frac{1}{2}$ ins. diameter and $1\frac{3}{8}$ ins. diameter. *Bedford Museum*

58   Rattle of stone. Egyptian. 1360 B.C.

59   Rattle in the shape of a pig. *c.* 3 ins. long. Pompeii.

Ethnological Museum, Cambridge

60   Pottery rattle. *c.* 2 ins. diameter. Mexican. Prehistoric

61   Striped pottery rattle. *c.* 2 ins. diameter. From Mohenjodaro, India

62   Clay rattle in the shape of an owl, light pinkish brown in colour. $5\frac{1}{2}$ ins. high. From the Mycenaean tomb at Enkonu, Cyprus. 1200 B.C. *British Museum*

63, 64   Two baked clay rattles in the shape of pigs. From Greece. 4th century B.C. *British Museum*

65   Crepitaculum, a little Roman rattle with bells attached to make a jingling sound. Pompeii

66   Seed rattle. Brown colour. West Africa. *British Museum*

67   Seed rattle. Brown. Equatorial Africa. *British Museum*

68   Ball rattle with bivalve shell and pebble, covered with silk. Japan

69   Rattle carved in the shape of a bird. Wood. South Africa. *British Museum*

70   Rattle of carved wood. Painted red and black. Made by the Tlinket Indians. South-east Alaska, America. *Wellcome Museum, London*

71   Rattle of the Chorotis. Shown open and closed. South America

72   Clapper rattles. 16th century. European

73   Rattle. 14th century. France

74   Hochet, sometimes known as a 'clacker'. Pompeii

75   *Crécelle*, or 'cressell', once used in Roman Catholic churches instead of a bell, during Passion Week. France. 14th century.

76   Rattle in the form of a doll. Wooden, painted white with red decoration, black spots and lacing. 6 ins. high. 18th century. *Folk Museum, Cambridge*

77   Bauble. A piece of peasant

jewellery for a child, consisting of a whistle and bells. Spanish. 18th century. *Victoria and Albert Museum, London*

78   Silver bell rattle with mother-of-pearl ring. *Given to R. E. M. Moore by Miss Marian Davis*

79   Rattle of straw work. 7 ins. long. *c.* 1850. *Peterborough Museum*

80   Hochet de la Folie. First Empire of Napoleon Bonaparte, 1804

81   Poupard. The doll and musical-box are twirled by a turn of the wrist. The music produced is from Faust. Doll has bisque head, plaster limbs, arms loosely fixed with cord. Cream net dress, gold trimmings, pale pink sash, painted shoes, ochre colour. Doll 6½ ins. high. Handle about 7 ins. high. The platform is covered with coloured paper, surrounded by a crimson and white satin flounce, edged with blue-green tinsel. Bought in Paris about 1860. French. *Bethnal Green Museum, London*

82   Ninepins found in a child's grave. Made of stone. From Nagada, Egypt. Later 4th millennium, B.C. *Ashmolean Museum, Oxford*

83   Set of ninepins. England. A.D. 1600

84   Playing kayles, i.e. throwing a stick at ninepins, at Smithfield. 13th century

85   Ninepins and balls. 18th century

86   Ninepins from an engraving by Chodowiecki. Note the 'captain' in the centre. 18th century

87   Elephant ninepin. One of a set cut from three-ply wood and mounted on stands, some stained darker than others. 3½ ins. high. Two wooden balls. *c.* 1942. *Belonging to R. E. M. Moore*

88   Top of glazed composition, a beautiful cerulean blue with deeper

blue markings. 2 ins. high. From Thebes, Egypt. 1250 B.C. *British Museum*

89, 90   Two tops with whip. 2¾ ins. and 2 ins. high. Greece *British Museum*

91   Spinning-top of bone. *c.* 2 ins. high. Roman. *Cirencester Museum*

92   Boy whipping a top. English A.D. 1400

93   Whipping a top at Smithfield, London

94, 95   Whip tops from manuscripts of the 14th and 15th centuries. MS. Roy. 2B. VII, Queen Mary's Psalter. *British Museum.* MS. Douce 6. *Bodleian Library, Oxford*

96   Medieval German top. From the *Hortus Sanitatus,* Antwerp, 1521

97   Carved wooden top which forms the shadow showing the silhouette of the head of Louis VI. From *Toys of Other Days* by Mrs Neville Jackson

98   Wooden top (*pia*) with whip. Swahili. *British Museum*

99   Pegtop of wood. 3 ins. high. 1820. *Salisbury Museum*

100   Top of polished wood in the form of a figure. *Victoria and Albert Museum Exhibition, 1967*

101   Humming-top of metal, unpainted. 'The New Choral Top.' Victorian. *Folk Museum, Cambridge*

102   TOPS
i   Humming-top of Japanese lacquer. Dark brownish black with cream markings and flat scarlet top. In Japan, humming-tops are sometimes known as 'thunder'. *Pitt Rivers Museum, Oxford*
ii   Top. Fawn colour. Drum 4 ins. high, stick 11 ins. long. From Sikaiana, Solomon Islands. *Horniman Museum*
iii   Top. Blackish colour. 3 ins. across. From the Simbo group,

Solomon Islands. *British Museum*
iv   Humming-top of bamboo. Ochre and brown colour. From Java. *Horniman Museum*
v   Top to spin on a cord, as in a print by Hokusai. Japanese
vi   Tops of stone. Stained white with pink figure. 4 ins. diameter, 9 ins. high. These tops are kept in special baskets, and the longer they spin, the more valuable they become. Torres Straits. *British Museum*
vii   Top. Dark brown colour. 2 ins. across. From Florida, Solomon Islands. *British Museum*

103   Three Japanese lantern tops

104   Top-spinning. Japan

105   Japanese top with whip

106   Spinning-top. From a print by Hokusai. Japan

107   Humming-top. Wood, painted in bright colours, reds, greens, browns, mauve and prussian-blue. 8 ins. long. Mid 19th century. *Bethnal Green Museum, London*

108   'La Toupie Magique.' Tissandier. 19th century

109   Top. German patent, No. 130596, by Joh. Heinr. Dreckmann in Münster. 1901

110   Tippe top. Wood, painted. As it spins, it turns itself upside-down and continues spinning. 1½ ins. diameter. Made in England, by Christie and Jay, Ltd. *Lent by Moreton Moore*

111   Antelope. Pottery from Chanhudaro, India

112   Bull. Stone from Mesopotamia. 2300 B.C. *British Museum*

113   Bull. Fawnish with red markings. From the Kulli culture. 2000–3000 B.C.

114   Nodding bull. Clay, worked by cords. 5 ins. high. From Mohenjodaro. 2900 B.C.

115   Monkey. From the Indus Valley

116   Mouse. Painted steatite, with moving lower jaw and tail. Brownish with black markings. 5 ins. long. 1250 B.C. *British Museum*

117   Deer. Folk toy from India, traditional and timeless, made by children

118   Bull-fighting. From a painting in the *Escorial, Madrid*. 18th century

119   Old woman with three wooden, painted horses, of different sizes. Traditional. Dalarna. 1956. More to be seen in *Pollock's Toy Museum, Scala Street, London*

120   Tortoise with nodding head. Mexican. Early 20th century. *Ethnological Museum, Cambridge*

121   Elephant. Carved from a log of wood. Tusks of wood, carved and painted eye, painted ear. 12 ins. long. From Somaliland, and purchased in 1935. *British Museum*

122   A pull-along papiermâché bulldog which snuffles and growls when the lead is pulled. The lead comes through a slot in the collar, the head wobbles and the jaw appears to go up and down. A deep buffish colour, red leather collar with badger hair frill. Dog, 1 ft. 5 ins. long. *From the Gilchrist Collection of Victoriana, Isle of Wight. (Now dispersed.)* This dog was sold for £45 at Sotheby's in December 1968

123   Wooden pig. Dark brown with white markings. Trobriand Islands. *British Museum*

124   Wooden hunter's hartebeest. Dark brown. Somaliland. *British Museum*

125   Snake. Articulated with a leather strip. Wooden sections painted green and yellow, with tongue of flat leather. 24 ins. long. Japanese. Similar to those bought in Mexico today. *Gunnersbury Museum*

126   Beetle. Tin, painted green and gold with black legs and red wheels. Made in Germany, pre-1938. *Gunnersbury Museum*

127   Cow of knitted wool. A home-made stuffed toy, known in our house as 'Uncle Rajah' after one of the cows on the Ovaltine farm. 8 ins. long. 1944. *Given to Moreton Moore by Miss Laura Jane Sydenham*

128   Frog. Tin, painted green with splashes of yellow, red eyes, black legs. Jumps by clockwork. $3\frac{1}{4}$ ins. long. 1948. *Lent by Moreton Moore*

129   Folk toy. From Prague. 1948

130, 131   A bull and a tiger. Each 5 ins. long. Chinese. 1956

132   A cheap plastic pig. 1967

133   Pig. German patent, No. 208992, by Franz Steiff in Giengen, A. D. Brenz, Würrt, 1908

134   Dog. German patent, No. 199213, by the Firma C. Wilhelm Meyer in Leipzig. 1907

135   Goat. German patent, No. 13951, by Casimer Bru junior, in Paris. 1880

136   Toy bird. Wooden, with hole in the top. On a modern stand. *c.* 3 ins. long. 12th dynasty, *c.* 2000 B.C. *Fitzwilliam Museum, Cambridge*

137   Toy pigeon. Wooden. 6 ins. long. 1st dynasty. *Fitzwilliam Museum, Cambridge*

138   Hawk. Bronze, a greeny brown colour. Excavated on the Temple of Artemis, Ephesus. Greek. 600 B.C. *British Museum*

139   Tomb pottery. T'ang dynasty. $5\frac{1}{4}$ ins. high. A.D. 618–907

140   Three clay birds with feathers added. Prague

141   Swan. Solid lead. $1\frac{1}{2}$ ins. long. With green curved rushes of lead, $1\frac{1}{4}$ ins. high. Swan very heavy. *c.* 1949. *Lent by Moreton Moore*

142   Parrot. Clockwork, moving backwards and forwards when wound up. Goose. Clockwork, with nodding head and backwards and forwards movement

143   Bird. Yellow paper and wool, with strip wood tail, to fly on a string attached to a bamboo stick. As it swings around, the tail revolves and makes a whirling sound. These birds gradually disappeared during the war. Japanese. *c.* 1939. *Lent by R. E. M. Moore*

144   'Chirpy, the Clock work Chick.' $1\frac{3}{4}$ ins. high, $2\frac{3}{4}$ ins. long. *c.* 1949. *Lent by Moreton Moore*

145   'Little Ookpik' made to look like an Arctic owl. The originals were made of sealskin and, by mistake, the prototype had webbed feet, but these were altered later. 6 ins. high. Made by Fort Chimo Eskimos

146   Wooden bird, coloured and varnished. A traditional Russian toy, made in the U.S.S.R. 1965. *Lent by Miss Janet Boorer*

147   Noah's Ark. Carved from a solid piece of wood. Scandinavian. Early 17th century. Exhibited at the Treasures of Famous Children Exhibition. *Lent by Sir William Lawrence*

148   The ring. From which slices are carved as in a cake

149   Plywood elephant. $2\frac{1}{2}$ ins. high. From a small ark. Five-ply wood with a picture glued to each side. *Lent by R. E. M. Moore*

150   Ark. Brown boat, red roof, fawn walls, with the animals mostly in plain colours. Early 19th century. *Aylesbury Museum*

151   Brightly painted ark. Red boat, blue roof, yellow and black decorations. 18 ins. long. Fretsaw animals, painted on thin wood and fixed to thin green stands. Japanese. Mid 20th century. *Lent by R. E. M. Moore*

152   Zoo animals. Tapir $2\frac{1}{2}$ ins.

long; Ibex $2\frac{3}{4}$ ins. high; Orang-utang $3\frac{1}{8}$ ins. high; Walrus $2\frac{3}{4}$ ins. long. Bought at Whipsnade Zoo about 1948. *Lent by Moreton Moore.* For a number of years we went to Whipsnade where he showed his birthday-cards to the tigers

153   Zoo animals. Metal. Giraffe $4\frac{1}{2}$ ins. high. Gate $3\frac{1}{2}$ ins. high. Made by Britains Ltd, England. The fence and arch entrance made by F. G. Taylor, England, F.G.T. standing 'For Good Toys'. *c.* 1950. *Lent by Moreton Moore*

154   A homestead. Consisting of a pottery sheep-pen with animals. Speckly green fawn colour. Han period. 200 B.C. *British Museum.*

155   Back views of figures on colour plate, facing page 192. Each 3 cms. high from head to foot, i.e. the Nuremberg scale. *Lent by Miss Janet Dunbar*

156   Tree. Lead, painted green with brown trunk. 3 ins. high. *Lent by R. E. M. Moore*

157   Farm figures. Wooden, painted. Made by Frau Emmy Zweybrück's pupils at a school in Vienna. 1926

158   Dog. Jointed wood, painted white, with white fabric attached; brown eyes, black nose, red mouth with flat white teeth. Dog 7 ins. long. The tub painted primrose and blue. This dog is part of a toy circus, made by C. Schoenhut, U.S.A. in 1903, but not invented by him

159   Farm animals of lead with goose girl in white apron. 2 ins. high. White geese, yellow beaks and legs; hen with red comb; green stands. All very solid and heavy. *c.* 1949. *Lent by Moreton Moore*

160   Rabbit-hutch. Lead, painted green and cream, with two white rabbits and coloured carrots, all lead. *c.* 1 in. high. Made by F. G. Taylor & Son, London. 1948. *Lent by Moreton Moore*

161   Horseman. Terracotta, with

horse. *c.* $3\frac{1}{2}$ ins. high. From Cyprus. 450 B.C. *From Mr Butcher's museum at his farm at Sturt Hill, Shipton Gorge, Dorset*

162   Horse and rider. Greek

163   Horse and rider. Pale green with ochre-coloured legs. $1\frac{1}{4}$ ins. high. Sung dynasty, A.D. 960–1279. *British Museum*

164   Horse and rider. Lead. *c.* 2 ins. high. Roman period. *British Museum*

165   Little white horse, with greenish dapple and scarlet saddle. From a picture by Boilly, 1761–1845. *From the Royal Academy Winter Exhibition, 1954*

166   Wooden horse on wheels

167   Horse with 'barrel' body. Red horse, grey saddle, yellow stand with scarlet rim, yellow wheels with red spokes. From a picture by Zoffany, 1734–1810. *From the Royal Academy Winter Exhibition, 1954*

168   Horse on wooden stand. The white horse is covered with real skin with slight patches of brown, black wooden hooves, brown harness. 13 ins. high. Possibly before 1860. *Folk Museum, Cambridge*

169   Horse on stand. 10 ins. high. French. 1780

170   Horse with barrel body. Austrian

171   Edwardian boy with wooden horse

172   Horse of painted wood, piebald. Man with red coat, yellow trousers, purple rug. Erz Mountains, Saxony. 19th century

173   Horse of painted wood, in flat pure colours. The tail is a whistle. Erz Mountains, Saxony. 19th century

174   Horse of painted wood, with rider representing Napoleon III. Erz Mountains, Saxony

175   Toy model of a man on a

horse. Benue River, northern Nigeria. *Horniman Museum*

176   Playing at tilting. Known as the 'cane game' when canes were used instead of lances. English. 14th century

177   A tournament game with hobby-horses. Flemish. Early 16th century. *British Museum*

178   Boy with hobby-horse. Japanese

179   Boy with lantern horse. Chinese. *c.* 1912

180   Hobby-horse. German. 1600

181   Hobby-horse. English. 1821

182   Hobby-horse. Chinese. Han dynasty. A.D. 25–221. Played on by boys of seven to 14 years of age

183   Hobby-horse with wheels. Brown head, red harness, green stand and wheels. French, the Second Empire. 1821

184   Rocking-horse. 18th century

185   Rocking-horse. By William Long of Pennsylvania, U.S.A. Cabinet-maker and carver from London. 1785

186   A Wallis playing-card from a picture set of 1788

187   ROCKING-HORSES
i   Rocking-horse. Carved and painted wood. 30 ins. high to back, rockers 5 ft. 9 ins. long. Between 1650 and 1700, with possibly the rockers of later date than the horse. The last Chapple boy died in 1730, and the harness was said to have been made in the reign of William and Mary. *Lent to Bethnal Green Museum by Lord Grantley*
ii   Rocking-horse. English. 17th century
iii   Rocking-horse. French. 18th century
iv   Rocking-horse. Danish. Early 19th century
v   Rocking-horse. U.S.A. *c.* 1800
vi   Rocking-horse. German. Early 19th century
vii   Rocking-horse. English. *c.* 1788

viii Rocking-horse. English. Late 18th century

ix Rocking-horse. English. Early 19th century

x Rocking-horse. English. 1800

xi Rocking-horse. English. 19th century

xii Rocking-horse. English. Early 20th century

xiii Cheap rocking-horse. English. *c.* 1915

xiv Rocking-horse with steel frame. English. 1961. About 20 guineas

xv Rocking-horse. Danish. 1966

188 Rocking-horse. Carved wood. Yellow eyes, red inside nostril, mouth and teeth marks, black ears, outlines and hooves. The black dappling on white has been renewed. Leather harness and wooden stand. 42 ins. nose to tail; 49 ins. height; 40 ins. height to saddle; 79 ins. knob to knob on stand. English. *Sketched at Hatfield House by kind permission of the Marquess of Salisbury*

189 Badge worn by rocking-horse at Hatfield House. The seventh Earl was created the first Marquess in 1789. The badge is leather, the two buttons are bright bronze; the heart, coronet, helmet and arrows are all of dull brown bronze.

190 Drawing from patent of William Kennedy, No. 578. English. 1861. A rocking-horse with metallic springs

191 Horse. By Brown and Eggleston, manufacturers of hobby-horses, etc. New York. N.Y. 1856

192 Horse. By Montgomery Ward. U.S.A. 1877

193 Horse. By W. A. Marqua. Cincinnati. 1880

194 'Mobo Broncho.' The weight of the child on the saddle causes the legs of the horse to contract, pressure on the stirrups shoots them forward, thus causing the horse to canter. The inventor was H. Sebel, the sculptor George

N. Morwood. Mobo Broncho's were for export and also for the home market. 1948

195 Animal on wheels. From Ur. Early Dynastic period. 2686 B.C. *British Museum*

196 Small pottery cart. From Chanhudaro

197 Bird on wheels. From Mohenjodaro

198 Toy mouse on wheels. Wooden, bored eyes. *c.* 2½ ins. long. Egyptian. New Kingdom. 1080 B.C. *Fitzwilliam Museum, Cambridge*

199 Chariot. The only original wheel has spokes suggested, blue with seven brown spokes and brown rim. 4 ins. long. Egyptian. Late New Kingdom. 1000–700 B.C. *Fitzwilliam Museum, Cambridge*

200 Rider on horse with wheels. Ochre colour with red and black markings

201 Wooden horse. Egypt. 500 B.C.

202 Clay chariot. Ochre colour with pink and brown markings. Cyprus. 550 B.C. *British Museum*

203 Man reclining on a cart. From Cyprus. 400 B.C. *Pitt Rivers Museum, Farnham, Dorset*

204 Bronze chariot, driven by a bearded Sūmerian and drawn by four wild asses. The solid wheels have studded rims, and it is the earliest known example of casting bronze by the cire perdue technique. From Tell Agrab. 200 B.C.

205 Clay cart. Painted to imitate wicker chariot drawn by two horses, one missing, the other with lower back legs missing. Wheels 6 ins. diameter with painted details. Roman. *British Museum*

206 Cart of bronze. From Crete. *c.* 200 B.C.

207 Two cocks pulling a chariot. Clay. From Benghazi. 2nd century B.C. *British Museum*

208 Horse on wheels. Red and brown marks of paint on the wood. From Akhmim. Roman period. A.D. 200. *British Museum*

209, 210 Two clay animals on wheels. From the Valley of Mexico. Pre-Columbian

211 Boys tilting at the quintain. From a manuscript. A.D. 1344. *Bodleian Library, Oxford*

212 Inset wheels on wooden toys. 19th century

213 Man riding a hobby-horse bicycle. Metal. 2¼ ins. long. A.D. 1820. *Cuming Museum, Southwark, London*

214 Man on hobby-horse bicycle. Wooden. 1839. Note horse's head

215 Pull-toy, German patent, No. 66131 by Gustav Schwabe, in Berlin. Note wheels will give up-and-down movements. 1892

216 Carriage and four. Wooden. Belgium. 1916

217 Stuffed camel. German patent, No. 66936, by F. Steiff junior in Grengen a Brenz, Wurtemburg. 1892

218 Animated frog showing a mechanism for toy animals. German patent, No. 69972, by Joh and Issmayer in Nuremberg. 1892

219 Two toys. Wooden. Made by Frau Emmy Zweybrück's pupils at a school in Vienna. 1926

220 Hay wain with horse and farmer. Painted lead. Length 7¼ ins. Farmer 2⅛ ins. high. Made by Britains, England. *c.* 1952. *Lent by Moreton Moore*

221 Wooden elephant with cart. Grey elephant, yellow wheels, cream cart with blue wheels. Cart 5½ ins. high; total length 12½ ins. English. *c.* 1948. *Lent by Guy S. M. Moore*

222 A 'Buzzy Bee'. Yellow and brown. 6 × 6 × 3½ ins. high. A Fisher Price toy. U.S.A. 1950

223 The 'Cackling Hen'. Wooden, covered with paper printed in red, yellow, grey and black. Two large red wheels, two white wheels. Red plastic comb and tail. A pull-along toy which cackles as the wheels go round. 10 ins. high, 6½ ins. long. A Fisher Price toy. U.S.A. 1959. Sign, white f on red circle, white p on blue circle. *Lent by Miss Alison Sarah Carter*

224 Pull-along tram. Made of natural colour wickerwork with paper floors, velvet-covered seats and iron wheels. *c.* 1 ft. long; 1 ft. platform to top. Probably French or Spanish. Late Victorian. *Lent to the Boston Museum, Lincolnshire, by the Pinto Collection of Wooden Bygones, now at Birmingham*

225 Wooden cab of 1915. Home-made with bought metal wheels

226 Tank, No. 14. Olive-drab colour. Metal with rubber caterpillar bands, gun rotates, tank moves along. Length 2 ins.; with guns 2¼ ins.; width 1 in. A Benbros Qualitoy. Made in England. One of the T.V. Series, in a box, 2½ ins. high; top 1½ × 1¼ ins. with picture of tank in green and red. *Lent by Moreton Moore*

227 'Genevieve'. A 1904 Darracq. Metal, with red body, yellow wheels, gold lamps, steering wheel and radiator, black wings and running-board. The wheels rotate. Length 1⅞ ins., width ⅞ in. One of Charbens Miniature Series, in a suitcase box, 2¼ × 1⅛ × 1½ ins. Made in England. A film with this car as the heroine was shown in 1953. *Lent by Moreton Moore*

228 A pedal-car in which to ride. Metal, painted fawn with red wheels. *c.* 1942. Camouflaged during the war with a mixture of mud and water. *Belonged to Richard E. M. Moore*

229 Steam-roller, with to-and-fro action. Made of brass, tin and

plastic, an interesting combination. A Tri-ang Minic Toy. Made in England. 5¼ ins. long. *c.* 1954. *Lent by Moreton Moore*

230 'Silver Cloud'. Boxed toy. A model of Yesteryear by Lesney. Pale green, black cushions and tyres, gold wheels, bonnet, lamps, headlamps silver. The wheels rotate. 3⅛ ins. long, 1⅜ ins. wide. Box 4⅜ × 2⅜ × 1½ ins. The Queen's Award for exporting in 1968 was won by this little model Rolls Royce of 1907

231 A jeep, in which to ride. Metal, olive-drab, white wheels, steering wheel, windscreen and star. A rubber dagger is behind the driver. 1969. *Lent by Master Stephen Ingle*

232 Panama railway train. 1854

233 Railway engine and tender. Tin. Gilt colour engine, black ends, black platform, green railings and tender with red inside, prussian-blue wheels with ridges, no buffers. Large wheel 1½ ins. diameter; tender 2 ins. long. Probably German. Mid 19th century. *Bethnal Green Museum*

234 Train. 1900. Similar to one in the London Museum

235 Toy engine. Pre-1910

236 'Looky Chug-Chug.' Painted scarlet with yellow lines. 14 ins. long, 5¼ ins. wide, 7 ins. high. A Fisher Price toy. U.S.A. 1950

237 'The Pioneer.' A Marx toy. 1967

238 Push-chair for a doll. Bamboo and cane. 28 ins. high, 8½ ins. across front, 12 ins. maximum at base. Four iron wheels 2¾ ins. diameter. Made about 1880 by Shrives, a local craftsman, at Peace Hill, Cambridge. *Folk Museum, Cambridge*

239 DOLL CARRIAGES
i Wagon. Wooden. U.S.A. *c.* 1870
ii Push-chair. Wooden. U.S.A.

c. 1870
iii Push-chair. Wooden with solid wooden wheels, padded arm-rests, wooden handle. Yellow lines on the paintwork. 19½ ins. from ground to top of handle. English. *c.* 1880. *From the Collection of Mrs Heather Fox*
iv Perambulator or bassinet. Note the curtains. English. *c.* 1884
v Wickerwork pram or bassinet, with wire spokes to wheels. U.S.A. 1888
vi Bassinet with wooden wheels. U.S.A. 1890
vii Mail-cart with wooden handles and basket-work seat surround. Two iron prongs. Wheels have iron rims but no tyres, 10 ins. diameter. Cart 29½ ins. long, 17 ins. high, 14 ins. wide. English. *From the Collection of Mrs Heather Fox*
viii 'Harrogate pram.' Wooden handles have two cross-bars. Victorian wickerwork, inset thin rubber tyres. Painted cream and pale blue. 31½ ins. long, 10 ins. wide, 32 ins. high from ground to top of hood. English. *From the Collection of Mrs Heather Fox*
ix Pram of wood, with 'well' for feet. English. 1890. *Bethnal Green Museum*
x Push-chair with wheels with wire spokes. English. 1908
xi Small push-chair with iron wheels, leather seat and back, such as were sold at English fairs in the early 20th century. *From Lechlade Museum, belonging to Mr Swinford*
xii 'Folding' push-chair. English *c.* 1890
xiii Pram. English. 1908
xiv Pram. U.S.A. 1910
xv 'Victoria' or bassinet. Canework with rubber tyres. English. Edwardian. 1911
xvi Pram, with inside front of hood edged with bobble fringe, 'well' for doll's feet, rubber tyres, brass fittings. *c.* 26 ins. long, 30 ins. high to the handle. English. *c.* 1890. *Formerly belonged to Mrs Heather Fox*

240 Pram. Wheels have thin rubber tyres, pram dark brown

with a kind of American-cloth hood with inside lining, and 'well' for feet. 33 ins. to top of handle; 29 ins. long. Supplied by Redgates Ltd, the largest toyshop in Sheffield. 1920. *From the Collection of Mrs Heather Fox*

241 Model boat. 2 ft. 10 ins. long. Egyptian. Middle Kingdom, 2000–1800 B.C. *City Museum, Bristol*

242 Boat from a leaf, with coconut husk hull. 7 ins. long. Trobriand Islands. *British Museum*

243 Warship of wood. *c.* 14 ins. high. Neuchâtel. End of 18th century. *National Museum, Zürich*

244 An atmospherical boat with section. Tissandier

245 Small boat. 12 ins. long. U.S.A. 1890

246 Pull-along boat, German patent, No. 66131 by Gustave Schwabe, in Berlin. The wheels give an up-and-down motion. 1892

247 Model of the *Queen Mary*. Metal, three red funnels topped with black, two rollers underneath. $6\frac{3}{4}$ ins. long. Does not float. A Cunard White Star Liner by Dinky Toys, England. 1934–35. One of a few reissued during the war. *Lent by R. E. M. Moore*

248 A Greek child with a dart

249 Trobriand dart with two feathers, and Trobriand bow. 15 ins. long. *British Museum*

250 Boy with bow and arrow. From an engraving by Chodowiecki. 18th century

251 Toy boomerang. Australian

252 Boys with windmills. From medieval manuscripts

253 Windmill. 16th century

254 Windmill. French. 16th century

255 Windmill with bladder attached. Dutch. 17th century

256 Small French windmill. 9 ins. high. 1890

257 Fugelman. Carved wood. $9\frac{3}{4}$ ins. high. From the Black Forest. The figure rotates and the arms go up and down with the wind, sometimes these are used as bird-scarers. German. 19th century

258 'Oskar.' Metal policeman rotates on little spike through a hole in stand, to control traffic. Blue uniform, painted face, white gloves, silver buckle and badge, black and white stand. $7\frac{1}{4}$ ins. high with hand up. Made in Italy. 1955. *Lent by Moreton Moore*

259 Toy parachute. 18th century. These were popular in 1875

260 An early kite. English. Drawing adapted from a wood engraving in the *Mysteries and Nature of Art*, by John Bate, 1635

261 Kite-flying in China. 19th century

262 Kite-flying in Korea. 20th century

263 Butterfly kite with watered paper effect, each end is turned up slightly. *c.* 12 ins. across. Chinese. Early 20th century. *Pitt Rivers Museum, Oxford*

264 The Aerial Screw Propeller. From Joseph Myers's *The Educational Uses of Toys*, 1854

265 Flying model. By Penaud. The first model aircraft to be driven by elastic. France. 1874

266 'Stick' model, with hollow spar fuselage, made from very thin veneer. These followed the original stick models. English

267 Tractor model. A popular type with single surface wings covered with oiled silk. English

268 Grimmer model 'A' frame. Made by Robert P. Grimmer. Kits and individual parts were also supplied by the firm of Mann and Grimmer. English

269 Frog aeroplane. Designed by J. N. Manson. English

270 Gaming pieces. From an Israelite city. 12th century. Pyramidal dice were also found in the royal tombs at Ur, *c.* 3000 B.C.

271 Bone dice. $\frac{7}{8}$ in. and $1\frac{3}{4}$ ins. long. Indian

272 'Dominoes.' 3 ins. long. Choroti

273 Nine ivory pieces. From the Eskimos of Alaska. They could be dice, gaming pieces, or merely ornaments. *Horniman Museum* and *British Museum*

274 Stone die. From the Indus Valley

275 Wooden die marked with clay. 4 ins. wide. 2000 B.C. *Fitzwilliam Museum, Cambridge*

276 Ivory die. 2000 B.C. *Fitzwilliam Museum, Cambridge*

277 Two dice. 1900 B.C.

278 Die. 1900 B.C.

279 Ivory die

280 Terracotta die. Lydia. 9th–8th century B.C.

281 Ivory counter. Four-sided. 2 ins. long. 8th–7th century B.C. *Fitzwilliam Museum, Cambridge*

282 Long ivory die. From Akhmim. Roman period. After 30 B.C. This is the kind of die which Jesus may have seen used in high places.

283 Die. From Ochyrynichus, A.D. 100–300. This is very interesting for this was the place where the little Roman rag doll was found. *Truro Museum*

284 Die. Made of steatite, blackish in colour. Greek or Roman. *British Museum*

285 Three bone or ivory dice. Regularly marked on six sides so that the sum of any two opposite one another, adds up to seven. The 'ones' are larger and deeper, and the 'ones' and 'fours' are painted red. Chinese

286 Two counters or four-sided

dice. Lightwood or ivory colour. 2 ins. long. Chinese. *Pitt Rivers Museum, Farnham Royal, Dorset*

287 Long die, showing the four sides

288 Three Greek and Roman dice. i Transparent, made of rock-crystal; ii Pale green, made of bone; iii Reddish colour, made of marble. *British Museum*

289 Roman die in the shape of a figure. *British Museum*

290 Roman die. Made of bone. A.D. 43–410

291 Medieval die. From an Israelite city

292 Die. From Temestar, on the Danube, Germany. *Pitt Rivers Museum, Farnham Royal, Dorset*

293 Dice box with bone die. From London Wall. Medieval. *Guildhall Museum, London*

294 Medieval die. Bone. From Little Bell Alley. *Guildhall Museum, London*

295 Playing with dice, on a summer evening at Smithfield. A.D. 1300

296 Gambling or divining dice. White with pink markings. Indian. *Pitt Rivers Museum, Oxford*

297 COUNTERS
i Pottery counters. Prehistoric. *Winchester Museum*
ii Romano-British counters. Two clay pellets used in a game
iii Five roundels used in a game. *Salisbury Museum*
iv Three counters. *Truro Museum*
v Bone counter. *Dorchester Museum, Dorset*

298 Three Roman tallies. Malest, meaning 'Bad Luck', made of ivory; Victor, for the winner, also of ivory; Nvgator, meaning 'Trifler', made of bone. *British Museum*

299 Bone counters in a little box. Early 19th century. *Salisbury Museum*

300 Teetotum, with numbers up to 12. Early 18th century. *Salisbury Museum*

301 Teetotum or trendle. Silver. Used for games during Chanucah. Probably German. 18th century. *Given by Mr B. Elkin of Johannesburg to the Jewish Museum, Bloomsbury, London*

302 Teetotum or dicing top, with letters. 1814. *Shaftesbury Museum, Dorset*

303 Teetotum with numerals. Ivory. 1814. *Hitchin Museum, Hertfordshire*

304 Teetotum (*Nsiko*). Made from a disc of an ochre-coloured gourd on a wooden peg. 4 ins. across. Wapokomo tribe, Zanzibar. *British Museum*

305 Dobeli spinning-top (*pia*). *British Museum*

306 Teetotum made from wild fruit. Swahili. *British Museum*

307 Top. From Florida. *British Museum*

308 Lottery set. Consisting of a bag of green silk, an ivory and wooden top, an ivory stick and black wooden ticket-holders. Tickets of green paper. Stand 4 ins. diameter. Top and stand *c.* 5 ins. high.

309 Stick with holder. 5 ins. long. The numbers are rolled up and put inside the black ticket-holders. Italian. Second half of 18th century. *Bethnal Green Museum*

310 'Gadget for Lotteries' used in 'better' homes about 1860 in Denmark. The metal thread which keeps the receiver in place is pulled away and when turned a number falls down and stays (so well are they made) in the receiver, which turns round itself also. The balls are of wood with red numbers. *From the Collection of Mrs Estrid Faurholt*

311 Game in the form of a coiled snake. 1 in. thick, about 16 ins.

diameter, raised sections. Stands on an alabaster base, half the length across. Egyptian. Third dynasty or earlier, i.e. before 2423 B.C. *Fitzwilliam Museum, Cambridge*

312 Board game, with onlookers. From a fresco. Egyptian

313 The game of senet. Egyptian

314 The game of tau or robbers. Egyptian

315 Game of the bowl. Egyptian

316 Detail showing complete circles with dice

317 'Hunn.' From Woodperry, Oxfordshire. From Murray's book *Games other than Chess*

318 Probably a Saxon Hnefatafl piece, similar to 'hunns' found at Woodperry in Oxfordshire. Made of bone, this one was found at Tokenhouse Yard, London. *Guildhall Museum, London*

319 Crib board. Carved in bone in the form of a seal. Ivory colour with black markings. *c.* 6 ins. long. Made in Alaska. *British Museum*

320 Ivory gaming piece with dog-head. 2 ins. long. Used on a board shaped like a table with holes and with a drawer below to hold the pieces. The game is of hounds chasing jackals. Egyptian. New Kingdom, 1250 B.C. *British Museum*

321 A pachisi board, the national game of India

322 A ludo board. *c.* 1896

323 Pope Joan board. Painted red, black, gold, with blue on the cards. The top lifts off. 11½ ins. diameter. *St Albans City Museum*

324 Squail counters. Wood painted in various colours and patterns. 2½ ins. diameter. Indian. 19th century. *Bethnal Green Museum, London*

325 The game of squails, a form of shove-ha'penny. 16 painted wood counters in mahogany box with lead weight and swoggle.

Counters 2 ins. diameter. Painted in bright pure colours. German. *c.* 1845. *Bethnal Green Museum, London*

326   Wooden solitaire board with pegs

327   Solitaire board. Rosewood with ivory inlay. 12 ins. long; pegs $\frac{3}{4}$ in. high. English. Mid 19th century. *Bethnal Green Museum, London*

328   Modern solitaire board. Wood or plastic with glass marbles. 1967

329   Two squares and a snake from a snakes and ladders game with morals. Good deeds take one up the ladder, evil deeds go down the snake. *Lent by Miss Ruth Wainwright*

330   Board game with pieces of painted wood, some blue helmets, some black and red. *From the Victoria and Albert Museum Exhibition, 1967*

331   Hoop-la. Cardboard 'board' with holes, paper 'hats'. Early 20th century. The hats are flipped into the holes by hitting the board

332   Two gaming pieces of blue porcelain, one supposed to represent a cat. 1491 B.C. *British Museum*

333   Three gaming pieces. The tall one about 1 in. high. *c.* 2000 B.C. *Fitzwilliam Museum, Cambridge*

334   Gaming-piece. Cerulean-blue colour. Egyptian. *Pitt Rivers Museum, Oxford*

335   CHESS PIECES
i   Pattern on chess piece. Whalebone. English. *Dorchester Museum, Dorset*
ii   'Bishop.' Whalebone. 5 ins. high. Found at the Manor House, Witchampton. English. 10th century. *Dorchester Museum, Dorset*
iii   Chessman. Walrus ivory. Found in Ivy Street, Salisbury. English. Late 12th century. *Salisbury Museum*

iv   Chessman. Bone. 3 ins. high. From Falcon Square. English. 12th–13th century. *Guildhall Museum, London*
v   Chessman. Bone. English. 12th–13th century. *Salisbury Museum*
vi   Chessman. Walrus ivory. 4 ins. high. One of 67 pieces. Isle of Lewis. 12th century. *British Museum*
vii   Chessman. Note the stirrups. Merovingian. A.D. 486–751. *Salisbury Museum*
viii   *a.* Chessman. Bone. From Falcon Square. English. 12th–13th century. *Guildhall Museum, London.* *b.* Pattern on the back of a 'bishop'. *Dorchester Museum, Dorset*
c. Chessman. Bone. From Falcon Square, London. English. *Guildhall Museum, London*
ix   Chessman. Carved ivory. Roman period. France
x   Chessman. Carved ivory. France. 14th century

336   Draughtsman. Made from a horse's tooth. Anglo-Saxon. *British Museum*

337   Bone piece. 2 ins. diameter. English. Christian-Saxon period, A.D. 650–1066. *Winchester Museum*

338   Ivory piece. Probably used in a game representing backgammon. Found at Poultry. Early medieval. *Guildhall Museum, London*

339   Bone piece. Same as previous one

340   Piece or counter. $\frac{1}{4}$ in. thick. 12th century. *Guildhall Museum, London*

341   Piece. Medieval. *Glastonbury Museum*

342   Chessman. Walrus ivory. Found on the Isle of Lewis. Probably Scandinavian. 12th century. *British Museum*

343   Board with players. English. 14th century

344   Chess pieces at the time of Caxton. English

345   Set of miniature chessmen. Orange and white pieces in circular red box. *c.* 2 ins. across. From the Valley of Mexico. *c.* A.D. 1825. *Pitt Rivers Museum, Oxford*

346   Wooden pieces. Light brown and blackish, on a board made of leather with reddish and ochre squares. Used by the Hausa Emigrates. *British Museum*

347   Two girls playing knuckle-bones. Terracotta. 8 ins. high. South Italian Greek. *c.* 300 B.C. *British Museum*

348   Counter. Showing the game of Mora, played with the fingers. Italian

349   The game of atep. Played with the fingers. In the painting, the checks show it is a game of pleasure, the surrounding purse that there is a money prize. Egyptian

350   Domino box. Carved bone with sliding lid. 6$\frac{3}{4}$ ins. long, including handle. Made by French prisoners-of-war between 1797 and 1815, at Norman Cross near Peterborough, and given to Peterborough Museum by the grandson of Captain Lincoln Bàrker, last Governor of Norman Cross Barracks in 1816. *Peterborough Museum*

351   Spillikins. Carved bone, set into a crib board about 6 ins. long on four bone wheels. Some have coloured tops, the flag being pale blue, white, pale blue. Made by French prisoners-of-war, the same as the domino box. *Peterborough Museum*

352   Spillikins. Ivory, with red Roman numbers. *c.* 4 ins. long. *St Albans City Museum*

353   A few Spillikins. Ivory. From a set of 40 including 'blanks' and two hooks. *c.* 4$\frac{1}{4}$ ins. long. Late 19th or early 20th century. *Lent by Miss Ruth Wainwright*

354   Rod and hoop game. From an Egyptian fresco

355 Hoops. From an early Flemish calendar, showing the month of February. 16th century. *British Museum*

356 Hoop. Made from a cane bound with string. Choroti

357 Hula hoops. One for beauty, one for fun. England. 1958

358 Yo-yo. Known as a 'bandalore', 'quiz', or the 'Prince of Wales toy'. Bought at Peckham Fair in 1821. c. 2¾ ins. diameter. *Cuming Museum, Southwark, London*

359 Yo-yo. Wooden. 2¾ ins. diameter. 19th century

360 Eleyo yo-yo with box. Made of plastic, coloured half in red, half in blue, containing a battery, which illuminates the yo-yo as it goes up and down on the string. About 2½ ins. diameter. Made in Japan and sold in the U.S.A. but not in Britain. 1967. *Lent by Master Robin Nately*

361 Diabolo set. English. 1812

362 Diabolo. 'The Flying Cone'. Chinese. Sometimes known as 'The Devil on Two Sticks'

363 'Le Diable'. 19th century, c. 1820. French

364 'Cup and Ball'. Primitive, made of plaited cane. c. 28 ins. long. From Hawaii, here known as the 'ring and ball' game. *British Museum*

365 Cup and ball. From Japan

366 A beautiful cup and ball. Turned and engraved ivory. From the Royal Nursery of France. Cream colour. Height 7 ins. Engraved on it are the royal arms of France, and *Menus plaisirs du roi Versailles, 1779*, with reference to Maria Thérèse Charlotte (born December 1778), eldest child of Louis XVI and Marie-Antoinette. *Victoria and Albert Museum, London*

367 Cup and ball. Boxwood, with a transfer decoration. Handle 8 ins. long. c. 1850. *Bedford Museum*

368 BILBOQUET or CUP AND BALL
i Black lacquer cup with ball of knitted wool. *St Albans City Museum*
ii Spike and ball. Ivory. 7 ins. long
iii Spike. Wood, ornamented with ivory dots and with feather shuttlecock, to be caught on the spike. *St Albans City Museum*
iv Cup and ball. Turned wood. 19th century. *Salisbury Museum*
v Cup and ball. Rice paper. Very light to hold, pale fawn and brown with pinkish stitches. 9 ins. long. Japanese. *Pitt Rivers Museum, Oxford*

369 Battledores and shuttlecocks. From an early manuscript. Harleian

370 Battledore. Wooden handle, stretched parchment bat, surrounded by wood covered with dark red leather, embossed with gold, with a small label marked 'Warranted Best Vellum'. 15 ins. long. c. 1750. *Leathercraft Museum, London*

371 Ping Pong bat. Wooden handle edged with red leather, tooled with gold, and the trade name 'Ping Pong' stamped on it. Made in the U.S.A. 'The new table game of Ping Pong or Gossima' is on the box, and the set in Bethnal Green is marked 'J. Jaques & Son Ltd and Hamleys Ltd'. c. 1900. *Bethnal Green Museum, London*

372 Battledore and shuttlecock. Japanese

373 Bat of scarlet plastic, and white plastic shuttlecock. Both handle and shuttlecock are hollow with 'strings' of bat slightly curved. British patent, Nos. 670147, 686059, 686403. 1968. *Lent by Master Christopher Prior*

374 Boy on stilts. Japanese. Known in Japan as 'Bamboo horses'

375 Battledore and doll combined. Wooden. English. 18th century

376 Cut-out picture by Lothar Meggendorfer. From *Always Jolly*, a movable toy book, published in 1891, by H. Grevel & Co., 33 King Street, Covent Garden, London W.C. and printed in Germany. This copy in the Victoria and Albert Museum Library is inscribed 'to dear Guy from his Godmother, Christmas 1892', and appears to be coloured by hand

377 Abacus, with wooden beads on a dozen wires. Twelve beads in each row, coloured in groups of threes, blue, red, yellow and white, backed by a piece of wood nearly half-way up. 16 ins. high, 17 ins. wide. *Folk Museum, Cambridge*

378 Cash register. A Casdon Luxury Toy. 1967

379 Building bricks, 'The New Alphabet Game'. Wedge-shaped bricks for building a circular cottage. Yellow walls with orange-coloured stand and roof, black windows and letters, all of wood. English. Mid 19th century. *Victoria and Albert Museum Exhibition, 1967*

380 Crandall's ABC Building Slabs. Each wooden slab is about 2 ins. high, 1 in. wide, ⅛ in. thick, painted with a black letter. U.S.A. 1867. *Bethnal Green Museum, London*

The cover of the original box for Crandall's ABC Building Slabs, brown, fawn and black. 6 ins. square. H. Jewitt marketed these in England, and William Rose was the negotiator, the R in the two entwined triangles standing for Rose. U.S.A. 1867. *Bethnal Green Museum, London*

381 Building bricks. Imitation stone, coloured fawn, dull red and dull blue. Wooden box 12 × 9 × 9 ins. One of Dr Richter's 'Anchor' boxes. Directions add 'Beware of Quicklime Imitations'. German. 1888. *Bedford Museum*

382 A box of Lott's Bricks, set No. 2. Stone colour bricks red or

blue windows and doors. Strawboard roof, covered with red painted paper. Squares $1 \times 1 \times \frac{1}{2}$ ins. Box $9\frac{1}{2}$ ins. $\times$ $10\frac{1}{2}$ ins. Cottage built with Lott's Bricks, No. 2 set. The same scale as an O gauge railway. *Given by A. E. D. Lott, Esq.*

383 Building bricks. Bakelite, strong plastic in pale colours. A Hilary Page design, the raised circles interlock the cubes. Bricks $1\frac{1}{4}$ ins. wide. English. 1939. *Belonging to R. E. M. Moore*

384 Building bricks. Cardboard. Nine cardboard cubes in cardboard box blue, yellow, orange and red. 2 in. cubes. 'Empire ABC building bricks'. Made in England. 1944–45. *Lent by Moreton Moore*

385 Apple tree. Green plastic with red berries and brown twigs. One of Britain's 'Make-up Models', suitable for use with most types of models including 'OO' railway layouts and Britains Ltd Garden, Farm and Zoo models. 5 ins. high. Cat. No. 1801. Made in England. Other trees include a silver birch, beech and Scots pine. 1967

386 Playing-card used during the French Revolution. Made in France. 1792

387 Misfit cards in sliding box, known as 'Changeable Gentlemen'. Aquatints coloured by hand. Cards $2\frac{1}{4}$ ins. $\times$ $3\frac{1}{2}$ ins., in a wooden box. Published by R. Ackermann. 1819. *Geffrye Museum, London.* Also a set in *Bethnal Green Museum, London*

388 'Building Cards and Pretty Pictures.' Lithographs. English. Mid 19th century. *Bethnal Green Museum, London*

389 Picture card. From a pack on Proverbs, where each word appears on a separate card, each proverb having one picture. *St Albans City Museum*

390 Two cards from the game of 'Panko', or 'Votes for women'.

$3\frac{1}{2}$ ins. $\times$ $2\frac{3}{8}$ ins. 'The Great Card Game, Suffragists v. Anti-Suffragists, Pictures by E. T. Reed of *Punch*.' Published by Peter Gurney Ltd, 2 Breams Buildings, London E.C. *Gunnersbury Museum*

391 'Society Misfits.' 'A peculiarly Interesting Game. Full of Hilarious Amusement.' Played with 12 counters. Cards $3\frac{5}{8}$ ins. $\times$ $2\frac{5}{8}$ ins. Also 'Golly Misfits.' 24 sets of 3 in each pack, i.e. 72 cards each. C. W. Faulkner & Co., London. Early 20th century. *Lent by Miss Ruth Wainwright*

392 Card Houses. 'Upon a novel plan, Alphabetical and Zoological. Suitable for children, Simple and Secure. Beautifully illustrated in Oil Colour.' 'J. Wisbey & Co., London', marked on box. 'J. W. S. & S. Bavaria', marked on instructions, with sign. Cards $2\frac{3}{8}$ ins. $\times$ $3\frac{7}{8}$ ins., printed by chromo-litho. *Lent by Miss Ruth Wainwright*

393 Tangram. A modern version of the ancient Chinese puzzle of seven pieces which were carved of ivory in lace patterns. Made in ivory coloured plastic by Palitoy, England. Box 2 ins. square. c. 1948. *Lent by R. E. M. Moore*

394 Highly polished wooden pear, forming a solid block of wood which takes to pieces. 3 ins. high. Japanese. 1923

395 Unpolished wooden puzzle. Strips fitting one into another forming an 'open' cube with a small red ball in the centre. $2\frac{1}{2}$ ins. across; ball $\frac{7}{8}$ in. diameter. Japanese. 1960

396 Scissors toy. Painted wood. Black hats, pink cheeks, pale mauve coats, red and black drum, natural coloured wood stand. 6 ins. high. *From the Lovatt Fraser Collection, by permission of Mrs Lovatt Fraser*

397 Scissors toy. Bohemian. Mentioned as 'Lazy Tongs' by Mrs Ewing

398 Scissors toy with seven soldiers. Saxony

399
i Man on Horse, registered by Henry Jewitt. No. 301891 in the Design Registry. English. Probably the original drawing used for one of Crandall's famous toys
ii Mechanical Rider, by W. Ziegler of Munich, Bavaria. German patent, No. 9800. 1879
iii Man Balancing on a Wheel. No. 301094 in the Design Registry. English
iv Acrobat. German patent, No. 59701, by Ernst Paul Lehmann of Brandenburg. 1891
v Clown. German patent, No. 69577, by the Firma Joh. Friedr. Wallmann & Co., Berlin. 1892
vi 'A New and Improved Toy' registered by Henry Jewitt. Patent No. 1866. His sign was registered in England in 1870. This patent was a communication from William M. Rose of New York

400
vii The same idea as the Man Balancing on a Wheel (iii above)
viii Mechanical monkey. German patent, No. 69040, by William Pitt Shattuck in Minneapolis, Minnesota, U.S.A. 1892
ix 'Wartime toy.' Wood and string. c. 1945. This is a version of the old traditional toy of Bohemia. *Lent by Moreton Moore*

401, 402 Two Merry Jacks. Carved in wood by peasants of the Erz mountains. Here a squirrel and a man. Traditional. c. 1880

403 Merry Jack. Carved wood, painted. Brown face, gold collar, olive-green coat, Venetian-red trousers. Monkey $4\frac{1}{2}$ ins. high, total height 15 ins. *Peterborough Museum*

404 Street vendor. Yee. Chinese. c. 1912

405 Blow toy. Paper, with feather. Bought at fairs

406 Street Pennyworths. Mostly of tin. 1915. Collected by Ernest

King. Sketched at Lancaster House. *London Museum*

407 'Jack-in-a-box'. Seems to be a poodle in a cardboard container for jam, perhaps used as a surprise. 4½ ins. high. Made in Germany. *Pollock's Toy Museum, Scala Street, London*

408 Street toys. Nodding heads and rubber toys to blow up. Sketched on the steps of St Martin-in-the-Fields, London. 1928

409 Toy broom. Made of wire, ribbon and cork. *c.* 6 ins. long. Hung on the wall of a home for good luck in south London. *Cuming Museum, Southwark, London*

410 Teddy bear. 8 ins. high. Called 'Little Tommy Titmouse', it looks more like a mouse than a bear. 1908. *Victoria and Albert Museum Exhibition, 1967*

411 Teddy Bear. Yellow bear with royal-blue ribbon bow and red label. 12 ins. high. A Chad Valley washable toy. Bear made of top-quality British nylon

412 Golliwog trade mark. Advertising Robertson's Golden Shred marmalade. Since the 1920s

413 'Wembley Willie.' Stuffed toy, flesh-colour-painted features, purple hat with black band, felt purple suit, brown shoes, white waistcoat and white spats. Height 14 ins. One of Dean's British rag dolls to commemorate the Wembley Exhibition held in 1924 and 1925. Patented in U.K., Germany and France. 1925. *Lent by Mrs Evelyn Harvey*

414 'Cheerful Desmond.' A soft stuffed dog. 10 ins. high. *Lent by Mrs George Boorer*

415 'Funnybun.' 4 ft. high. Shown at a trade fair. 1957

416 Easter eggs. The egg is coloured and the pattern scratched away, or the pattern may be drawn in wax, the egg dyed, and the wax washed off, leaving the

light pattern. From Yugoslavia

417 Nest of woven baskets. In two colours, fawn and brown. From a 4 ins. wide basket to one of ¾ in. wide. Madagascar. *British Museum*

418 Money-box. Made of earthenware. Found in the Catacombs. *c.* 4 ins. high

419 Back views of pottery banks, showing slots for money. *Victoria and Albert Museum, London* Colour plate facing page 167

420 Model of the first Post Office letter-box erected in London in 1855, showing the distance from the main Post Office

421 Iron bank. In the form of a house, decorated with brass. 7 ins. high, 5 ins. wide. *c.* 1860. *Folk Museum, Cambridge*

422 Money-boxes of pottery. *c.* 3 ins. high. Made in Peru. 1930

423 Tilting toy. Stiff paper or cardboard painted red. 'Man with Fan.' Chinese

424 Tilting toy. Made to rise quickly for luck. Japanese

425 Tilting toy. Chinese. 1956

426 Tilting toy. To represent a monk. Spanish

427 Tilting toy. Swedish

428 Tilting toy. U.S.A.

429 Tilting toy. French

430 Detail of Oriental acrobat. 1762. See coloured plate, facing page 170

431 'Pantins Automatiques.' Described by Tissandier, showing side view and front view. France. 1850

432 Three acrobats. 'Les pantins de sureau de l'électrophore d'ébonite', by M. J. Pfeiffer, described by Tissandier. France. 1885

433 See-saw. Lord Salisbury and Mr Gladstone on the political see-saw. English. 1860

434 Man walking down a plank. English, Patent No. 61. by Marcus Brown Westhead, being a communication from James Noe Crow of Motthaven, New York, U.S.A. in 1864

435 Balancing figure by Georges Carette & Co. in Nuremberg. German patent, No. 53643. 1890

436 Balancing figure by Karl Standfuss in Deuben, Dresden. German patent, No. 238219. 1910

437 'The Hilly Billy drinking Ducks', Dilly and Dally. Each bird contains a volatile liquid, which evaporates under room temperature. A Magnetex product. 1948

438 PRIMITIVE WHISTLES
i Whistle. Pottery, in the shape of an alligator. *c.* 10 ins. long. Chiriqui. Prehistoric
ii Whistle. Pottery, in the shape of a sheep. San Salvador. *Horniman Museum*
iii Whistle. Pottery, in the shape of a sheep. San Salvador. Prehistoric
iv Whistle. Decorated bone, 11 ins. long. Chiriquano
v Whistle. Pottery, in the shape of a bird. Costa Rica. Prehistoric

439 Two bird whistles. From Chanhudaro, by the Indus. 2700 B.C. *British Museum*

440 Whistle. Pottery. Medieval. *Winchester Museum*

441 Whistle. Painted wood. Folk toy from India

442 Bird whistle. English patent. 1879

443 Water whistle. In the shape of a bird. Plastic, in all colours, the yellow being the prettiest. Water is put inside, the whistle blown into and a bird noise is made, a kind of warble or twitter. 4 ins. long. Made in England. *c.* 1950. *Lent by G. S. M. Moore*

444 PAINTED WHISTLES
i Whistle. White with coloured stripes of red, green, red, maroon. North Portugal, *c.* 1950. *Horniman Museum*

ii Whistle. Painted pinewood, primrose colour with red and viridian decorations. North Portugal, *c.* 1950. *Horniman Museum*

iii Cuckoo whistle. In the shape of a fish. Primrose with red and viridian decorations. North Portugal, *c.* 1950. *Horniman Museum*

iv Whistle. Glazed pottery, yellow and pinkish, with green and indigo markings, blue cap. North Portugal, *c.* 1950. *Horniman Museum*

v Ocarina flute. Magenta with scarlet and prussian-blue markings. An ocarina is a small musical instrument made of baked clay with finger-holes and mouthpiece, which gives out a low and flute-like note. It is sometimes in the form of a bird or the head of a goose. Italian. *Horniman Museum*

vi A whistling bird. Bright yellow with green and red wings. *Pitt Rivers Museum, Oxford*

445 Cuckoo whistle. Carved wood. 7¼ ins. long. By giving two blows through the whistle and by lifting up and down, the two notes of the cuckoo are realistically imitated. From Montreux, Switzerland. *Belonged to Mrs Fred Rowe*

446 Drum. Lizard skin. From the Trobriand Islands. The lizard skin membrane is stretched across the top. *British Museum*

447 A Penny toy whistle. From the Ernest King collection. 1915. *London Museum*

448
i Buzz toy. Ivory with sinew cord. Eskimo. *British Museum*
ii Buzz toy. Eskimo (after Culin)
iii Mou mou. Rio Parapite
iv Bun bun. Bamboo. 2½ ins. long. Japanese

449 Bull roarer. Made of wood, painted white with a green snake with black outline. A hole at the tail end. 8 ins. long. Pueblo Indian. *British Museum*

450 Musical toy. Tissandier. 'Coupe d'un bijou électrique et de la pile qui le met en mouvement'

451 Under view of bristle figure, showing legs. See colour plate facing page 177

452 A musical sewing party. The animal reading the book was originally the conductor. The animals are white, the cloth and stool tops crimson, the box edges vermilion, multi-coloured varnished paper and blue flowers on front of box. Varnished wooden legs to four stools and chair and table with wires underneath passing down through box lid. The animals may be Pomeranians, as Queen Victoria patronised the Fancy Pom about 1888.

A similar animal stands atop a musical-box in the Edinburgh Museum of Childhood and is labelled 'Jura-made French automaton' with musical-box 1880.

Jura is a province between France and Switzerland. The owner of the 'sewing party', Miss Ursula Radford, puts the date about 1890, and says that she always understood that it was of German make

453 Nursery clock. Three automatic figures play a tune when the hour strikes. Case painted cream with pink roses and green foliage. Width of case 12 ins., height 19 ins. *St Albans City Museum*

454 Four figures at a forge. An automatic toy. 16th century. From *Une encyclopédie allemande du XVI siècle*

455 Squirrel in a cage. German patent, No. 88120, by William Jerome Wilcox in Cornwall, Connecticut, U.S.A. 1895

456 Clockwork toy. Black tin figure with box-like body and plaster head. Dressed in a black cotton gown with white

neckbands, piece of white cotton on head, black and white check trousers. Red box with yellow stencil pattern, top covered with blue velvet. The circle denotes some object which is missing. The figure holds a book in his hand, and moves forwards and downwards. Figure 6¼ ins. high. Top box 3¼ ins. high. Bottom box 3 ins. high. The toy probably made by the Automatic Toy Works, New York, U.S.A. in 1875, who produced a similar Negro preacher at this time. *St Albans City Museum*

457 Peepshow. 'The Seige of Gibraltar' (note spelling). 1728

458 The Thaumatrope. The disc is rotated rapidly by means of threads and the bird then appears to be inside the cage. Introduced in 1826, generally attributed to Dr J. A. Paris. The bird is coloured in pale colours. *Science Museum, South Kensington, London*

459 Part of a paper strip to fit inside the Zoetrope, below the slots. Pale mauve ball, black imp with green eyes. Strip 4 ins. high. The Zoetrope in Bethnal Green is marked Milton Bradley, Springfield, Massachusetts, U.S.A. 1867

460 The Zoetrope. Black tin with white paper strip with coloured pictures. *c.* 1860. *Folk Museum, Cambridge, and many others including the Science Museum, South Kensington, London, Bethnal Green Museum, London and Pollock's Toy Museum, Scala Street, London*

461 Magic lantern. Lit by a candle. Black tin. Total height 6 ins. *Folk Museum, Cambridge*

462 Magic lantern. Burning oil. Glass top, orange colour lamp, brass fittings, black tin screen. Total height 6 ins. *Folk Museum, Cambridge*

463 Boy with a bow and arrow. From an early 14th-century manuscript

464   Figure disguised as a stag. 14th-century manuscript. *Bodleian Library, Oxford*

465   The Hobnob, of the Merchants Tailors of Salisbury. *Salisbury Museum*

466   Toy jousting shield. With aperture for lance, and engraved with the cross of St George. 15th century

467, 468   Toy gun. 3 ins. long. 17th-century. Toy wheel-lock pistol. *c.* 4 ins. long. 1607. Found at Clarendon. *Salisbury Museum*

469   Boys playing soldiers. From an 18th-century engraving by Chodowiecki

470   Bean- or pea-shooter. Choroti

471   Outfit for a boy, by Schoenhut. U.S.A.

472   Boy dressed as 'Batman'. Outfit comprises 'Large cape, shaped cowl, plus pants with belt to fit age 3–10. In extra reinforced shimmering P.V.C. with contrasting Bat decorations.' 1966

473   Warrior with club. 3 ins. high. From an Italian tomb of the Stone Age. Bronze Age figure. *British Museum*

474   Roman soldier. Tin. A legionary of the Imperial period. Found on the Rhine. A.D. 9. *British Museum*

475   The quintain. 14th century

476   Knight. Wooden. Mid 14th century. *Guildhall Museum, London*

477   The well-known figure of Frederick the Great, by J. Hilpert. 5 ins. high. 1777. *Nürnberg Germanische Museum*

478   Lead 'flat' soldier on stand. $3\frac{1}{2}$ ins. high. Belgian. *c.* 1830. *Bethnal Green Museum, London*

479   Tin soldier. With 'gold' bugle, and 'gold' sword. Beautifully painted, natural colour face, black peaked hat with red top and black plume, blue tunic, white band and collar, red cuffs, gold epaulettes, red line on blue trousers, blue roll behind him, red rug with yellow edge, green stand. White horse. 4 cms. high. 1867. *St Albans City Museum*

480   Tin soldier. With lance and pennon, red, white and blue, lance-tip gold. Red top to black plume, black hat with peak, gold badge, red cuffs, red stripe on blue trousers, blue centre to roll. Soldier has a moustache. Black horse. Green stand. $2\frac{3}{4}$ cms. long, overall length 6 cms., 4 cms. high. *St Albans City Museum*

481   Lead foot soldier. Grey helmet, brown pack, red tunic, silver sword-stick, blue trousers, green stand. One of a set belonging to the cavalry soldier on colour plate. 4 cms. high. *St Albans City Museum*

482   R.A. Gun, No. 1201. Lead alloy, colour olive-drab. $5\frac{1}{4}$ ins. long, 2 ins. wide. Wheel $1\frac{7}{8}$ ins. diameter. Made by Britains Ltd, London. Patent No. 34218/30. 'This gun is also designed to fire a shell by an Amorce Cap. Pull back breech cover as for ordinary firing, place Amorce Cap in circular depression, insert shell and depress firing lever. Note, the gun is more powerful and realistic by this method.' *Belonging to R. E. M. Moore*

483   'Spacemen'. Coloured plastic, one colour to each figure, red, blue, pale blue, orange and green. $2\frac{1}{2}$ ins. high, including removable transparent helmet. Given away in packets of Kellogg's Corn Flakes. *c.* 1958

484   Lancer, by Fabergé. $5\frac{1}{4}$ ins. high. A captain of the 4th Harkovski Lancers bearing the mark of the workmaster Henrik Wigstrom, with lapis lazuli tunic and breeches, top-boots of black onyx. 1914–15. This figure was sold for £6,950, in March 1965

485   Chair. Made of lead. *c.* 2 ins. across, $2\frac{5}{8}$ ins. high. Roman.

A.D. 100. *British Museum*

486   Woman with rolling-pin. Working model of pinkish clay. Greek. From Rhodes. 5th century B.C. *British Museum*

487   Doll's house. Being a child's wardrobe of painted wood. 6 ft. $6\frac{1}{2}$ ins. high, i.e. 200 cms. English. 1712. *Victoria and Albert Museum, London*

488   Doll's house. Made in the U.S.A. 1744–74. *Van Cortland Museum, New York, U.S.A.*

489   Dumb-waiter. Mahogany. 12 ins. high, with set of pewter. 18th century. *Similar to one in Bethnal Green Museum, London*

490   Furniture. Made from horse chestnuts (conkers), pins, cork and green D.M.C. Height of table-top from floor, $1\frac{3}{8}$ ins., height of chairs $1\frac{1}{2}$ ins., length of sofa 2 ins., placed on a brown velvet carpet 5 × 7 ins. All home-made. *c.* 1911. D.M.C. stands for Dewhurst's Mercerised Cotton, almost unobtainable in 1968. *Lent by Mrs Muriel Green*

491   Doll's house. Made by the Jouet Belge, showing an old house in Ypres destroyed during the First World War. Dutch. 1916

492   Two vessels. 1 in. high. Iron Age. *Salisbury Museum*

493   Three Phrygian vessels. Painted. From the child's tumulus at Gordium. 500 B.C.

494   Toy tea-service. Staffordshire salt-glazed pottery. Palish greeny cream, with sap-green decorations, very thin pottery, cups with no handles. *c.* 1750. *Newbury Museum*

495, 496   Kitchen set. With cooking-stand, oil-container, stool, and various utensils all made in brass. Indian. *Lent by Mrs J. C. Bishop*

497   Doll's dinner-service. Showing how it is cast in lead, from *Lead Toy Casting* by G. F. Rhead. 1948

498   Decanter with glasses. Glass and metal, sherry colour glasses. Decanter 3 ins. high. Six glasses, tray, and decanter were inside an Easter egg from Hamleys in 1912. *Lent by Mrs Muriel Green*

499   Silver with black handle, by David Clayton. English. 1720. *Victoria and Albert Museum, London*

500   Chocolate-pot with molinet. Silver with black handle, by David Clayton. English. 1720. *Victoria and Albert Museum, London*

501   Silver teapot. English. 1730. *Victoria and Albert Museum, London*

502   Silver Pikeman. Marked F.S. From Amsterdam. Dutch. 1730. *Victoria and Albert Museum, London*

503   Silver dog and kennel, by A. van Geffe. From Amsterdam. Dutch. 1738. *Victoria and Albert Museum, London*

504   Silver chestnut-roaster. Marked B.I. From Amsterdam. Dutch. 1746 *Victoria and Albert Museum, London*

505   Silver gridiron with fish. From Haarlem. Dutch. *c.* 1750. *Victoria and Albert Museum, London*

506   Silver mousetrap and cat. Dutch. 18th century. *Victoria and Albert Museum, London*

507   Silver pan with brown wooden handle, by David Clayton. English. *Victoria and Albert Museum, London*

508   Gold table with coffee-pot, six cups and saucers with spoons. Perfect with lid opening, etc. and hinge to table, less than 1 in. high. 1800. *From the Margaret Tarrant Bequest. Victoria and Albert Museum, London*

509   Shabti box. Wooden, white box on red base, red and green lids, and red, yellow, blue, green and blackish decorations. Containing shabtis made of wood, clay or wax, which are not dolls but which could be mistaken for such. Egyptian. New Kingdom, 1250 B.C. *British Museum*

509*a*   Detail of decoration

510   Old woman sewing. Made of wood with a cord to pull which raises her head and moves her right hand to and fro. Plaster head, dressed in bonnet and red and white check neckerchief. A flowery cotton gown of clovers and apron of same material. No underclothes. She is 7 ins. high when bending over. *St Albans City Museum*

511   Oven. Metal. Complete in every detail, taps turn on, lids come off, kettle handle hinged, doors open, etc. 10 ins. wide, 14 ins. long, $6\frac{7}{8}$ ins. high, 16 ins. to funnel. Kettle $4\frac{3}{4}$ ins. high, $3\frac{1}{4}$ ins. diameter at base. Black and silver colour. The oven formerly belonged to the Misses Dickinson of New Farm, St Albans, Hertfordshire. *St Albans City Museum*

512   Singer sewing machine. $7\frac{1}{4}$ ins. high, 7 ins. long. Made in the U.S.A. *c.* 1914. Given to the author by her grandmother, Mrs John Sebastian White, and used for perforating notebooks in addition to sewing

513   Doll, showing heroin smuggling. Chinese. 1960. Adapted from *Airline Detective Drug Traffic*, by Donald Fish

514   Female doll. Pottery, on a pottery bed or cradle. White figure with pink face, black hair, and pink bed. From Tel el-Amarna. 18th dynasty, 1550 B.C. *British Museum*

515   Sand toy. Metal, red truck, blue hopper. When empty the truck is pulled up by the weight. 16 ins. high. 1950. *Belonged to G. S. M. Moore*

516   Section showing lines of woodcut with raised printing surface
Section showing metal with incised lines for holding the ink

517   Stone showing greasy surface to hold ink, and wet surface to repel it

518   Woodcut of a wagon. French. 1587

519   Woodcut of a cradle. German. 1600

520   Marble showing white on black as in a wood engraving. English

521   Straw horse with white lines cut away on scraper-board. Mexican. 20th century

522   Engraving on copperplate after Chodowiecki. End of 18th century. Note cross-hatching and dots

523   Initial letter. Designed by Kate Greenaway to be cut by professional engraver. *By permission of Messrs Frederick Warne*

524   Halftone or three-colour process block of a Jack-in-a-box. From a watercolour by Alice B. Woodward, illustrating the *Land of Lost Toys* by Juliana Horatio Ewing. Naturally the dots will not show in this reproduction. 1910

525   Jack-on-strings. A modern version made with wooden beads. 7 ins. high. Austrian. 1969. *From Galts Toy Shop*. When made of card these toys are named pantins, after the French town Pantin in which they originated

Sources

These toys are in the following museums:

Ashmolean Museum, Oxford, Nos. 56, 82;

Aylesbury Museum, 150;

Bedford Museum, Bedford, 57, 367, 381;

Bethnal Green Museum, London, 81, 107, 158, 187 (1), 233, 239 (9), 308, 309, 324, 325, 327, 371, 380, 387, 388, 459, 473, 474, 478. Colour, opp. page 3, No. 7; opp. page 64, No. 2; opp. page 192, No. 10; opp. page 208, Nos. 7, 9;

Bristol City Museum, 241;

British Museum, London, 4, 10, 11, 12, 34, 35, 51, 62, 63, 64, 66, 67, 69, 88, 89, 90, 98, 102 (3), 102 (6), 102 (7), 112, 116, 121, 123, 124, 138, 154, 163, 164, 177, 195, 202, 205, 207, 208, 242, 249, 273, 284, 288, 289, 298, 304, 305, 306, 307, 319, 320, 332, 335 (6), 336, 342, 346, 347, 355, 364, 417, 439, 446, 448 (1), 449, 473, 474, 485, 486, 509, 514. Colour, opp. page 49, Nos. 1, 2, 3, 4, 5, 7, 9;

Cambridge Ethnological Museum, 59, 120;

Cambridge, Folk Museum, 44, 76, 101, 168, 238, 377, 421, 460, 461, 462. Colour, opp. page 192, Nos. 2, 3;

Cirencester Museum, 9, 91;

Cuming Museum, Southwark, 213, 358, 409. Colour, opp. page 3, No. 5; opp. page 160, No. 1; opp. page 192, Nos. 7, 8;

Dorchester Museum, Dorset, 8, 297 (5), 335 (1), 335 (2), 335 (8b);

Fitzwilliam Museum, Cambridge, 136, 137, 198, 199, 275, 276, 281, 311, 333;

Galerie Royal, Dresden, 17;

Geffrye Museum, London, 387;

Glastonbury Museum, 341;

Guildhall Museum, London, 293, 294, 318, 335 (4), 335 (8a), (8c), 338, 340, 476;

Gunnersbury Museum, 48, 125, 126, 390. Colour, opp. page 192, No. 1;

Hitchin Museum, Hertfordshire, 303;

Horniman Museum, Dulwich, 102 (2), 102 (4), 175, 273, 438 (2), 444 (1, 2, 3, 4, 5). Colour, opp. page 49, No. 8;

Jewish Museum, Bloomsbury, 301;

Leathercraft Museum, London, 52, 370;

Lechlade Museum, 239 (11);

London Museum, 235, 406, 447;

Newbury Museum, 494;

Nuremberg Germanische Museum, 477;

Peterborough Museum, 79, 350, 351, 403. Colour, opp. page 3, No. 4; opp. page 160, No. 3; opp. page 208, No. 6;

Pinto Collection, Birmingham, 224;

Pitt Rivers Museum, Farnham Royal, Dorset, 203, 286, 292;

Pitt Rivers Museum, Oxford 102 (1), 263, 296, 334, 345, 368 (5), 444 (6). Colour, opp. page 49, Nos. 10, 11; opp. page 177, No. 7;

Pollock's Toy Museum, London, 119, 407;

St Alban's City Museum, 23, 323, 352, 368 (1), 368 (3), 389, 453, 456, 479, 480, 481, 510, 511. Colour, opp. page 3, Nos. 2, 3, 8; opp. page 177, Nos. 1, 3, 4;

Salisbury Museum, Wiltshire, 2, 99, 297 (3), 299, 300, 335 (3), 335 (5), 335 (7), 368 (4), 465, 467, 468, 492. Colour, opp. page 14, No. 4;

Science Museum, South Kensington, 458;

Shaftesbury Museum, Dorset, 302;

Sturt Hill, Shipton Gorge, Dorset, 161;

Truro Museum, 283, 297 (4);

Van Cortland Museum, New York, U.S.A. 488;

Victoria and Albert Museum, London, 18, 77, 100, 330, 366, 376, 379, 410, 419, 487, 499, 500, 501, 502, 503, 504, 505, 506, 507, 508. Colour, opp. page 3, No. 1;

Wellcome Museum, London, 70;

Winchester Museum, 297 (1), 337, 440.

These toys have been lent by the following owners:

Mrs J. C. Bishop, Nos. 495, 496. Colour, opp. page 208, No. 8

Mr D. Blaylock. Colour, opp. page 14, No. 1

Mrs George Boorer, No. 414

Miss Janet Boorer, No. 146

Mr Butcher, No. 161

Miss Alison Sarah Carter, No. 223

Miss Janet Dunbar, No. 155. Colour, opp. page 192, No. 6

Mrs Estrid Faurholt, No. 310. Colour, opp. page 3, No. 6

Mr J. D. Fordham. Colour, opp. page 14, No. 3

Mrs Heather Fox, Nos. 239 (3), 239 (7), 239 (8), 239 (16), 240

Mrs Lovatt Fraser, No. 396

The Lord Grantley, No. 187 (1)

Mrs Muriel Green, Nos. 490, 498

Mrs Evelyn Harvey, No. 413. Colour, opp. page 14, No. 2

Master Stephen Ingle, No. 231

Mr A. E. D. Lott, No. 382

Mr A. Moreton Moore, Nos. 110, 127, 128, 141, 144, 152, 153, 159, 160, 220, 226, 227, 229, 258, 384, 400 (9). Colour, opp. page 14, No. 5

Mr Guy S. M. Moore, Nos. 221, 443, 515

Mr Richard E. M. Moore, Nos. 78, 87, 143, 149, 151, 156, 228, 247, 383, 393, 482

Master Robin Nately, No. 360

Master Christopher Prior, No. 373

Miss Ursula Radford, No. 452

The Marquess of Salisbury, Nos. 188, 189

Mr George Swinford, No. 239 (11)

Miss Ruth Wainwright, Nos. 329, 353, 391, 392. Colour, opp. page 64, No. 3; opp. page 177, No. 2

The Author, Nos. 394, 395, 445, 512. Colour, opp. page 177, Nos. 5, 6; opp. page 192, No. 9

Bibliography

Books in which toys are mentioned

Adam, Leonard. *Primitive Art*, 1940

Allan, Mea. *The Tradescants*

Beaumont, C. W. *The Mysterious Toyshop*, 1924

Bell, R. C. *Board and Table Games*, 1960

Cassell, J. *Book of Indoor Amusements*, 1882

Cooke, C. W. *Automata, Old and New*, 1891

Craig, G. *Book of Penny Toys*, 1899

Cremer, W. H. *The Toys of the Little Folk*, 1875

Crouch, H. *Complete View of British Customs*, 1724

Crouch, H. *Complete Guide to Officers*, 1732

Culin, Stewart. *Games with Dice*, 1889

Daiken, Leslie. *Children's Toys throughout the Ages*, 1963

Daiken, Leslie. *World of Toys*, 1963

d'Allemagne, H. *Histoire des Jouets*, 1903

Dongerkery, Kamala, S. *A Journey through Toyland*, 1954

Ewing, Juliana H. 'Land of lost Toys', from *Brownies and Other Tales*, 1910

Falkener, E. *Games Ancient and Oriental*, 1892

Faurholt, Estrid. See under Jacobs, F. G.

Fraser, A. *A History of Toys*, 1966

Garratt, J. G. *Model Soldiers*, 1959

Gibson, Cecil. *A History of British Dinky Toys*, 1966

Gomme, A. B. *Games for Parlour and Playground*, 1898

Gordon, Lesley. *Peepshow into Paradise*, 1953

Gosse, A. B. *Civilization of the Ancient Egyptians*

Greene, Vivien. *English Doll's Houses*

Gröber, Karl. *Children's Toys of Bygone Days*, 1928

Gurney, Beham W. *Playing Cards*

Hammond, Alex. *The Book of Chessmen*

Hampe, Theodor. *Der Zinnsoldat: ein deutsches Spielzeug*

Harris, Henry. *Model Soldiers*, 1962

Hartley, D. and Elliot, M. *Life and Work of the People of England*, 1925

Hawkins, J. *General History of Music*, 1776

Hercik, E. *Folk Toys of Czechoslovakia* Prague, 1952

Hibbert, Christopher. *The Court at Windsor*

Hillier, Mary. *Pageant of Toys*, 1965

Jackson, Neville, Mrs *Toys of Other Days*, 1908

Jacobs, F. G. and Faurholt, Estrid. *Dolls and Doll Houses*, 1967

Joseph, A. S. *The Practical Building Toy*, 1854

Kiefer, Monica. *American Children through their Books*, 1948

Landells, E. *The Boy's Own Toymaker*, 1859

Landells, E. and A. *The Girl's Own Toymaker*, 1860

Latham, Jean. *Doll's Houses; A Personal Choice*, 1969

Leaves from a Journal. Queen Victoria

McClintock, Marshall and Inez. *Toys in America*, 1961

Meggendorfer. *Always Jolly*, 1891

Morley, H. *Bartholomew Fair*, 1858

Mukhopadhyaya, Ajita-K. *Folk Toys of India*, 1956

Muir, P. *English Children's Books*, 1954

Murray, H. J. R. *History of Chess*

Murray, P. *Toys*, 1968
National Federation of Womens Institutes. *30 Crafts*. Article on Toys,
    Gwen White, 1950
National Geographic Magazine
Nordenskiöld, Erland. *La Vie des Indiens dans le Chaco*, 1942
Nordenskiöld, Erland. *Spiele und Spielsachen in Grand Chaco und in
    Nordamerika*
Patent Office Library
Papouskova. *Lidove*. 1948
Piggott, Stuart. *Prehistoric India*
Pollock's World of Toys, 1969
Rabecq-Maillard, M. *Histoire du Jouet*, 1962
Remise and Fondin. *The Golden Age of Toys*, 1967
Rhead, G. F. *Lead Toy Casting*, 1948
Seyffert, O. and Trier, W. *Toys*, 1923
Sy, M. *Die Thüringer Spielwaren*, 1929
Tissandier, G. *Les Recréations Scientifiques*, 1881
Tissandier, G. *Jeux et Jouets*, 1884
Waterer, J. W. *Leather Craftsmanship*
White, Gwen. *A Book of Toys*, 1946

Booklets and catalogues

Belgrade Exhibition of Children's Toys, 1958
Bonds of Euston Road Catalogue
Cambridge and County Folk Museum, 1951
Children's Books of Yesterday. Percy H. Muir. National Book League
Children's Paradise Exhibition
Children Throughout the Ages Exhibition, 1934
Changing Face of Childhood Exhibition, 1967
Children's Toys. Rottingdean, Sussex. Booklet
Davy, M. J. B. *A Science Museum Handbook on Aeronautics*, 1935
Docker och tennsoldater. Nationalmuseum, Finland. Booklet
Dolls' Houses. Victoria and Albert Museum booklet
Doll's and Dolls' Houses. Victoria and Albert Museum booklet
Dukke Samlingen. Legoland, Copenhagen. Catalogue
Jeux et Jouets d'autrefois. Institut Pédagogique National, 1961
Fisher Price Toys. New York. Catalogue, 1950
Model Soldiers through the Ages Exhibition, 1958
Origins of the Motion Picture. D. B. Thomas. Science Museum Booklet,
    1964
Period Dolls' houses from Many Lands Exhibition, 1955
Popular Carriages. C. Hamilton Ellis. British Transport Commission, 1954
Readers' Digest articles
Titania's Palace. Major Sir Nevile Wilkinson. Booklet. 1926
Teaching Toys. Rachel M. R. Young. Norwich Museum booklet
Treasures of Famous Children Exhibition, 1931
Toys. Victoria and Albert Museum booklet, 1967
Toys & Games. London Museum booklet, 1959
Two Hundred Years of Jigsaw Puzzles. London Museum booklet, 1968
Various catalogues from sales
Warwick Doll Museum booklet, 1955

Index